Hearts Entwined

The Love Letters of Therapist-Soulmates

Kathryn Elliott, Ph.D. &
James Elliott, Ph.D.

Anthetics Institute Press
PO Box 81097, Lafayette, LA 70598
(337) 234-8221, Fax: (337) 233-6534
anthetics@aol.com
www.antheticpsychology.com
Facebook/Anthetic

ISBN: 978-0-9644220-2-5
Printed in the United States of America
To order, please contact
Anthetics Institute Press
P.O. Box 81097, Lafayette, LA 70598
(337) 234-8221
E-mail: anthetics@aol.com
Fax: (337) 233-6534

Contents

THE FINDING   7

THE FIRST TWO MONTHS   33

PAWLING   227

ENGAGEMENT!   411

JIM & KATHY'S WEDDING   493

EPILOGUE   505

Part 1

The Finding

OUR MEETING STORY

What happens when you combine a full moon, the breaking waves of a California ocean side, a most romantic retreat center, and two people who've spent their lives longing for a great love?

We're James Elliott & Kathryn Elliott, therapists and soul mates. And those were the ingredients of our meeting so many years ago. Perhaps they explain why I sat down right next to this strong, intelligent man at a conference table full of empty chairs. And why during those first ten days of our intense meeting, I asked him to inseminate me. And why I had an anxiety attack when we had to part.

But, let's start from the beginning…

Kathryn's Story: When I headed to California for my doctoral colloquium, my position was, "This is my Ph.D. I'm here with the sole purpose of obtaining my doctorate in counseling psychology." I went there with no conscious thought of meeting a man.

In fact, I had been thinking for a number of years, "I'll never find a man who would be what I want." I was disillusioned by past relationships. My first husband had fallen madly in love with one of my friends. He was "supposed to be" my husband for life. I was bitter; I even hated to go to weddings. When I had to attend a wedding, I looked on cynically.

Once I got over the acute pain of that breakup, I opened myself to another relationship. This time I wouldn't pick a nice guy. This time I picked a bad boy — a cocaine addict. You can imagine where that ended — in trouble, along with him with the law. This occurred in my last semester of graduate school for my master's degree in counseling and the probationary period of my first counseling job. Fortunately, my clean history cleared me. I never picked a bad boy again.

Back to nice guys...My next boyfriend was sweet, kind, faithful, but weak (when my father died, he didn't come to the funeral home for the wake.) I couldn't face a lifetime with a guy who wouldn't be there when I most needed him. Grieving my dad, I thought, "That's it. I give up on guys. There's no good guy out there. I'll be roommates with this supportive female friend, devote myself to my work (college instructor); and fill my life with activities with my friends and support group (Peace Time—a non-conventional spiritual group of great friends). Thirteen years passed between when my marriage ended and my new life began.

MY LIFE IS UPENDED

With my life back in place, I was determined to protect and maintain the stability I had achieved. When I realized that I would have to earn my Ph.D. in order to obtain tenure to do the thing I loved (teach counseling and psychology), I looked for a doctoral program that would be least upsetting to my life. I talked to my therapist, Evan, who said, "Have you considered a non-traditional doctoral program?" I said, "I've never even heard of it." So, I read up in Baer's Guide to Non-traditional Colleges and Universities and learned of one such university in Los Angeles. I applied and was accepted. I went to see Evan to celebrate. But he said, "Wait. You know you tend to jump into things impulsively. Have you checked to see if it's accredited?" Whoa. I did. They weren't.

So I searched for an accredited doctoral program and found the Union Institute. They even had a faculty member, Della, who also taught at a university only an hour away from where I lived. I went to see her. She was wonderful, warm, supportive. I was accepted to Union. My first step was to choose an entry colloquium date and site. To my relief, there was one at the perfect time for me, Jan. 6-15, my winter break between semesters. When I read where it would be held, I was excited. It was Asilomar Retreat Center on the Pacific Coast near Carmel, California. Perfect. I had lived in California during my first marriage and loved it. It was a magnet for me. So, I invited my roommate, Cali, her mom, Bella, and my mom, Lorraine, to travel with me for a pre-colloquium pleasure trip to California.

A FATEFUL SUNSET
CUTS A CHINK IN MY ARMOR

We had a beautiful trip up the 17-mile drive past Big Sur and on to Monterey. It was the last day of a lovely trip up the California coast, January 5, 1989. We neared Carmel at sunset over the Pacific Ocean, and the beauty of it was stunning.

We stopped the car at a roadside cutaway to savor

it. It was a high vantage point with a panoramic view of the flaming sun setting over the ocean. In our field of vision, a dozen yards in front of us sat a couple close together on a blanket on the ground, their heads together watching the sunset. I think at that moment, some part of me felt a pang of longing. A tremor went through the well-constructed armor I had created for myself. Life was all in place. And so was my shield against intimate relationships, born of disillusionment and despair. But when I saw the couple on the blanket, some locked away place in me wanted what they had. Perhaps God or the universe was priming me for what was to come the following day.

JIM'S QUEST

Two hours north of that spot on that same day, Jim was preparing to drive down from his office in Berkeley to Asilomar Retreat Center. He would be entering his doctoral program in psychology. He had long been on a quest for a life partner; a colleague to share his life and work. This excerpt from his letter to Kathy dated November 20, 1994, describes his search:

I began my search in 1941, in Detroit, little knowing that you hadn't been born yet. Let's skip now to November 1951, the first time there was a possibility of finding you. In that month I was back in the Navy in Pensacola, still searching. You weren't there. I went looking for you in Mobile but all I found was the girl from Meridian. You weren't in New Orleans, either.

In 1952 I was in Philadelphia with my ship, and in 1953 (when you were 2), I was back in Detroit, working for Ford Motor Co. In 1954 (you were 3) I began working as a magazine editor. If you had gone dancing at the Greystone Ballroom, I might have found you and taught you to dance. In 1956 and 1957 (you were 5 and 6) I was at Wayne State University, finishing my undergraduate degree. Then I went back to my job as editor.

In November 1960 (you were now 9) I went to California. Surely I'd find you there. But of course, not yet. I began leading groups in 1964 (you were 13). I was hoping you'd come to one of my lectures or groups. In 1969 (you were 18 now) I began leading professional training groups. You didn't sign up, even though I led two groups in New Orleans. (Something seemed to be attracting me to Louisiana.)

I couldn't find you in my master's program (1985, when you were 34), but I had high hopes of finding you in my doctoral program. This would be a nontraditional school, and I wanted a nontraditional wife. By now I had a list of criteria: first, a colleague; then 56 other items.

I'd developed a custom before attending a professional event–I would check out the women's names and their affiliation. So when the university sent the list of learners who'd be attending the colloquium (the opening learning event), I'd read the women's names with a mixture of hope and curiosity. There was Svetlana — sounded exotic, majoring in psychology; Ann — nice solid name, also majoring in psychology; Rebecca, majoring in English, not in my field, but I liked the name; and Kathy Vermillion, majoring in Occupational Counseling (they'd made a mistake in her major). I dismissed that last one, because her major indicated someone who wouldn't share my interests.

My erratic 20-year relationship with Amelia had recently ended. I'd decided to break my pattern of pursuing her for one more reconciliation. I was free, and with hope in my heart, on January 5, I drove down to Asilomar to begin my doctoral program.

EPIPHANY

Kathryn: The next day I saw Mama, Cali and Bella off at the San Jose airport. I felt a sting of tears — I'm on my own, removed from all the structures I've created for myself. That passed. I got in my rental car and drove to Asilomar. January 6 was our first official meeting for the 14 doctoral students. It would last ten days, provide us with an orientation to our learning process and to our dissertation, then we would each return home to pursue our studies.

When I walked in the room (it was a free standing building, named Curlew, very cute, redwood and stone, glass windows with the sun streaming in at every corner, a huge stone fireplace; a set of meeting tables and chairs); one man sat there alone. I saw him from behind, sort of in profile. He had light brown hair, a full beard, a tweed jacket. He had a pen in his hand and was thinking and occasionally making notes on a small pad. I immediately thought, "He looks like a psychologist; probably wouldn't be interested in me." Then with 14 other empty chairs around the table, I went and sat in the chair next to him. That man was Jim.

(Some part of me that had been tucked away all those cynical resigned years came back on stage. She was still very much alive. She saw her man.) I placed my briefcase on the floor between us, and it promptly fell over on to his leg. I said, "I hope I'm not invading your space." He said, "No, not at all." He told me later that he thought, "Invade my space! Invade my space!" That part that was re-emerging was very careful to not let the scared part that had created a firm cocoon back home know what she was doing. She spent the next ten days on the fast track; getting to know this excellent man; checking him out. Jim did the same.

I CHECK JIM OUT

It was a strange and wonderful thing to meet this intriguing man, Jim. I was incredibly attracted to him. But some cautious part of me said, "You'd better check him out. He might be an alcoholic or drug addict. " (For nine years, I had worked as a counselor with people with substance abuse problems. So, I was very aware of the pain that could bring to a relationship.) In addition, these strange wonderings were, I think, an artifact of meeting a man over a thousand miles from home. There was no normal social context in which to find out about him. No common friends. No relatives. Not even a professional community. At Asilomar, we were lifted totally out of our normal lives. And that was part of the challenge in getting to know him. But it was also the magic. So, as I got to know him, the "checking him out" began.

Every day, one of us learners would present our doctoral study plans to the group. The day that Jim presented, he stated that he had written books and would use his dissertation as the basis for another book. So, at the break, I asked him, "Would you teach me to write books?" (He told me later that he loved that I saw his expertise and wanted to learn from him. He felt my respect and admiration for him.) We later agreed to meet in his room during the break.

When I got to his room, I noted right off the bat that it was toasty warm. (Though sunny, it was a cold January day outside.) I told him, "Mmm. I love that you keep your room warm." He said, "I love to keep it warm." So, we both noted that we were compatible in terms of the environment we liked. Then he walked over to the drapes and started to draw them across the wall of windows. I said, "No, don't close the drapes. I'm not comfortable with that." (I was still unsure whether I could trust this man.) So, we talked. And he told me about writing books. At one point, I thought, "This is the perfect opportunity to check him out." So, I asked him if I could use his bathroom. While in there, I looked at all the bottles on his counter. No alcohol. No drugs. Good! He checked out.

JIM CHECKS ME OUT

Jim had come to the colloquium not only to pursue his doctoral work but also to find a life partner. He'd been searching for years for a great love. And he had a list! He'd developed 56 criteria for an ideal woman. So, he knew just what he was looking for. His notes from Asilomar reveal his thought process:

> KATHY: I'd like to talk to you about how you write books.
> JIM: Okay. Let's get together.
> KATHY: (Later) When can we get together? (She's highly motivated.)

This dialogue was significant. One of Jim's criteria was a woman who would respect and value him. His ideas. His opinions. By my request to learn from him, he had a big indicator that he'd found that woman.

WHAT HAPPENED IN JIM'S ROOM

Lots! In fact, 3 First Things. #1-I had my first experience of Jim beholding me. I had been the first colloquium participant to present my doctoral learning plans. They had to do with the concept of Callings; that is, being called to the work you do; something archetypal and transcendent. In his room, Jim said to me, "That's a work of genius." I was stunned. And affirmed. And warmed. He'd paid attention to me. And actually seen me. I told him later that for me that was a

Day of Naming. I was now more than ever falling hard for this man. He was relating to me in a way no man had ever done before.

#2-Jim became my teacher and guide into the world of closeness. He had a map. And he took me on that first step of the path to having intense connection. He began by disclosing a feeling he was having. And a vulnerable one at that. He said, "I feel scared." My immediate impulse was to want to soothe away his fear. "Oh, don't feel scared." But that's not what he wanted. He wanted to have his feelings. And go deeper into them. And explore them for the growth to which they could lead. So, he said to me, "No, I don't want you to say that. I want you to say, 'Can you tell me more about that?'" Hmm. This man didn't want a conventional connection. He wanted more. I liked that. So, I said, "I can learn that." And I did. And it certainly led to an intense connection.

#3-Our first hug. When we finished our conversation, and I got ready to leave, we walked into our first hug. I don't remember who initiated it. But it was awkward. Jim seemed stiff. I was surprised, because he was such a warm man. I think now that the intensity of the setting (his room with that bed undeniably there) and the rising voltage of our attraction to each other formed an undercurrent that colored everything we said and did. This wasn't just a friendly hug. This was a prelude to a Relationship.

18

WHAT HAPPENED IN MY ROOM

Jim and I were spending every moment possible getting to know each other better. One day he and Ann and I met in Ann's and my room. We lay on the two double beds like girls at a slumber party. (I think Ann in her bed and Jim and I across my bed, but not close.) We talked and talked. Then Ann had to leave for a meeting with someone else. As she left, we stood up to tell her goodbye. (I think lying alone on the bed together would have been more than we wanted to handle at this point.) I must admit I felt a mixture of relief (I wanted to be alone with Jim) and an anticipatory thrill (I wondered what would come of this intimate time). The energy between us was intense.

Well, we hit on a sensitive topic right away--Jim's stiff hug of me in his room the day before. I said, "Jim, I have some words to give you." (I didn't know about the communication skill of feedback. Jim would more formally teach me that later. But, without knowing it, I was diving into it.) "You are strong, and that's wonderful. Yet I noticed certain stiffness when you hugged me in your room."

He was listening openly and intently, "Yes."

So, I continued. "I want you to be less stiff; to instead take in my femaleness. Yes, my female lubrication." He said, "I'm imagining right now that I'm going inside your body, bathing myself in your juices, soaking up the sheer niceness of your femaleness." (We were both becoming transported to a place of depth connection we hadn't been before.) From that same transported state, I spoke.

"If God were speaking, he would say: 'You are my son in whom I am well pleased. Incorporate the feminine. When you see Ann and Kathy and others, drink them in and let that part of yourself be nourished.'" I had had my eyes closed while I had said this. But now I opened them and told Jim, "I didn't know what I was saying. That just flowed out of me."

So, that's how Jim and I began to swim around in spiritually and sexually infused imagery. It was as if some high-voltage energy was being tapped in each of us. It was electrifying. But we weren't backing off.

WE GO SHOPPING AND
MAKE SOME SURPRISING DISCOVERIES

Our doctoral colloquium was packed with activities and learning, so we were grateful on about the fifth day to have a good break. Jim and Ron decided to do a little sightseeing and told me they were going out in Jim's car. I asked if I could go too. They both said, "Sure."

So, Jim, being from the area, took us to Carmel and to the cutest place, The Barnyard Shopping Center. We browsed in the bookstore there. I saw a number of books that I wanted to order for my doctoral work and thought I'd write down the titles. But I didn't have anything to write with. I asked Jim, "Do you have a piece of paper?" Then, (because I'd found a little scrap in my purse), "Oh, that's okay."

But Jim said, "I need to have you ask me for things. Here's one. (And a pen.)" Every- thing we were saying to each other was steeped in revelation of who we were and what we wanted from a relationship. Jim was telling me, "I don't want you to be self-sufficient in our relating. I want you to tell me what you want." Wow! And he proved it with the next thing he did.

We briefly parted to go into separate shops. When we met up again, Jim had a little paper bag in his hand. He handed it to me. When I opened it, I was surprised and charmed. Inside was an adorable little stuffed sea lion. He told me he wanted me to have something to remember our meeting by. I couldn't believe he had bought me a gift. And one that was so in keeping with my personality. This man was truly getting who I was. He was beholding me. Among the things I had told him about myself was that I had some special stuffed animals at home–a soft stuffed brown elephant with soulful eyes as well as a floral bear with his arms ready for a hug. The sea lion told me that he had listened to me. And had noted that if he wanted to give me a gift, the little stuffed sea lion was just the right thing.

And we had one more exchange that capped off this establishing of how we would relate. After we left the shopping center, Jim said he needed to stop for gas. As we pulled up to the pump, Ron said to Jim, "I have a need to give. Here's some money to help pay for the gas."

But I said, "I have a need to be given to." And I didn't offer any money. I was saying, "I sure love being with a man who will give to me. I gladly receive what you are giving."

THAI FOOD AND
WHAT HAPPENED ON THE CAR RIDE

On Wednesday, the sixth day of the colloquium, we were all exhausted. So, we were given the afternoon off. I went to the group's picnic lunch on the rocks at the edge of the Pacific. Jim didn't go; he wanted to make photocopies of the sample dissertations. Besides, he was from the area and had visited the local sights before. Still, I missed his company. After lunch, the group went to the Monterey aquarium, where we saw the adorable sea otters playing in the bay.

At suppertime, we all met outside the aquarium. Something in my spirit lifted when I saw Jim there. The group had decided to go to a Thai restaurant for supper. Jim sat across the table from me. It was a convivial meal. But I'd never eaten Thai food before, didn't know how to order, and I went hungry. Jim said later, he wished he'd known; he would have helped me order or would have shared his food. As we left the restaurant, Jim asked the group, "Anybody want a ride?"

I said without hesitation, "I do!" No one else said anything. I think they were starting to see the connection he and I were making and didn't want to interfere.

So, we got in his car, and he said, "I want to take you somewhere to show you something I think you'll really like." I said, "OK." I was intrigued. Once again, he was implying that he had beheld me and could see into me and what I'd like. He drove us a few blocks and parked the car near a building that I couldn't tell yet what it was. As we were moving to get out of the car,

I reached over and unlatched his shoulder belt, along with mine. I couldn't stop invading his space! I felt a little bold doing it, but that bold part of me didn't want to miss a golden opportunity to communicate that she wanted closeness.

As we walked from the car to the building nearby, I could begin to see what was inside. It was a carousel! The Monterey carousel. Oh, my! First, the sea lion, and now this. This man truly was seeing that inner child that longed for a man to see her; to play with her; to love her. (I didn't articulate this to myself at the time, but I see it now.) The carousel wasn't running that night, but we took pleasure in walking around, looking at all the fanciful horses. It was magical.

I TOUCH SOME FEAR AND
CHECK JIM OUT FURTHER

As wonderful as things were going between Jim and me — he was incredibly caring and empathic — it couldn't stop my getting some stuff triggered. (Stuff is just a word for emotional baggage.) As part of our learning, we were shown a video on sexual harassment in graduate school. I started feeling afraid. It was that primal fear of strange men that women have. So, after the video during the break, I told Jim, "I'm having bad feelings about the film. It's made me think, 'We don't know each other; you might even be a rapist.' I don't want to come from fear with you." He said, "Is there any way I can help?" I told him, "Yes; I need reassurance about safety." His response: "I can only say, 'I'll work on my stuff; there will be some risk.'" Oh, no, that wasn't reassuring! So, I said, "No; I need a statement about your intentionality." This time he said, "I'm disgusted with men like those in the video. I've known men like them. I would never be that way. Your freedom is precious to me." That did it. That was the right answer. He'd checked out once again.

I MAKE A REQUEST: FOR INSEMINATION

The next day, before lunch, I said to Jim, "I have something I want to ask of you. And it may take some explanation." He said, "OK, let's talk after lunch."

At lunch, Jim sat across the table from me. When we'd both finished eating, we looked across and smiled a secret smile at each other. Jim nodded. We got up and left. As we walked along the boardwalk to the beach, it was bright sunshine. I had on sunglasses. When we stopped among the rocks near the water, Jim said, "Take off your sunglasses." I did, looked directly into his eyes and dived in, "I have a request of you. I want you to inseminate me with your presence; with your strength—with a belief in myself. I want you to be inside me to give me faith in myself. I want to take that home with me." His response: "OK, if it comes, I'll do it."

After my boldness in making this outrageous request, I had some inner critic backlash (for more on this, read our book, Disarming Your Inner Critic). I shared it with Jim. "I'm afraid you'll see my request as a physical come-on. My inner critic says it's phony; it's just sex I'm wanting." Jim surprised me again with, "But even if physical sex were to be involved, it would be symbolic of deeper insemination." (Oh, I began falling even harder for this man.) (Jim wrote in his notes that day, "This girl has fears I've never heard of because of this new depth.")

Later that day, Jim told me, "OK, I've thought about your request. And I can do it." We agreed to meet in the lodge after supper. It was dark outside, but the lodge was warm with lamplight and firelight. We sat on a love seat facing the fireplace. People were all around the room, some playing ping-pong, some just talking. But all that dropped away when Jim looked into my eyes. He told me, "As boys, we learn through one experience after another to be strong. We play games to toughen us up…" And then he told me more about his history. And as he spoke, I followed his journey into strength. And he somehow transmitted that strength to me. And I took it in. And something magical happened. Something transformative. And I have never been the same since.

THAT FIRST KISS

After Jim's transporting insemination of me, I was floating. And exhausted. So, we headed off to our rooms together. Yes, we were leaving the warm glow of that firelit lodge. But I didn't feel the clear, cold night air. I was warmed from within by Jim's strength. When we got to the top of the path, we paused. Then he did it.

Jim took my face in his hands, and then slowly, and so tenderly kissed me. I had never been kissed like that before. That kiss spoke volumes—his cherishing of me; his caring attitude toward me; his honoring of my need to be romantically connected with. He poured the essence of masculine love and tenderness into that kiss. And with that a bond was formed, from which there was no turning back.

OUR CONVERSATIONS: CREATING CLOSENESS

Jim made notes of our conversations at Asilomar. As we spoke, we were creating more closeness. How?

1: Requesting Feedback:

JIM: What do you like about me?

KATHY: Your affirmation; you named my book a work of genius. Your warmth, closeness, the energy between us.

JIM: I want reassurance that you like me.

KATHY: I'm GLAD you sat next to me.

JIM: What about me do you find sexually attractive?

KATHY: Well, your sensitivity is real appealing to me. And maturity. And not having to explain things to you. Your immediacy.

JIM: What do you mean by maturity?

KATHY: You were able to be with pain and those other feelings. That's the level I want to relate on.

2: Giving feedback:

> KATHY: You were endearing, giving your presentation. I like your eyes; the way they crinkle when you smile. I've been watching your hands. Your nose. Your hair. Your hands are so warm. We click emotionally, intellectually, and spiritually.

> JIM: You are a spiritual teacher.

These bits of feedback were important. We were beholding each other. And in each other's eyes, we found respect, admiration. And growing love.

THAT FINAL NIGHT

It had been a mere ten days. Yet for Jim and me it was the high point of our lives. Everything before was our longing; our search. It was also our preparation. This was our Finding–each other, at last. Our twin; our soul mate. Everything forward would be a fulfilling of this, working it out, living it. A Finding is an archetypal thing–something transcendent that lifts us out of our ordinary lives. This colloquium had it all–everything we each loved: intellectual sharing, collegiality with warm people, the beauty of the ocean, cozy fires, great food–but most important, our meeting; the beginning of our fulfillment.

And so that final night was a celebration of all this. And did we celebrate—all of us learners with Della and Rodrigue, our faculty leaders, gathered in Crocker Dining Hall, enjoying prime rib and wine. Afterward, we all went back to Curlew, our special meeting room where we'd spent those ten days learning and sharing. This time, the meeting tables had been put away. Instead were chairs in a circle and a warm fire crackling in the fire-place. We left the room dark, only the firelight reflecting on our faces. It was wonderful. We talked about our impressions of each other and of what the experience had meant to each of us. And then we began to sing! Song after song. But two songs stand out in my memory. First, Jim and Svetlana joined their beautiful voices in HaTikvah, ("Kol ode balevav P'nimah–Nefesh Yehudi homiyah"), the national anthem of Israel.

I didn't know the translation, but it was haunting, then rousing. At one point, as they sang, they began to dance around, their arms in the air. We were all clapping in rhythm.

Then I sang–a song written by a dear friend. Its first verse was my blessing to the group and my love song to Jim: "The same stars that shine on me shine on you. And the moonlight that fills my sky fills yours too. Even though we're miles apart — in the spirit of the Lord — my love and my prayers keep me close to you."

We'd have one more meeting in the morning, but it would be brief, then we'd be returning to our homes. But tonight, I was on a cloud.

PARTING

The Asilomar colloquium had been our Finding. What we had discovered led us to realize that we valued each other highly. But where would this lead? On the tenth day, Jim drove me to the San Jose Airport so I could fly back to Lafayette. When it was time to board the plane, I had an anxiety attack. I was puzzled and asked Jim to hold me. I realize now that I was afraid that I would lose this man; that I would never see him again. We hadn't made any commitment to each other. I still hadn't faced the changes that would take place if our relationship developed into a committed one. All we had said was that we would write. He didn't know if I would just return to my home and all my embededness there. It was scary. I didn't want to lose what I had found.

I wrote my first letter to Jim on the plane home; he wrote his to me the next day. Those would be the first of 130 letters we would write each other over the next six months. Through those letters and through the phone calls we fell deeper and deeper in love; got to know each other; and risked greater and greater closeness. The letters chronicle the challenges we faced—our mutual longing for profound closeness; our fears of revealing ourselves, both the best and worst in each of us; and the negativity of others toward our love. And through those challenges, the letters contain how we used every concept and skill we knew to overcome them and to grow and change through them. They tell of how we were swept along into greater depth, deeper intimacy, and in six months, marriage.

OUR MESSAGE TO YOU, THE READER

The letters contain our most intimate thoughts and feelings. When we wrote them so many years ago, we had in mind only each other as audience. We know the language of our letters is strong, poetic, even provocative. That's because we both hungered for closeness so much, that we dived into a place inside all us humans that is extraordinary. It's a place full of archetypal energies. (It's the same place where the heroic soldier goes to tap what it takes to fight to save his buddies or to defend his country.) We think it was that archetypal energy that empowered us to love in such a way that it can be a beacon to others of what's possible. That is, we don't have to settle for distance or just longevity in our marriages. We can have an emotional closeness beyond anything we've ever seen.

Now something has happened to lead us to publish our letters. In May 2008, after 19 years of marriage, Jim suffered a devastating stroke. For three years, he remained with me, cared for at home until his death in 2011. As he lay in bed, I read our love letters to him. Not only did they remind us of all the magic of our first six months together, but they touched those around us (caregivers, family, and friends) who overheard them. They identified with that first blossoming of love; with our passion; and with our struggles. When I wrote about wanting Jim to inseminate me; to be inside me, one said, "I know that feeling. I've felt that. Early in our relationship, my husband and I were so close that even when he was working out of town, we felt like we were inside each other, communicating with our thoughts and feelings." But she added, "Now we've lost it. And I would like to find it back." She and many others said, "You have to publish these. We want to read them." And we began to agree.

Our work together had been devoted to helping couples bring deep closeness back to their relationships. We believe we have found a way to continue that work by sharing our letters with you. For those of you who have longed for a relationship that could fill your hunger for closeness, we want our letters to give you hope that you can find it just as we did. But more than hope, we want to model for you how to have specific criteria in order to find the right partner. For those of you who say, "I've never even seen a good relationship, much less a deep passionate love," we want to show you what a deep love looks like and feels like and sounds like. For those of you who have had deep closeness but have lost it, we want to reassure you that you can create it again. And more important, we want to show you what it takes to keep a deep love alive—how to overcome your own internal blocks to this closeness just as we did. You'll read how we did it. In addition you'll see how to master getting free from the negativity, cynicism, and even contempt of others toward your profound love as we did. You'll read how we struggled to do it.

Most important, for all of you, we want to tell you that inside you is a great reservoir of magical energies for loving in a deep way, even in a mythic way. We tapped that reservoir. Our letters tell about what tapping it did to us; how it profoundly changed us. And fulfilled us.

May our letters inspire you, give you hope, and begin to equip you to have your own mythic love.

With love,

Jim & Kathy

Part 2

The First Two Months

MONDAY, JANUARY 16, 1989 7:00 PM

Dear Kathy Jo,

(How nice to type your sweet name.)

The first thing I want to say to you is that I didn't know that the experience we had would be so powerful. After I left you, I ate a McChicken sandwich at Stanford Shopping Center in Palo Alto, bought a sweater (light brown), and slowly drove home, and thought only peripherally about you. But that night as I lay in bed, all kinds of images came to me: your dear face, your empowering words, the song you sang, and on and on, a succession of images, one after another.

Well, this is good, I thought, and I wonder how long it will last.

When I awoke this morning, there was a new kind of thing happening: first, I again saw your face clearly, the face you showed me as I was telling you the things I said in response to your request—your face deeply moved and touched by what I was saying (and you assured me that my words were indeed powerful, and I had not been sure, and because you are sensitive, knew that I would want to know, and you in any case would want to tell me, so again there was one of those remarkable marvelous connectednesses that we had, as though we were one person and one part was reassuring the other part, much greater than anything I had ever experienced before and only now am beginning to meditate on and perceive the magnificent splendor of).

In any case, I was seeing images of your face, and the word lubricate came to mind, and I said to myself

Okay, I will let myself be lubricated by your femaleness and your love and other things you offered that I'm only dimly aware of, and I began to relax and ask myself what was this lubrication stuff, what was it about?, how would it work its way in my life, and I felt juices and fluids gathering at the joints of my body, and in the space of about a half hour, I began to relax, with your presence still with me in a powerful way, almost as though you were here watching me (perhaps even more powerfully than if you had really been here?) — it was as though I was indeed carrying you with me, you were attending me, and it was much more than a simple image of you, it was your sweet and full Presence itself. The precious essence of you that you had given me — more than a mere thought, which was all I thought I would have, invading all parts of my being and infusing them with something that is now making them all glow.

So I said to myself, what will this lead to I wonder; it's an interesting experience; and it felt like there would be more to come. I was driving to go shopping for groceries, and a car cut in front of me, and I was about to get angry when I said wait a minute, and I was now speaking from some deep place in me, deeper than I had been before (and I had gone pretty deep at times), with your face still accessible any time I wanted to look at it, and the episode of the other driver now seemed quite insignificant, compared with something else that was more important, like it was a little ripple now on the surface, but now I was living from a place much deeper than the surface, and it was just a little ripple way up there, not very important at all, and I could love the driver of that other car, and suddenly I relaxed more and said that all those things that used to matter so much don't matter anymore, those little irritants, and now nothing jangly that is happening is having its former impact, and I walked more slowly at the supermarket and sauntered around, buying this and that, and outside carrying the groceries to the car, felt the sunshine warming my body and just looked at the people scurrying about and felt at peace and knew at last the beginning of what you meant by becoming less stiff (less frantic, I would call it).

I had been wondering about your note, feeling a bit defensive, not wanting to decide about it for a while, though, keeping open on it and having faith that you surely had some- thing to teach me that I was not yet ready for but would be soon, and now I was indeed less stiff, at least beginning to be, and I felt centered in this deeper part of myself and now knew what the note meant, and knew that you were right (and that I was right when we talked in my room and you asked about writing books, and I told you that I wanted something from you but I wasn't sure what it was but it was very important to me, and it had something to do with just experiencing your Presence, from which my intuition told me some great good, some great wonderful splendid benefits would come that I would not know in advance but if I would just be open to it and patient, It would happen, because I had been prepared for it). So I now felt that serenity that I hadn't known at all that I was lacking (or knew but thought it was okay). And you had evoked that in me by giving me the gift of your female lubrication, which sounded exciting and wondrous and strange at the time you used the words, and now I was beginning to know what it meant. I think there is more to come.

And then something happened: instead of being an image with me, one that I could bring to mind whenever I wanted, you flipped — into a place inside me, and you were now in my head, an inch or so behind my eyes and looking out at the world through them, as though I had a twin inside me, a companion, with your being permeating every part of my mind in the precious and sweet way that you are and that I had surrendered to.

And there you are now.

And you say things to me, some in words but most in gentle attitudes and little steerings, and you are beginning to guide my life, and this is what I had wanted without knowing exactly what it was on that day you asked me about writing books.

I Love you Kathy Jo,

SUNDAY, JANUARY 15, 1989 9:15 PM

Dear Jim,

I'm on the plane back from Dallas to Lafayette, writing furiously some new ideas and questions that have come of an incredibly sweet, synchronistic encounter on my San Jose flight. A guy had the seat next to me, but since the plane was relatively empty, he said, "I'll sit behind you, so we can both spread out." Well, the flight was especially beautiful — over the snowy Sierra range, Las Vegas, and the Grand Canyon. I guess we both needed to talk about the beauty we were seeing, because we began to interchange comments of appreciation. That led to "why are you flying, etc." The blessing occurred as I told him of my project, and darn if he didn't start unbeknowingly processing with me, giving me his thoughts and questions; surmising my spirituality without my declaring it; he's a Christian. So I want to share with you some of what came about in my thinking about my work out of that meeting:

I declared, "I want to see if archetypes within us (e.g., the "helper") might exist, which if identified and named, could empower the person to work of satisfaction in any number of jobs, as long as it offered opportunity for expression of that archetype. Also, "As opposed to formal traditional vocational tests which intentionally limit options to measurable qualities (e.g., realistic, artistic on Strong-Campbell test), I want to open the inquiry of vocational choicemaking to more possibilities." I'm just thinking that I'd like to personify, name or "something" those possibilities so that they have life, personality, and power. A question I now have is, "were callings (defined as spiritual urgings toward certain work or activities) just for a past time and for a particular people (religious) or is it possible that non-religious persons may have a similar experience in which there is some urging from an inner place to do a certain work? And what does that imply for a spirituality of all vocational choice making?"

(New day, Monday) Well, today was reentry day for me, and despite literal and figurative cold showers, I remained centered and steadfast re: my project. A lot of that steadfastness came from a fertile place in me, full of you and your gift to me. So already our interchange has been called on to strengthen me, and I can tell you, it did. Thank you. Your voice, your words, your eyes were vividly there for me. To explain about the cold showers, I got ready to step into the shower this morning only to find out that our hot water heater went on the blink during the night. Figuratively, I had to interact with a couple of colleagues who don't relate at the level of respect and love that I've just spent 10 days basking in.

On the other hand I've had a wonderful homecoming from Cali, Mama, and Hale and from my students. They've all listened enthusiastically to my gushings about the colloquium.

It's really been an up and down day now that I think about it. Up with awakening to a sense of how precious an experience I've just had; down with a 7:00 am call that my favorite beloved uncle had died last night. Up with a wonderful lunch with Mama at my favorite seafood restaurant; down with the news that the extra pay course at the local C.D. unit did not make. Up with a wonderful time with Hale telling him all about colloquium; down with a devil's advocate interchange with a colleague. Up with a new John Sanford book (What Men are Like)) at the library; up with a call from the gifted program affirming my summer course proposal; down with a disquieting slosh of water in my hatchback of my car. It's amazing I'm not motion-sick! I'm having crawfish for supper and king cake for dessert—immersing myself in Louisiana cooking.

Thank you again for the loving support in seeing me off Sunday. I went from your loving arms to the dear interchange with my co-traveler to the loving arms of Cali. Total cushioning all the way!

I hope that your reentry has been gentle and fertile, that your writing is blessed, that your UGS process unfolds with inspiration and love.

You are very special to me, Jim. Be assured that you are in my thoughts, heart, and prayers. You are cushioned in those.

Call or write as you can.

I love you,

Kathy

SUNDAY, JANUARY 22, 1989, 1:30 PM

Dear Kathy Jo,

This will be a more task-oriented, less rhapsodic letter, but I want you to know that the loving energy we created still burns within me, giving my life a warmth and splendor.

I have some questions.

What we did was affirm one another. What was that? How did we do it? Have you ever done anything like that before? As deep? With the same content? (Am I leaving any questions out?) Any comments you can make about what we did will be greatly appreciated.

We also introjected each other. Same questions as above.

A couple days ago, I thought: I wouldn't want to do this with any other person. I would want to do it only with a person whom I can trust to be purely loving.

New topic: I would like to call you on Saturday or Sunday. What would be the best times? (Best times to reach me are Saturday morning 9-10 a.m. — unless I have a group then — or Sunday evening, 10-11 p.m. That's Pacific Time. Other times to reach me are 6-6:30 p.m. Mondays and Wednesdays, just before my groups, which start at 7.)

I'm enclosing some photocopies of material on writing books. Since I'll be sending you more photocopies from time to time, let me tell you that I always mark things that seem important to me, and if there's an X in the margin, it means I disagree. An ! or an * means I agree strongly or find the material very important.

As a good style to borrow from, I recommend the Bry book mentioned in the enclosed booklist.

Now some comments about your project. You're focused on archetypes, but I wonder if symbols might be a better concept. I've always thought of archetypes as being limited in number (according to Jungians), but symbols could be anything. If you'd like to explore this concept, I recommend the books of Ira Progoff (list enclosed). I recommend them anyway, and I'm enclosing a little piece I wrote about Ira. The last paragraph especially has great meaning for me. Note that Progoff does a Dialogue with works, which I think you might find useful to explore. I've been in his workshops, and I've given similar workshops, so if you want to know more about this, let me know.

In your letter you say "as opposed to formal traditional vocational tests." Do you mean to replace them with archetypal work? Or use them to supplement archetypal work?

I like your explaining callings as spiritual urges. They are indeed, and they can be ignored only at our own peril; the price of squelching them is deadness, & chronic depression (perhaps mild but pervasive and destructive). Callings, I think, are not just for religious people but for anyone. In fact, spirituality must be divorced from (maybe not divorced from; just separated from) traditional theories; must come to each person, religious or not, as in the final Progoff paragraph; will come (as it did to one member of my group who is now an atheist and was once a Southern Baptist) as "intuitive impulses coming from a deep source." "That is spirituality," I told him, and he is now mulling that over. We must, I think, encourage a spirituality which is freed from any constrictions of Scripture; it must be our own, based on our own experiences, not on something we are given as either dogma or theory. We must meet God (or whatever we wish to call IT—and there may even be more than one It) face to face.

I love you,

FRIDAY, JANUARY 20, 1989 11:40 AM

Oh, Jim—

I was hoping to be hearing from you soon, missing our frequent interactions, and last night your incredible, beautiful letter arrived. So, sandwiched in between getting home late and leaving again for my Peace Time group, I read and re-read your letter (3 times). That is the most beautiful letter. I was moved to the core, as I seem to be with you. Today, as I sit in my office (and I want to describe it to you later), I have some insight into what this experience with you is for me.

The experience goes back to that first day in your room—a day of real significance for me—a Day of Naming. I've known the power of naming for a while and have even taught my classes about it, but it is an amazing, transforming thing to be the one who is named. You named me first—"Kathy, do you know you have a work of genius here?" Do you have any idea what it is like to tenuously offer some work so close to your heart, sensing its giftedness, but not daring to trust that anyone could see it. And then to have someone without hesitation speak a word of affirmation, blessing, and receiving of it? Well, I tell you, it is life-changing, core-empowering. Then you not only named my work, but you told me that apart from my work, the essence of who I am was so powerful and impelling to you that you wanted it for your own life. My God, that is beyond my describing. Now your letter comes and I am more deeply moved into an experience of the Goddess within myself (as Svetlana has named me). For me, this is a humbling, esteem-building paradox of an experience. To have inspired you enough to change your behavior/reactions is one thing; to have touched you/met you at the level of being in you to guide you is mind blowing. For me that is part of what was meant by "The Word became Flesh and dwelt among us." All I can say is Thank you, Jim, for naming me, loving me, seeing me and receiving Me. It's a transforming experience for me. And I'll tell you how it's been evidenced: I have been a powerhouse of activity on my UGS work; others have sensed some aura of spiritual openness in me and have shared things of themselves I have never heard from them; one of my colleagues who defends his own vulnerability/spirituality with chronic clowning sat in my office and offered to open the door verbally for me to do workshops on spirituality and vocation at the center where he consults; and Hale observed, "You are so womanly!" So you see how powerful your touch on my life has been.

As to your gift of strength and all the other wonderful attributes of yourself which you have spilled into me, I am quite concretely experiencing it as a solid, strengthening rod within me — an unshakable place of centering and grounding and trust in myself. I don't understand this Mystery of relatedness and mutuality we are sharing. But I revel in it and absolutely cherish it.

I want you to be able to image me in my office, so let me describe it for you. I think it must have been a bland place before I moved in: putty colored walls and blinds over the three tall windows to match; one institutional green 7-foot bookshelf; one scarred old bookshelf; two army green file cabinets; one cypress typewriter table; an oldish wooden desk and even older wooden swivel chair. But I live here, and I must create a space that nurtures and inspires me; welcomes and blesses others. The putty walls are transformed with framed posters by Edna Hibel (my favorite artist). One of a profiled mother and child as if behind a veil; one called "compassion through the generations" of an intergenerational family of sort of Indian (as in India) looking women; and one called "a celebration of life" of a girl swirling with a bouquet of flowers. The blinds are raised to let in the beauty of a live oak tree outside my window, covered in resurrection fern (Joey, my inner little black boy gets to feel like he's living in a tree house). The green bookshelf is full of chemical dependency, etc. books, special awards I've won, and a holy card icon of a white pelican on a cross, ripping its breast in sacrifice, plus a little framed picture of the happiest little mouse dressed in suspenders and tripping his way across the clothesline of a cranky Mrs. Spider! (Both were given to me by my friends at my former job.) The cypress table has a wicker tray with green teapot and flowered mugs. My desk has a brass lamp with navy lampshade. (I hate to work just in fluorescence; incandescence warms my heart.) I also have a candle, silk flowers, crystals given me by a student, and some beloved books. So this is where I'll be doing much of my doctoral work and all of my schoolwork and where I'm writing you today.

New subject: My baby sea lion is a joy; he sits on the night stand by my bed. Cali loves him too. Each time I see him, I think of you and your utter support to me. I am also still chuckling and celebrating that wonderful vignette of solid masculinity as you handled the security guard at the airport. What a delight! And a moving picture of your response to me (as I talked to you about it afterwards) nodding your head in your own special way and saying, "You're goddammed right!" and, "Is that okay for me to say to you?" Utterly delightful you are.

I'm now in my car outside the post office, and the wind is blowing hard from the north. I just had a couple more things I wanted to say to you, and I'm trying to retrieve them (on a full stomach of Chinese Shrimp Delight)…Let's see, I'm thinking…Oh yes.

There is a sacred, secret place in me that I can't and don't want to even touch with words. But I want you to know it's there. It's the place created and filled with you and your response to my request from you. You gave perfectly, I want you to know. And that's part of what makes it sacred. I won't continue talking about it, lest I bruise it. I just trust that the soul communion and sweet empathy we share will confirm it to you.

Oh, and the final thought I wanted to share is of the spiritual gift you've given me. You see, I've gone through a time (several years now) of moving away from some former fundamentalism. I don't go to church; I don't (and can't) read the Bible; I'm turned off by fundamental Christianity. Yet, I am God's to my core. It has not fit my pictures, nor does it fit those of my more fundamental friends. And here you come, saying you see living spirituality in me, and you want it. Thank you. It confirms to me that I am integrating my spirituality and sensuality. Joy! You have been my priest in a way! Any my daddy! And my friend! And my love! And my soul mate!

You have my love —

Kathy

TUESDAY, JANUARY 24, 1989 7:30 PM

Dear Kathy Jo,

Your wonderful letter arrived today, and I drank it in. I love feedback from you; for example, about the security guard at the airport. To me that seemed quite ordinary, what I did; your writing about it gave me a new perspective on myself. I also like the fact that you can spell not only incandescence but fluorescence! And I like the way you respond to the things I say and do; that is, that you respond to each of them, giving a personal reaction, instead of writing, for example, "That was a nice letter; now let me tell you what I did today." You are aware.

New topic. As boys, we men learn about things like electric motors, and I want to suggest a metaphor. A motor needs what is called a load—some work to do. Otherwise, it spins and spins and quickly burns itself out. With a load, the motor is fulfilled, so to speak. You are that for me: a something (I surely don't want to call you a load) that receives what I offer, that affirms and welcomes it, that provides a place for it (as a woman has a secret loving place for a man's sperm).

And so I don't have to spin uselessly; you are willing to receive what I offer. And I do the same for you; I receive your fullness. And as we do this mutually, we are both enriched, and little tender green shoots in each of us are drawn forward and encouraged to grow, basking in the other's acceptance, soaking up the life-giving waters the other gives.

Now, if we want to continue doing this, and I

think we do, it will require taking risks, and I want to encourage both of us to do that.

My declarations of love for you are no longer risky (though they once were). And I sense some risks that you have taken: Can I really be close to him? Can I trust him? Can I really call him, or will he be too busy? Dare I ask him to inseminate me, or will he take it the wrong way? Good risks.

What I'm saying is that I want us to take even more risks—say things about which we might think, Oh I couldn't say that! Risk making mistakes. Risk triggering stuff in the other person (because we're willing to work on it if it comes up, right?). As an example of my risk-taking, I mean the sentence above where I talk about sperm. Will she feel repelled? Will she misunderstand? Maybe I should tone it down.

Now, if you ever feel uncomfortable with anything I say or write I want you to tell me. THIS IS VERY IMPORTANT TO ME. That is, I want to take more risks in saying things to you, but I'd like an agreement from you that you will tell me of any negative reactions. Okay?

We are not ordinary people. There's no book where we can look up information on how to have the kind of relationship we're developing. It's sui generis. We are indeed inventing it as we go, and I'm so happy with the way it's going, and I want more, and I want us to see our relationship as a THING in its own right, with a need to unfold in its own way, as we nourish it and look on with awe and surprise, perhaps, at what will happen next.

If all goes well, I'm suggesting, we're going to get

into some deep places with each other. I don't know what they are, but I sense them there—a potential, an opportunity that you and I have the courage to explore.

Is this something you'd like to do? (I ask that, I know, without your knowing exactly what I'm talking about.)

In connection with this, I want to say that there is something else I can give you, something that will indeed strengthen you. It is the ideas, concepts, principles, and skills that I have learned in my work. They are designed expressly to give people strength and structure to handle very deep, very intense feelings. I want to give you that, if you wish.

I hope I have said the above clearly.

New topic. I'm impressed at how our letters that cross in the mail seem to respond to each other. Your talk about non-orthodoxy, my comments on Progoff.

Thank you for telling me about the place deep inside you where I live. I have such a strong sense of that. (Aren't we unusual people? I think there has been nothing like us before.)

This letter of mine is not as poetic as a former one, and my inner critic is chastising me for that, and I'm challenging it by saying, "I have the right to write a prosaic letter, so shut up. Kathy Jo and I have lots of ideas to talk about; we're just getting to know each other."

I'm enclosing a copy of a little newsletter I used to publish, with an article on dreams which, at the time I wrote it, had only a minor meaning for me but now has much more.

And here's a poem from my scrapbook I'd like to

share with you. It's by Brendan Gill:

WICKLOW

Things by our sharing them put on sacredness.
Even an ill chance can make holy for us
Places and occasions. See how these hills
Are hallowed by our having been lost among them?
We walked in merriment till we were tired,
Lay down, and slept them into being blest.

Isn't that nice? Let me know if you'd like more poems.

The ending of your letter was so warming for me. I do want to be priest-like for you; daddy; friend; your love; and especially your soul-mate. And perhaps at times your little child (when I need comforting), your mentor and teacher (as you are mine), your stalwart companion in our great work.

I Love you,

FRIDAY, JANUARY 27, 1989 10:10 AM

Dear Jim,

I'm frustrated! I'd really like to talk to you more. I've wanted to write you before this, but this is the first chance I've had all week. I guess the core thing I want to communicate is that I think of you very often; think about processing some event or idea with you. So may our spirits commune even when I can't physically stop to write or call. The feeling I'm getting right now is an assurance that they do. There. That's better.

I am so revved (reved). Two meanings: 1) revved, as in my engines are roaring — I'm going a mile a minute internally and externally. That is a trip for me, because I am usually so calm and even-energied. I feel like I am in a swiftly flowing stream, being whooshed along by the current. But let me tell you I am not resisting. I am enjoying the heck out of the ride! There is great joy in this for me. 2) The other meaning is reved — one "v" as in reverence. I do reverence this process. It is holy for me. The image I have is that I am like a puzzle piece that has found its place. I was made for this. It is awesome. Do you know the prayer posture, "I fall on my face before God"? Well, that's where I am living. Each day brings such a rich offering of synchronistic events, it is almost beyond my flesh to endure. For example, Evan my friend and counselor has come across two articles in professional journals that absolutely contribute to my study (e.g. "Mental Imagery in Career Counseling & Life Planning: A Review of Research and Intervention Methods" — complete with about a hundred references). Books have come to me with no apparent effort on my part. And (this is so sweet, as in succulent, you'll love it) more confirmation from my students. The other night during class break, one of my students gave me a glowing-faced affirmation, "Kathy, being in your class, I feel like I've been to church." And she meant it in its best sense, I could tell. Then you send me that beautiful packet on writing (bless you!). Ron sent me an address of a publisher who has requested book-length manuscripts on Jungian topics. I'm filing that away as a promise. And there's more. But you get the picture. Now, I want to communicate with you about your questions and about the article you sent me.

First, thank you for your sensitivity in opening your task-oriented letter with an affirmation of love and connection for me. That was perfect; warmed my heart, connected with me at that deep place. Thank you, Jim. You are truly a soul-mate for me. By that I mean, someone who connects with me at my deepest need, knows just what to say, and meshes in a dynamic interactive interchange at each turn. It is a joy. And a mystery to me. Yes, we did affirm each other. I don't know that I can definitively answer your sweet questions. But, I'll just give you my thoughts. Irene de Castillejo in Knowing Woman (I love that book) says that there is a phenomenon called meeting. In it, two people see each other, connect with each other, and give life to each other. Veils drop away, distractions drop away, and a core meeting takes place. I think we had (and have) a deep meeting. She talks of this as an ideal, rare, yet attainable human interaction. How did we do it? I don't know. To tell you the truth, it totally took me by surprise. If I was looking for that, I didn't know it. We must have both been prepared for it, in a very open and loving place within ourselves. For me, it came like a dawning of recognition. I have an image of you and I sitting in our places

54

in Curlew — you to my right, at the end of the table — me not knowing you. And then, I slowly, very slowly, turn in my seat, and with a comfortable, warming, thawing, I settle into a place of recognition: I receive you. I know you. Why, I love you! Purr. And that's as close as I can come to explaining it. It's really not an explanation at all. Just a knowing. I have had "meetings" with others before. I had a meeting with Cara there. But it wasn't the same. Cali and I live a lot of our relationship in meeting. But then, the mundane everydayness weaves in and out of it too. I have meetings with my students and with my prayer group friends. But they're all at different depths. You are special. Unique. Touched a spot in me that seems to have been prepared for you to touch it. So how can I compare it to any other? That would be a sacrilege. How can I compare them to you? That would be a sacrilege.

Yes, we introjected each other. For me, that was a truly creative act. And one of the highest order of which I'm emotionally, psychically, and spiritually capable. There was an exchange of essence that contained the matured, fertile goodness of what we've each gained through our lives. We chose to give it to each other to fill some gap in each of us. A mutual need. But again, I almost feel like I'm profaning it to talk about it. It's strange. I want to talk about it, and I'm glad you do too. But mostly I think the words I use should just celebrate it, not analyze it. So forgive the analytical stuff. I do celebrate and am deepened and enlivened by what we share. Thank you, Jim. Thank you, God. Thank you, generous Universe. Thank you too for honoring this by saying you wouldn't want to do this with any other person. Do you know how to warm and melt me, or what?

Now for some content. I have to take issue with your

saying that there are a limited number of archetypes. Jung and other archetypal psychologists have said that there are as many archetypes as there are experiences in life. But that's sort of nitpicking, because I do plan to use symbols and archetypes in my study. Thank you for the Progoff article. It was new information to me. I love his premise of not "diagnosing and reducing to normalcy." You tell 'em, Ira! I loved his describing his groups as having a reverence and spontaneous spirituality with love and unity like "buoyant water" that holds people up. I also agree with entrusting people with their own processes. And yes, I agree, the spirit comes through the individual. We have experienced that, haven't we?

I guess I have a place in me that is "opposed" to formal traditional vocational tests. But I don't want to take that stand in my work. Thanks for sharing the light. I'll really want to moderate that in my work to "in adjunct to" or as "alternative to" traditional vocational tests. Thanks. I'd like to hug you right now. Here.

"We must encourage a spirituality free from constrictions of scripture." Yes, I have experienced scripture as constricting and as freeing. So, I've put it down for now (as in laid it aside). Yet, inside of me, verses come to feed me: "I have called you by name." "Fear not, little flock, it is your father's good pleasure to give you the kingdom." As you say, we must meet God face to face. Our spirits are at one about this.

I am reading your "Anthetic Values." I love the way you write. It's like being with you.

I like your idea of Anthetic self-acceptance. I have learned (and dynamically deal with in my own life) that what works in transforming my life is to be willing to include and embrace what I see in myself, even if I don't like it at first.

It has been life-changing for me. But I know about trying to repress too—Yuck! I am fascinated by your info on Anthetic processing—not transforming one feeling into another—but maintaining each with its own integrity, then tracking and working with them. I like the integrity (that's the word I want to emphasize) you give to each feeling. So, I'll continue reading and interacting with you.

I want to get this in the mail, so just a couple things more. Time to call me: Monday night (6–6:30 is good); 6:30 Wed. (your times). I have class Tuesday & Wednesday, but I get home by 6:00 your time, but then I haven't eaten supper and really need to (8:00 pm my time). Saturday 9–10 good usually (unless I'm out running errands). Friday nights are good, say 7:00–8:00 your time. Sunday night 10–11 is too late for me. I crater! Sunday mornings are great. Can you talk then? I guess we'll just have to negotiate. It seems you're most free late at night, and I'm not a late night person, so we'll have to work around that. Anyway, let's talk soon. I'll probably call you tomorrow, so you'll talk to me before you get this.

I am enclosing a copy of my colloquium evaluation. I thought you'd enjoy it. You'll see and hear yourself in it, of course!

For now, receive a great bathing of love and feminine warmth from me, Kathy Jo style! Be empowered to be you—

I love you—

JANUARY 30, 1989 9:30 A.M.

Dear Jim—

I am so hungry to talk with you. Your letter offered an opening to more risk taking. O here's more from me—a need to process with you my inner struggles. (Will he think I'm neurotic? Immature?) There is discomfort in being home. I've come back expanded, changed. Well, actually, maybe not changed so much as deepened into places I haven't accessed. I am strong, in touch with my personal power and magnificence; named; inseminated. All my loved ones have received me back with love. Yet we're having to negotiate our relationship with my growth. That is so uncomfortable for me. Somewhat of a feeling of a suck toward backsliding into hiding my light under a bushel. But there is a roar in me that will not stand for that. The three major people in my life here are, of course, most affected. Hale and I talked last night, and he really put light on it for me. He said, "Kathy, you came back changed—a woman; in touch with your power. It is awesome and I've been jealous of your growth, your experience." Yet he's inspired by it, so we'll work through that. Cali is a little afraid of my relationship with you—ambivalent. She sees the love, bonding, and power and fears a sexual outworking. My mother called and tried to put a guilt trip on me for not calling her this weekend. (I don't usually call her anyway on weekends.) So I get her fear of my individuating—afraid I'll emotionally abandon her. All sorts of other close friends and acquaintances have expressed that they're watching me, seeing the power, and putting their lives up to the light of my experience. So the outcome for me internally is some turmoil; perhaps a little growth ambivalence. And the strain of again detaching from taking care of my loved ones emotionally, making sure they don't feel discomfort and hurt. I know you can speak to me on this. I wish we were together as you do. But with a letter, I'll be able to read it over and over till it soaks in. Anyway, thanks for listening to this right off the bat. I would prefer to start with loving, connecting words, but I had to clear this out first. A final word on this: I set you free of having to take on my discomfort and make it go away. I ask only for your wisdom, your brotherhood, and your teaching of me. I think that I got the message at colloquium from the seminar people that this would be a common experience; that we'd need support and that our loved ones would have their own journey in conjunction with ours. So that comforts me.

Another note of business. You'll notice that I've included the reference list from the Religion Index. It's purely a request. Please just look for these if you have time and energy. But let me know, okay? If you can't get to them or can't find them, I'll go to New Orleans. (Don't they sound contributory to my study? I hope I can find them.)

Now to more connecting things… I read your letters over and over. I too love your specific references to things I say. (More interconnectedness.) I love your motor load metaphor. It was beautiful. You should have seen the process that went on in me as I read that paragraph. First, resistance! "What is he talking to me about boys and motors for?" Then, oh melt, you translated perfectly to me. For me, this represents how you translate the masculine for me, make it meaningful and relatable for me and even delightful. Thank you. And I am so happy to be a load for you. I love your talk of a "secret loving place for a man's sperm." You didn't offend me. That was precious. Please don't apologize for your prosaic letter.

Whether in prose or poetry, you touch me deeply. (You can give your Inner Critic a kick in the ass for giving you trouble on that one!)

More risk...I will tell you my negative reactions as they arise. We can work through them, so be assured I'll risk that. Yes, we are inventing this relationship. It blows my mind. (Does he think that statement is too trite? Juvenile?) We are nourishing it and allowing it to unfold. It doesn't fit any pictures. It's long-distance, yet paradoxically (I had to look up the spelling on that!) deeply intimate. My mind wants to do traditional things with it. I think, oh, he must too. He'll go away, because I'm far away, not moving geographically, not sexually consummating. Are you really willing to create something new, extraordinary? And to be with the pain/joy of it? Am I? This is scary to me to write. My stomach is tense. I'd rather skirt it. But I refuse to prick-tease this relationship. The power we've shared is in the utter honesty and out-frontness with which we communicate. I refuse to be sucked into a lesser, shallower relationship. Please address these thoughts, okay?

Yes, I do want your strengthening gift to me of skills to handle intense feelings and experiences. I guess that's what I was asking for early on.

I love the poem you sent. "Things by our sharing them put on sacredness." Exact description of Asilomar and us. & "Slept them into being blest." Ah...

Yes, you can be all the roles to me. (Thank you for accepting.) Including my little child & mentor & teacher (as I shall be for you) & my stalwart companion. Beautiful.

Well, I was blown away by your bulletin with the dream article. My god, 1982?? You articulated questions & issues that are exactly what I am studying. "Because we internalized the negative messages and decided to buy into them, we learned to cover up our Dream." "What we must do is go back to when the Dream was still alive." That's exactly what I want to do in my workshops. And will be trying out the last two Thursdays in February and 1st two in March when I offer my workshop to the community. Bless me, father in this. I also liked Levinson's ideas of the mentor and the Special Woman. Am I that for you? May I be?

So in that vein, I'm anxious to hear more of your doctoral processing. I want to know more details of your work. I read the copy of your letter to Della and would like to hear her response. Could you tell me more or again about your concept of noetics? Also more on the spirituality in your work. I would love to hear these things and to give you my feedback and empowerment.

Some personal feedback now. When I talk to you on the phone, I love the way your voice gets all warm and happy when you find out it's me on the phone. I love the way your voice sounds. And that there is always laughter and joy rippling right under the surface. That is a delight. I love that you want to tell me you love me. Well, I love you!

How did your workshop go? And Sunday's day with your group? I prayed for you and sent support your way. I do that a lot.

I had a breakthrough while talking to you. Remember my dream at Asilomar? The Swedish woman needed another weapon to defend herself against the hoods. (My need to have a weapon to protect myself, my feminine, and my work.) Well, I told you, I think that I have a sword now. And there was an immediate connection with my dream. I now have my weapon. And you should see how beautiful it is—a gleaming sword with a gold handle very shiny and very lethal! Hooray! Your touch on me has helped produce it and Bruce's (my adjunct) is going to help me hone its use. You will too.

Yes, please send me more poetry. I love it and the connection with you.

Here is a quote I ran across this week and want to share with you: "It is a high inducement to the individual to ripen, to become something in himself, to become world, to become world for himself for another's sake; it is a great exacting claim upon him, something that chooses him out and calls him to vast things." Rainer Maria Rilke

Beautiful articulation of my study and of my relationship with you.

I love you,

Kathy

FRIDAY, FEBRUARY 3, 1989 6:00 PM

Dear Kathy Jo,

All week I have been functioning up near the surface — at the ripply part of life, where there are jangly things to do, checks to write, announcements of groups to put in the mail, etc., and now that I begin writing to you, I move down into that deeper part where love and peacefulness enfold me — that place that you have somehow led me to, just by speaking from your own depths. What a marvelous thing.

One of the many things I like about you is that from you I get immediate feedback about what I do that you like, which is a very new thing for me; in most of my close ("close") relationships, the woman did not have that freely-flowing responsiveness that you have (you see, I actually like comparing you with others), and I want you to know how much I treasure it. For example, when you wrote that you liked the love and connection I offered as a preface to my task-oriented letter. What you are doing is teaching me how to love you, and I am a willing pupil. Loving you is so good for me.

The same day I got your letter I went to the John F. Kennedy University library and photocopied several pages from de Castillejo's book Knowing Woman. Now, this might seem like a perfectly ordinary, mundane thing, but it is quite extraordinary. First, that you suggested the book. I'm not used to such responsiveness. (At Asilomar I asked one of our colleagues about an important issue for me: should one's close relationships be with those in the field? She said yes — not only so you can get input, but also so you don't have to explain so much. So I'm happy that I have both from you.) I talked the other day to my friend Ray Vespe, and he added a third advantage: so you can share your work; not only by talking about it but also by working together — doing, in his case, couple therapy; to which I mentally added, and leading groups together. So that issue is now settled for me: I will seek out friends only from within my field.

Now, where was I? (I'm thinking…) Oh, yes: all I have to do is mention something, and you introduce me to an author I've never heard of. Input. So my photocopying those pages symbolizes my decision about friends. (That's the second point.)

I found de C's words on meeting to be illuminating, though I would prefer the term communion. What you and I have is more than meeting. I think of it in terms of permeability: we are permeable to each other. Most people are impervious: our words bounce off their hard, shiny surfaces. But we let each other in. It's a joy.

(I love your image of me at Curlew, you turning to receive and love me. That is indeed it, and I look up and smile and become open to your love.)

As to our mutual introjections: I have actually received in the mail a review copy of a book about such things! Photocopies of selected pages enclosed. I'm not sure I like the word kything, nor do I agree with everything the authors say, but I like the concept. Any reactions?

Now, you ask me to forgive the analytical stuff; you wonder if you are profaning what happened by talking about it. I want to argue in favor of talking. (Of course, you do say, "I want to talk about it, and I'm glad you do too.")

Words are extremely important to me. I come from a family of origin where no one explained anything to anyone; things just happened; there was no discussion. Moreover, I happen to be a highly verbal person. I need words. And I believe that words can encourage the process of growth. For one thing, we both agree that naming empowers. Words are expressive, and when expressed (especially if voiced), leave space for the next thing to emerge. If not voiced, one is stuck; one's process is blocked. Do you agree?

Words serve as a kind of scaffolding that permits deeper exploration, too. First I have an experience. Then I describe it with words. Next time, I can move deeper, following the words I have already constructed. So I get farther and farther. (The analogy breaks down here.) It's sort of like building a bridge out over the water: I go to the end of the words I have made and dive in, then return and build further out, and so on. Does this make sense?

But there are two dangers with words: One is if the inner critic uses them as grist for its mill, in its attempt to stifle creativity. The second danger is when one loses contact with grounding experience and flies off into abstractions, where almost anything goes.

But if one can overcome these two dangers, words can be useful.

Here's a quote from de C: "Woman is vaguely aware of being herself in direct touch with the mysterious source, but her awareness is so diffuse that she can seldom even speak of it. She needs, passionately needs, the animus's torch (that's me) to light up for her the things which she already innately knows, so that she can know she knows them." (Well that's not really me; that's the masculine aspect; but I know how to do it.) That's on page 84.

On page 86: "Through man, woman finds the animus who can express the soul she has never lost. Her burning need is to trust her own diffuse awareness, to know what she knows and to learn to speak of it, for until it is expressed she does not wholly know it."

Words will not profane an experience if they are gentle and caring. Please, sweet Kathy Jo, let me encourage you to learn not to fear words.

Now, about vocational tests. I've found that tests of ability are useful for me. It was good to know what my IQ was, to know that I have really good clerical and verbal abilities, to know that my math is good but not as good as my verbalness, that my ability to use logic is a bit worse but still okay, and that my ability to organize data (Minnesota Form Board, I think) is superb. All these test results have been important to me in positioning myself: finding my place among others and deciding whether I have the ability to do the work that has called me. So I hope you won't be opposed to them. Interest tests, on the other hand, have been nearly useless to me, or useful only as checklists of possibilities. Once I got the blocks out of the way and once I permitted my inner symbols to appear and transform my life, interest tests were irrelevant. I knew exactly what I wanted to do.

And now something about which I am absolutely

ecstatic: the responsive way you reacted to my booklet! Oh, how nice that is! I hope to hear more, especially critical comments you might have — and engage you on an intellectual level, as I have been doing in this letter What joy to find both love and intellectuality in one person! *** (I stopped typing for a minute and sat and meditated on your lovely face — and smiled, the way I have been smiling so often from time to time while thinking about you.) And I miss you.

Love,

MONDAY, FEBRUARY 6, 1989 11:30 AM

Sweet Kathy,

I have just gotten released from a "should" — I can write you any time; I don't have to respond to a letter. And I can write a short letter, too, responding only to some parts of your letter, reserving others for later, more thoughtful treatment. (Be assured I will try to respond to everything, especially the things you ask particularly about; and if I ever don't, do let me know right away.) Anyway, here's a brief note, written in the middle of writing you a much longer letter, which longer letter you will get soon.

About dependency: One might say glibly that we are after all all dependent on each other, so what's the fuss about dependency? But you and I mean dependency as emotional, not physical. There are two meanings of emotional dependency: dependent on the other person's love and approval for our own self-esteem; and dependent on the other for deep connectedness. The former is a buffer and must be used with great caution, as one would take a drink to feel good and get relaxed but be careful not to get so dependent on alcohol that one feels good ONLY when having a drink, or two, or a whole lot more (of course, your work touches on this). But an alcoholic drink, for those who like it (I happen not to, though I once did), is not in itself a bad thing. What I say about buffers is: Enjoy as many as you can get but don't get addicted to them.

The other kind of dependency — on connectedness — is different. It's a non-buffered pleasure, it seems to me. I have it with my son Kevin and daughter Carol, and I feel good when I make contact with them (by telephone now) and so I feel good when I make contact with you, too. More than good. And if you should say, "you know, Jim, I've been thinking it over, and I guess I don't like you anymore," I would feel some intense pain (and my guess is that you too felt a twinge when I typed that), but I would survive, and my life would still go on glowing from your touch, because the flame (remember my symbol at Curlew?) is now self-sustaining, the flame you and I kindled together (I guess it was on the beach, when you asked me to inseminate you, and I had asked you to take your glasses off; and also when you bestowed upon me your lovely femaleness), but the pain would be sweet, and I welcome it if it's there, because it means I have loved deeply, more deeply than ever before, and that in itself is precious; that in itself is, would be, enough, more than I've ever had.

So dependency? Sure. Some pain involved? I'm willing to take the risk; I'm an old hand at working with pain; it's just a feeling; anyway. Better to risk and feel some pain if it comes than remain closed up and safe.

Another thought on dependency: It's not like with my love-addicted clients, who become dependent on emotionally unavailable people, and who yearn for little crumbs of affection ("Why can't you tell me you love me?"), constantly hungry for more. We do not give each other crumbs, precious Kathy, darling Kathy, we offer each other huge feasts of affection, great banquets of self-opening ideas; and I come away stuffed to the gills with the joy we create. I am always willing to express my love fully (as much as I dare, anyway), as you do too. We do not constrict out loving feelings; we are not afraid of opening to the other (or not much, and we are both dedicated to taking bigger and bigger risks in this); we are not stingy with our feelings; we are willing to let out love gush forth in wilder and wilder ejaculations (yes, let us not fear to). The love that you have unleashed in me frisks through my life, romps in my soul, making every moment glow. I could not give up that marvelous state of being. (Ah, this is becoming another rhapsodic letter; how nice!)

The metaphor that I alluded to at Asilomar was that I was on some sort of vehicle (chariot? Stagecoach?) drawn by three charging horses, high-spirited, which I must control with the reins, who threaten to plunge out of control, one in either direction, or all three carrying me away into God knows what dangers, and I'm doing pretty good at controlling them, damned good in fact, at this new task I never planned for myself, but was indeed ready for, and maybe even planned for, wondering who it would be. Who the girl would be. Yes, girl, if that's okay.

A second metaphor I mentioned is more apt now: I have gotten on a boat or raft of some sort that was floating down a small gentle stream and it was very pleasant and I could get off whenever I wanted, the banks where so close, but then the stream widened, and the water got rougher and faster-moving, and now I must steer carefully to avoid the whirl-pools and rocks and submerged logs, and it takes all the skill I have amassed (which is plenty) to keep it from foundering, but it's exciting, and I love it, and I exult in my mastery of it; it exercises my muscles (some that have been unused for years). It evokes feelings, and ideas, and images I never knew were there.

But now the stream is so wide that I couldn't disembark if I wanted to, and for an instant I feel trapped. If I am trapped, it's in a sweet, precious trap that brings forth much goodness in me and energizes my life like no other trap! Trapped, perhaps, in the way I have trapped myself in my work (being unable now to choose such things as stock market analyst or advertising executive—and glad of it!)—happy to be trapped in such a great trap. Life-ennobling. Enfolded by love.

So here I am on my raft or boat, and the current rushes me faster and faster, and it's so thrilling, and the scenery is so exciting—and I wouldn't trade it for anything. This image is my journey with you, dear Kathy, and I am now committed to something that will take me I know not where, except that I am so willing to go where it wishes, because it is something that my soul has thirsted for all my life. Like a man on the desert, thirsting for water, coming across a lush oasis with green grass and palm trees swaying and clashing in the wind (but is it a mirage? Maybe. No. No! It's the real thing!)—and there's even (in my image) a fine bakery with luscious pastries and a good French restaurant that serves Creole foods with gravy on the rice! And here I'll stay with a sigh of relief at having found it—at last!

I love you, Kathy Jo,

P.S.: I have signed up for the March seminar in Pawling, NY. Jane ("Adoption" Jane) is also a registrant.

P.P.S.: How I wish I could have seen you in your gold and wine silk dress, flashy, projecting your womanliness out into the world, letting others drink it in, presenting your power and your beauty as great wonderful splendid gifts for others to share!

MONDAY, FEBRUARY 6, 1989 9:30 PM

My love, my sweet Kathy—

I want to begin by responding to your request for processing. About your new growth that was triggered by the colloquium and our relationship, and the responses of the important people in your Lafayette life.

Yes, the colloquium is having a profound effect on us, and I suspect others. We have it seems, taken a quantum leap into a new way of being, with its own requirements, which are unfamiliar to us yet. You have reminded me that this is the case. (It was just a sort of orientation session, and all we did was talk about our deepest concerns and then shared our love—and that doesn't, on the face of it, seem so powerful, but the ripples from that are still spreading though our lives; it was a big bang emotionally speaking.) So we've got to talk about it a lot so we can understand it and use it constructively. We need to integrate it in our lives so it can be fully transforming.

And I want to tell you a story that is important to me. A joke, sort of. It seems that there was this tailor and his wife who lived in the back of their shop and saved their money and invested it wisely and built their business, and after many years, they had enough money to buy a big department store. So they went to inspect Macy's, which was for sale, and the man looked over the whole store, top to bottom, after which the real estate agent said, "So what's your decision?" And the man said no, he wouldn't buy it. On the way home, his wife asked him why, and he said, "Because there's no place in the back where you can live."

The moral, of course, is that we carry old assumptions of limitations into new places and decide not to move into those new places because of old assumptions. Change often involves loss of something which we discover, when we make the change, we don't really need any more. But before we make the change we think we do, so we fear the change.

An employee doesn't want to be promoted to supervisor, because she or he would no longer enjoy being one of the guys, or because there would be too much responsibility. When I was 18, I didn't want to go to college too far from home. I felt too insecure. So growth means doing scary things, stretching, as you say, oneself—pushing a bit further than one feels comfortable with. And learning that while growth means giving up some things, it means adding some new things, mostly individuation, exercise of personal power, full development of one's potentials.

Now, one of my lifelong struggles has been to find my position in the context in which I live. As a child, I got many messages from mom and Dad (mostly Dad) that I was defective and inferior. But even mom, who said I was smart and some day would amount to something, for now (she didn't say this, but this was what it added up to): "Go play in your room and invent the atomic bomb, but don't bother the grown-ups." I seemed to get a lot of other negative messages from people as I grew up. To my first therapist, I mentioned wanting to be a psychologist (I was 17), and he said, "Every patient wants to be a psychologist," with a little laugh. Since I was unusually sensitive, this had a great impact on me, although I did declare psychology as an undergraduate major (at University of Illinois), then got my BA (at Wayne State University, in Detroit). I talked to some fellow students about graduate school, and they said, "Watch out for that Miller Analogies Test; it's a tough one!" — I thought I probably couldn't make it.

At the same time, I had gotten very high scores on IQ tests (142 general, 168 verbal), which I conveniently forgot. What I had done when thinking I couldn't get into graduate school was to think I was like other people.

It took me a while (years, in fact) to learn that I was special. That the psychologist's words were appropriate for ordinary people but not for me. That the student's warnings about the MAT were correct for average people but not for me.

Blocking this feeling of being talented was the feeling that if I thought I were special, I was being elitist — putting myself above others — being too big for my britches.

So I did apply for graduate school and was accepted, despite a terrible undergraduate GPA because I was mostly depressed (without knowing it) and unfocused (I did know that). That acceptance was the first step in placing myself correctly. At least, I said, I'm good enough to be admitted.

Throughout graduate school I compared myself to my fellow students. I gradually grew to see that I was much better than they at knowledge about psychotherapy. I got all A's with one exception, an A-minus. So now I knew more about my position. My thesis advisor by the way, confirmed my position, which felt good.

Then I dared to compare myself with my professors! What chutzpah! Slowly, I realized that in ability and general knowledge, I was superior to them all! "How dare you think that," my inner critic said.

And then I began critiquing (i.e., thinking critically about) writers of books on personal growth, and by God, I was better than most of them!

And now at UGS I am finally thrown in with my real peers. Now I know what my position is. So I have had to change my self-image drastically.

The change has also been in my Dream. Once it was, as I mentioned, to have a wife and kids and house in the suburbs; then it became to be a really good clinician; but now (especially after my communion with you) I think I have a world-historical mission. I thought I could bring a new philosophy of life to people (and still do), but after experiencing you and your powerful presence, my calling has now been revealed as much more profound—a spiritual calling of some sort—a calling to be the beginnings of something that will ultimately, perhaps, transform the world. (What hubris! What a swelled head! Shut up, inner critic!)

I am important to the progress of human culture. Or can be. And if I fail, I will at least have tried. Which is enough.

So no longer is my dream that of a wife, kids, and suburban home—a job at Ford Motor Company— retirement at age 65. My dream is my work, and I can say to you, "My work is more important than you,

Kathy," and you, because you are my Special Woman, will say Oh yes.

Maybe not everyone will be ready for receiving my mission, but I am destined to produce it, to implement it. I can do no other.

So now I know my true position. And like the tailor, I no longer ask where's the place in back where I can live—where's the wife and kids (happily I already have those) and house in the suburbs. I have this great mission, which must be served. And if I died tomorrow, it would be okay, because I have recognized my true purpose—which is all-important.

At times I use this as a buffer, but most of the time I feel it as a great calling to which I must be responsible, must serve with integrity and diligence. It is an honor to be the one called for this. If Plato was right, and we choose our lives before birth, then forgot we have chosen, this would have been exactly the right life for me, even with all its problems and hassles and mistakes and pains and lack of material things. They're just ripples on the surface.

But the pursuit of my Dream has entailed some losses in human relationships. First, my ex-wife, Gail, whose dream was the husband-kids—suburban home one. The divorce (which she got) was a painful loss for both us and I cried about it (mostly about what was not to be, a dream that had vanished).

Another loss was my friends in Detroit. They were two or three couples that we invited over, or who invited us, and we talked about surface things, while I thought this was really living. But after coming to California, I have grown away from them.

In California, I thought it was just that it was difficult for me to make new friends, but what was happening was that my ideas about friends were up for grabs now; I didn't know what I wanted in a friend, what standards I had (or even that I could have standards!). I was willing to be friends with whomever wanted me, for whatever reasons. Recently I've been more careful about the reasons people like me and want to associate with me. Some of them like my caring and sensitivity, but not only can they not be caring in return, they become indignant when I ask them for caring. I could have made a lot of "friends," but have deliberately avoided doing that because I didn't know who I was yet and didn't want the pain of having to say goodbye again; one man in Berkeley still likes me and feels hurt and angry that I don't want to associate with him and can't listen to me when I complain about his self-centeredness and judgmentalism.

So now I want to be very selective about who I want for friends (I'm glad you're one of them), because I don't have an infinite amount of time and energy. And because I am no longer content to follow the wife/kids/house model. Or even the model of the clinician who works all day and wants to forget about psychotherapy when he comes home and says, "What's for dinner?"

I am serving a cosmic purpose now, and I must be careful with my time, prioritizing it cautiously. I have a sacred trust that absorbs my whole life, and I must choose my friends in relation to it and not merely in relation to the fact that they are really good people or need me or would be hurt if I didn't give them some time. I cannot personally take care of all the people who would benefit from my caring. I must nourish my personal life so that I can reach thousands, hundreds of thousands, with what I can give.

(Of course, I must keep monitoring myself so I do not become egocentric; it's a difficult and tricky thing I'm trying to accomplish; it would have been easier to follow the Ford Motor Co. model.)

Nor do I want to hurt people's feelings (so to speak) unnecessarily, and if those feelings do get triggered, I will always be ready to help them see the hurt as an opportunity for growth (which they, of course, will not always see the way I do).

To put this another way: I can live only for others, in which case, my great work will go undone, and I will feel resentful (i.e., only to make sure they don't feel bad).

Now, I say all this to you to tell you how I have grappled with some of the issues you are (or may be) facing. I can't give you advice on this, of course; it's too crucial an issue. As one grows, one has some choices with relationships:

Give them up, and feel the pain. (Or make them less consuming of time.)

Incorporate them into the new growth; bring them along; give them some opportunities to learn, to grow; make new demands; trigger their stuff; help them process it. Maybe give them even more importance now.

The turmoil you feel is, of course, a good sign. It means that some old patterns are dying (or about to die) and are fighting to stay alive, perhaps. And that new ones are being born. Whatever has happened at the colloquium to open you up, to deepen you, to expand you, will call you to a new destiny, which the old reactive patterns will fight. However you resolve this struggle, I will be with you, your steadfast friend and companion. Please call on me any time; in the middle of the night I will be there for you, whenever.

I do not want to attenuate your feelings, I want to encourage you to deepen them, to let them blossom. I know how to work with them.

No, I don't think you are neurotic or immature to have this struggle; you are my fellow-struggler, like me; we will do battle together, side by side, you with your gleaming sword, I with my skill and knowledge, shoulder to shoulder, against whatever we need to be against, (such as the inner critic). Yours is the natural struggle of a person in an exciting and painful growth process, and I cheer you on.

Though I did not of course know you before UGS (B.U.G.S.?), I can imagine what you mean by being changed; I do get a sense of that; and I want to assure you that many people may not like the new you, because they fear power and envy it and resent it; they like people who keep a low profile, who are subservient, who are willing to give love and caring but are not expected to express any needs or wishes.

There's a saying in Japanese that goes a long way in explaining their culture (and parts of ours too): "The nail that sticks out will get hammered down." You will begin doing greater things than before, and will be open to criticism now, and misunderstandings, and I can help you with that. Because you and I know we must do what we are setting out to do; we cannot turn back now. There is power inside us that must be honored. And I am with you.

I love you, Kathy Jo

P.S. Let me give you some revised times to call me: 8:30-9:00 a.m. Saturday or Sunday mornings (or any morning for that matter, but rates are cheaper Saturday or Sunday)—Pacific Time. I'll leave my telephone bell turned on.

P.P.S.: I have much more to write but will get this letter in the mail immediately.

SUNDAY, FEBRUARY 5, 1989 10:25 PM

My dear Jim,

It's that cold wintry night. I'm all cozy inside, thinking of you and of our wonderful conversation today. It amazes me that I can risk showing you my broken places and find that you have space for them in your love for me. Thank you. I knew I loved your maturity and the extraordinary way you flesh out your masculinity – gentle strength.

Well, I want to spend the rest of this evening with you and with your work. I've had a cup of coffee so I can stay awake and I'm curled up in a chair with "Anthetic Values" by James Elliott and with my lap pad and lap desk. So here goes, I'll respond as I read along…

Page 9…Childhood Programming…Are "primary" and "secondary self" your terms? Yes, a baby does need that balance between love and security and permission and encouragement to become separate. I would like to see this taught to future parents, to teachers, and to school kids. But then the authorities don't want to have to deal with too much autonomy. It makes for creativity and unboxiness. Schools still are too boxy. I don't think California schools do this, but in Louisiana, older schools with big beautiful windows are now keeping the shades drawn so the kids supposedly won't be distracted. Absurd!

On to inner critic…I love this part! I like your expansion of the idea to emphasize its driving power: "harsh conscience," "internal oppressor," "inner saboteur," "inner propagandist." You see, what you're doing is the masculine gift at its most healing: shining the light on specific things in order to show them up for what they are. Images that fit this are: the mechanic with his hood light, looking for problems in the engine and a good daddy with his flashlight showing the kids that what they thought was the bogeyman was only some branches of a tree.

Inner critic and its coloring of the self as flawed and defective is a powerful image to use with adult children of alcoholics who have damaged self-esteem, and really with anyone from a dysfunctional background (95% of us?).

I like your descriptions of the compensatory self, the replay self, and the defensive self. Have you thought of marketing this for alcoholic/adult child/recovery audiences? It is so apropos. You'd just have to gear your title to that sector: "Disarming the Inner Critic: A Guide to Recovery of the Devalued Self" or something like that. And market to publishers of recovery literature…big business. And an audience hungry to hear what you are saying.

(I am loving this dialogue (?) with you and with your work. I am into it!)

From Self-condemnation to self-acceptance (p. 13) — yes, here's the rub. That value that self-condemnation serves us. I've found that you are right — it's a poor, ineffective way to live. For me, I know it was a real struggle to trust that, "Now there is no condemnation in Christ. " Yet when that broke in upon me — what freedom! So many Christians don't get that — so a great healing contained right in their guide, the scripture, is lost to them.

Unfolding…Premature interpretation — "aha" inside me. I do that. And then I have to repair the damage that does to get to healing. Thanks, Jim, for that explanation. You talk about noetic material coming from a "cramped, folded up" state. Have you ever noticed that some pain/discomfort/

awkwardness is involved when we physically come out a cramped position? Perhaps you may want to address that as part of the process; reassure the reader that that can be expected (that psychological discomfort/pain/awkwardness).

Your talk of processing feelings reminds me of the term "stack attack" that I use. Anger/hurt/etc. at some event often has a whole stack of earlier events underneath and usually has some precipitating occurrence.

Yes, "including feelings in my acceptance bag" humanizes me. I don't think I would have had the power to work with my clients with chemical dependency problems if I hadn't faced and included my own experiences I told you about while we drove to the airport.

Empathic Involvement (p. 20). Strong yet flexible ego boundaries and yes — I find that many of my graduate students are attracted to counseling out of strong empathic personality traits in themselves. The ego boundaries aren't always/even not usually there. They must develop them as they practice caring. I know I did.

Depth Communication — that's us (you and me) isn't it? We just dove (dived??) right in — both of us swimming down to deep waters with each other. Part of why there is so much aliveness and power in our relationship.

I like your Anthetic framing and think it's vital.

p. 26 — This is important. Anthetic relating. There is some unease in me about the Frank and Mary example, feminizing it, Kathy-izing it or whatever. (And I want you to understand that I am not taking issue with your point. I think it's good. It's valid.) But there is some abruptness in "Just because you love me, that doesn't mean I have to do anything." I think some bridge is needed. I think "Just Because" are the offending words for me. Perhaps (and I'm just brainstorming here. Try it on for yourself), "I hear and acknowledge that you love me. And I affirm that I don't have to do anything in response." I guess I like some acknowledgement for Mary and I like an "and" statement, "You love me, and I am free." See what you think.

Anthetic caring and reactive caring — I guess that's what scared me — when I touched the reactive part of myself toward you. Thanks for accepting me in that. It's very healing and freeing. It doesn't have to run me.

Anthetic caring for larger groups…You might read Scott Peck's work on community for further research. I think the book might be titled "A Different Drummer." Or something like that.

Responsibility disengagement — good stuff, good term — strong term (term with strength).

P.37 as you talk about critical thinking, it reminds me of a book I'm reading, Women's Ways of Knowing. The authors (Belenky, et al.) are involved in describing ways women think and construct reality. Critical thinking as you describe it is similar to their description of "constructed knowing," thinking in context, integrating all of the truth. I recommend this book to you to expand and support what you're saying here.

Phase III of training program (p. 39) Yes having similar values is a powerful state for a group to get work done. I know in my prayer group, we've gone through times of value rapport and of non-rapport (when a group of new people come in with different values). It was a real strain in the latter.

I like p. 42–43 Anthetic relaters — nice and concrete. As I read your list, I see you, Jim. You have really introjected/

practiced/made your own this system/way of living. I like it. You left me hungry for more detail — more how to — more examples of Anthetic relating and self-care.

Please explain "orthogonal technique" for empty chair work. I don't know that term.

Well, it's 12:50 a.m. I can't believe I'm still awake after midnight. I've finished your manual. I wish now that we could sit in a cozy coffee shop booth over coffee and doughnuts and dig into a dialogue on all this. Let's do that sometime, okay?

I want to hear more of your work as you progress. It delights me. It teaches me. It connects me with you core to core, and I love that.

Be affirmed, dear heart. You are special, precious. I love your thinking and your feeling, and your spirituality.

I love you, Jim

Till we speak again,

Kathy

P.S. I am enclosing $15 for copies. Thanks again for serving me in this way. And take your time.

THURSDAY, FEBRUARY 9, 1989 9:55 AM

Dear Jim,

And I do mean dear. Your wonderful letter arrived yesterday. Shall I tell you how it touches me? Yes, indeed. I am touched at how you express that deep peaceful loving place that I have led you to. And I love that you in turn give me specific immediate feedback. Thank you for all the naming you do of me. "Freely-flowing responsiveness," you "find both love and intellectuality in me." I love that you notice, receive and celebrate all of me. Yes, I am teaching you how to love me, and I am core-touched that you are a willing pupil (learner!). And I am warmed that "goodness" is connected with your loving me. And you said one of the "many things I like about you." I love that. And I love that you tell me what you treasure. I am very touched by that word, treasure. And I love that you honor the references I am giving you: going the same day to find Knowing Woman. The give and take in our relationship is remarkable. The mutual intellectual and loving interaction is a joy. As you spoke about Ray Vespe's contribution to the advantage list for having close relationships in your field, I thought, gosh I wish we could do some work together. Then right before I drifted off to sleep, or maybe it was when I awoke in the night, the reality of that possibility hit me. I would love to collaborate with you on a book sometime or to lead a workshop or group together. (One idea is a book, handbook, manual and/or workshop on disarming the inner critic for chemical dependency audiences.) Would you be open to something like this? Wouldn't it be great? Perhaps we can be open to a topic that would be mutually satisfying.

Now, on to content in your letter. I think you have a

wonderful point that communion is a better term for what we share than meeting (de C.). (I love the way you think and reason.) The permeability idea is beautiful. Yes, we are permeable to each other. Yes, it is a joy.

I also love the synchronicity of the kything book arriving. Thank you so much for copying these things to share with me. That is very special to me. I have never connected with anyone like this before. (Hale and I do read the same books and talk them over, so I've experienced something like it. And Cali and I do the same. All precious to me.) But I've never had a written correspondence at this depth. This is a gift to me, you know. Because I am learning (getting to practice, experience) giving voice (written and spoken) to my intellect and to my heart. And you receive and honor it so dearly. Thank you for your correcting me re: talking. I honor your need for words; for naming, for voicing. What you said confirms the book I am reading, Women's Ways of Knowing. The authors make the point that women have been silenced, have not had a voice, and have not been listened to when they have tried to express themselves. Yet women are learning to have voice; to work through ideas, to risk expression. I think this must be my lesson and my encouragement and my affirmation for my doctoral work. (I must include this in my personal growth portion of the Learning Agreement and Project Demonstrating Excellence.) I accept the loving lesson from the book and from you. I will learn not to fear words; not to fear my own thoughts, my own voice. And I will be practicing that learning with you. I know you lovingly receive it. And honor it enough to affirm and to reason with me. For example, your defense of vocational tests. I like your voicing of specifically what they gave you, "finding my place among others and deciding whether I have the ability to do the work that has called me." Beautiful. May I quote you? I am not opposed to tests. I use them and have used them. But I want you to understand that my heart and mind are turned in another direction. And the passion I express about that direction drives my work and gives me courage. I believe I am a voice (and will grow in being that voice) for the legitimacy of inner guidance for vocational choice making. So it may look like opposition to tests. No. It's taking out the sword to defend a way that has been ignored, denigrated, and neglected. Would you speak more to me about "the work that has called you?" I mean speak about your experience of being called to a work. I am hungry to hear this from you.

You could not have quoted a more perfect portion of Knowing Woman. It perfectly describes my current position ("her awareness is so diffuse she can seldom even speak of it"). I know what I know inside, but to put it in words is my challenge. To articulate the gift and the knowledge I have to give. My need is described exactly ("she passionately needs the animus's torch to light up for her the things she innately knows"). You shone your torch on me and my work when you said, "Did you know you have a work of genius?" And at that point recognition and affirmation dawned. Yes, I do know. Deep thank you, Jim, for that. And it describes what you are doing for me, and I trust will continue to do. (Sometimes I think you are shy about saying things directly to me. It's okay. I'm shy too sometimes.) Did you give me these quotes, because they apply to you and me? My inference is that you did. Am I right? You did say, "The animus's torch (that's me). I know how to do it." I inferred, "that's me toward you, Kathy." Right? "Through man, woman finds the animus who can express the soul she has never lost. Her burning need is to trust her own diffuse awareness (this truth makes tears come to my eyes), to know what she knows and to learn to speak of it, for until it is expressed she does not wholly know it." Exactly my journey. How did you find the most applicable statement to my journey out of that whole book? That's incredible. You are my soul mate to do that. I'd like to cry on your chest right now. (I have a precious image of you holding me at the airport with my head buried on your chest/shoulder, and that's what I'd like again right now. I know you would gladly give it. So I think I'll appropriate that experience right now… I just sat back and let myself feel that until a deep releasing breath came from me.)

Which brings me to the kything article. I love, "to show yourself without any disguise or mask," as you would to your kith and kin. We are doing that with each other. Also "to present your soul to another." I know we are doing that. I think that these will grow. I think we've had some bit of caution about relating "without any disguise or mask." We haven't shown all the glory nor all the pock marks we each have. Yet that's appropriate. It will unfold. I know I want it to. What a precious Indian love charm, "Let her put her soul into the very center of my soul, never to turn away." "Your soul has come into the very center of my soul, never to turn away." Ah… So true. (By the way, and this is an aside, I checked out a book on transpersonal psychologies by Tart. I'll be reading it and wanting to discuss it with you.) This article has some ideas I'd like for us to use. It comes at a needy time inside of me. I've been grieving not getting to be with you in the flesh more and not knowing what to do but bear it. What a flash of possibility to think that we might be able to connect in this deep way. There is intentionality to it I hadn't considered possible. Some ideas I'd like to try with you: 1) intentional meditation to link mentally for a few minutes at a given time each day (they call it triangles). I do think it's possible just for us. I don't care to add a third right now. (2) Coinherence kything – imaging your two bodies as one, your mouth, my mouth are as one mouth, etc. (read p. 125-126 again). It sounds powerful. It makes my heart pound!

P. 139 really seems to describe the mutual introjections we've done. They speak of the issue of self-esteem, but we've done it on the lubricating/strength issues. But you certainly have other qualities I'd like to introject. For example, your easy laugh. I can see you doing it at the colloquium (can't remember content) and over the phone when I said I had spoken to my class on models for rehabilitation, and they said it was so spiritual. And your ability to disarm the inner critic with the question, "What is the truth here?" I like their statement (p. 140) "the truth about who we are is usually far more than we would ever imagine." I want us to reveal that truth to each other and to give that to the world. I also agree with "divine indwelling of the very presence of God within us." Yes, Yes, Yes. I see spiritual (religious) people as missing this. "He/she is still out there somewhere. God's surely not in me." That's unthinkable. My mother and I talk about this. She is aware. I want you two to meet. "Courage." The ability to carry on despite discouragement, etc. Yes, to stand with the negatives bombarding us. My dad modeled that for me in his dying. A very courageous facing of death. You model that courage for me too. So, I'll also be introjecting that. So thank you for the article. I got some good ideas out of it. And tell me your thoughts in response to what I've said.

Thanks too for the copy of your colloquium evaluation.

My dear heart, did you hear the similarity in the way we perceived the experience and in the way we wrote about it? Your language is so rich, and your heart is open. (Do you feel loved by me? I seem to gush all over my letters to you. So you should be getting it!)

I also like your letter to peers. Thanks for elucidating your thinking on various issues. My friend and counselor, Evan, is applying to UGS with a PDE study on conflict resolution. Ya'll might have some contribution to make to each other. He's also worked with oil companies, couples, and attorneys re: conflict resolution. You know I want to do some peer days with you. So look to New Orleans and your certification meeting. Also if you come to Houston (and Lafayette) we could do one with Della in Lake Charles. I'm waiting to see what seminars I'll do this year. I can't remember when the research one in Minnesota is, but I'm pretty sure it doesn't fit my schedule. I'm enclosing a non-UGS conference I'll be doing in May. Want to come? I'm going to use it for internship time. It's for me to do. These guys have stuff to teach me. (They're giving me a break on room and board—$100 off since I'm a student.) I'm sending a copy to Ron and to Elizabeth too. I'll be buying tapes of the sessions so I'll send you any that I sense would interest you.

Have you ever taken the Myers-Briggs? I haven't but I've done a shortened version, the Kiersey Temperament Sorter, and I type Introverted, Intuitive, Feeling, and a mix of Judging/Perceiving. No surprise, really. Does typing bother you? I'd like to know if you have leanings on type. I'm not big on labeling or typing but it's kind of fun to do. I don't live by it. Because even though I'm introverted, I love teaching my classes, even the big ones. I think I access other parts of me—exercise my feeling/intuition and intellect to contribute to my students.

I hope you're enjoying the tape. Let me know if you'd like more music or if my taste is just too offensive to you! I'm really okay if you don't like all the same music. I figured you'd enjoy the tape just as a glimpse of me, even if you didn't care for the music for yourself. Am I right? I'd like to know what you like too. I can still hear you and Svetlana singing and you by yourself. You aren't shy about that, are you? You have a wonderful voice, both speaking and singing.

Now I have a request to make of you: If we were both in a Judeo-Christian (really a Christian) vein, I'd say, I want you to pray for me. And I still want to use that word—pray for me. Yet my sense is that it will be something like holding me consciously in yours and God's heart; sending loving, supportive, empowering vibes my way. And I have a specific time. I'll be doing a workshop starting Thurs., Feb. 16 from 5:30 to 7:30 CST. It's called, "Vocational Choice Making: An Inner Journey" and will incorporate and risk offering my ideas on inner work for vocational choices. I want to relax into this risking, this challenge. I want to be open to what I can learn from the participants. And I want to trust the process. So if you would support me in prayer, I would feel very strengthened and loved. Thank you.

I think I'm through for now, and I must get to my reading (Womanspirit Rising and Women's Ways of Knowing). I love visiting with you like this. And I miss you too.

My love to you,

Kathy

FEBRUARY 11, 1989

Dear heart,

Just a quick note in order to get a copy of my letter to you that had not made it to you yet. I was so upset! I just knew that you had it Thursday and that we'd be able to speak about it some when I spoke to you today. Please let me know if the original got to you, because it had cash enclosed for copies, and I'll want to send you that money if you didn't get it. This also leaves me insecure about whether you are getting other correspondence from me. So...did you get the letter on notebook paper with a bookmark enclosed? And did you receive my tape and Valentine card? Let me know. Elizabeth sent me something that took about 6 days to reach me, because it went to Mississippi first, even though she had typed the address clearly and correctly.

Also, let me rhapsodize (I like your word) about our phone conversation. It left me elated; enraptured; enfolded. I was hyper for about two hours afterward! You stimulate me emotionally, intellectually, spiritually and physically. You love me as I would hold the ideal of how I would want to be loved by a man. That is an awesome thing to experience in reality! Thank you for being you and for sharing yourself with me. I loved your questioning of my spirituality, giving me an opportunity to attempt to articulate what I know. I was so touched by your spontaneous prayer to God for me. That was precious to me; beautiful. My gut is so moved and warmed right now just thinking about you. I cannot yet put it all into words. Sigh.

As for our mutual inspiration to work together, I am ecstatic. There is not the least bit of doubt in me that it would be wonderful. So I am ready to talk seriously about your San Francisco workshop idea on spirituality. Can you speak in more detail about it? You were so fearful to say it, and I was so beside myself to hear you offer it, that we both just touched it and ran, like two excited children touching some fascinating beautiful piece of crystal, then streaking off.

Well, I want to get this in the mail to you so more later. I am enclosing a copy of Ben's (my adjunct) newsletter. I loved the Lily Tomlin quote. It captures my experience beautifully. Also, let me know what you think of his words on gender differences. I love this interchange with you. In fact, I love you.

Kathy

WEDNESDAY, FEBRUARY 8, 1989 6:30 PM

Dear One,

I've just come from a lecture entitled "The Impossibility of Psychology," by a PhD from Yale (philosophy), at Wright Institute (a school for PhDs in clinical psychology), and I felt nervous at first during the question-and-answer period, or as it began, but I was the first to speak, and I asked a complex and trenchant question (which the speaker did not understand, as a matter of fact), and I was able to do so relatively comfortably because a few minutes before I asked it, the following thought came to me out of the blue: I am wrapped in the enfolding love of my beloved; there is nothing here to fear. I felt it very concretely, something I've never experienced before with anyone. This is the first time I've felt your love so powerfully. (I thought I was the one giving you strength.) I'm going to meet with this philosopher and press my point further. (Thank you.)

Here's some material on Progoff. Let me know if I can suggest some ideas for your workshop; I've had a lot of experience in this area.

I kiss your letters and read them over and over, especially the little one where you said you needed a connection with me and opened your mind and heart, inviting me in (I did go, and it is warm and soft and luscious there).

I'm re-reading Women's Ways of Knowing and would like to discuss it with you.

We are daring to confess to each other the tenderest

expressions of out innermost loving feelings, taking risk after risk. What a fine thing!

I love you Kathy Jo,

FRIDAY, FEBRUARY 10, 1989 2:00 PM

Precious Soul Mate,

I want to address two issues (plunging right in), dear one. The first is composed of your statements and questions as follows:

"He'll go away because I'm far away."

"He'll go away because I'm not sexually consummating the relationship."

"Are you really willing to create something new, extraordinary?"

"And to be with the pain/joy of it?"

To begin with, I want to say flatly that I want as much of you as I can possibly get. Having said that, I am willing to enjoy whatever parts of your life that you are willing to share with me. Your love. Your fine mind. Your tenderness and sensitivity. Your spirituality — that which first attracted me to you. And all the other things about you I cherish. They are so precious to me.

In other words, I WILL NOT GO AWAY BECAUSE YOU ARE GEOGRAPHICALLY DISTANT. I WILL NOT ABANDON YOU BECAUSE WE DO NOT HAVE A SEXUAL RELATIONSHIP. Period. You may wonder about this now, but you will come to trust it in time.

And yes, I am willing to create something new and extraordinary with you, and I am willing to go wherever this new thing leads us. I am indeed willing to be with both the joy of it and whatever pain it might bring. There, now.

Second issue. You have not mentioned this, but I want to imagine your asking me: "Jim, is it possible to love more than one person?" My answer of course is yes. Possible for some people: for those who are clear channels for love. For our love, Dear Kathy, is not our own. It comes though us from some transcendent Source. We both know how powerful it is (even how dangerous it could be if not handled properly), and I'm happy that you and I are willing and eager to accept the task of channeling it. It's so sweet. We are learning, you and I, something that few people have had the good fortune to learn. To learn, that is, to deal with this powerful force. Most people simply cover it over, it's so dangerous. Let us give ourselves lots of credit for handling this so well (even though, I suspect, we could do no other than open ourselves to each other the way we did, given the kind of people we are).

I love you Kathy,

SATURDAY, FEBRUARY 11, 1989 10:45 AM

Kathy, my love,

Thank you for the cute little bookmark; I use it to keep my place in the books I'm working with for me PDE. Here's a Valentine gift. Will you be my Valentine?

I send my love to Cali, too.

Love,

MONDAY, FEBRUARY 12, 1989 11:00 AM

Dear Kathy Jo,

I must begin by saying I am feeling closed up now; the only warmth in my life is my work and my precious relationship with you; let me see if by writing it out I can reconnect with you. Yes, already I am feeling your sweet presence.

I went to a workshop on the inner critic yesterday, and something in me cried out, "They're doing it all wrong!" but I said little; I wanted to learn what they had to say.

I want you to know that every little thing you do, I notice. For example, even the way you unbuckled the seat belts in the car! Notice and take delight in.

When we spoke on the phone Saturday, I got a new sense of your slow, soft, gentle voice—infused with Southern lushness. I need what it projects. "Just take it easy, Jim," it says; "Just relax, my love." Oh, I need that! I need some of the harsh edges of my male roughness smoothed and gentled, and I think you know that and are willing to do it.

I got your letter about my booklet, and it was a delight. I've only read it three times, though, and later I'll respond in detail. Just for now I want you to know how nice it was to picture you curled up (like a cat) with your cup of coffee, reading it—happy, contented, warm, soft, loving, relaxed, easygoing (how nice to type those words, to re-evoke your presence!).

What a treasure you are!

Remember when I spoke of your incredible niceness?

And I get to partake of that!

I feel more connected with you now; I'm writing myself into connectedness.

I'm enclosing the first of the photocopies; you sent way too much money, unless you want even more items. It's such a joy to serve you this way!

I'm also enclosing some rough notes (almost free associations) on my spirituality ideas—for your comments, corrections, feedback, etc.

And here's another poem:

IN DEFENSE OF MYSTICS
BY LEONARD BACON

Man can be taught. But those adroit in living
Search for a truth as different from learning
As simple kindness from routine forgiving,
As heat is different from and more than burning.

Beyond mere seeing, they desire discerning,
And may discern what they may never see—
Despite all stillborn certainties, returning
To things impossible that yet must be.

For something that they never could have proved,
And that it was not in their power to test,
Was always with them. And it lived and moved,
Compelled them and possessed them and obsessed,

Till they who had been blind and reason-ridden
Learned their reality from what lay hidden.

(And now I am fully connected with you.)

Della says she did not get my letter (she called), but on the phone said yes, put as little as possible into your learning agreement; you can always add later (but it's more difficult to subtract). So I'm going to present two areas:

Cognitive Therapy and Psychodynamic Theory (which will result in my book, How to Stop Sabotaging Yourself). I will probably make this two independent study courses.

Psychotherapy and Spirituality. I'm less sure of this topic, but this is what I want to do my peer days on. Maybe I'll know more when you give me feedback on spirituality. (Any books I can read?)

I would love to do a workshop in Lafayette (and see you again!). I could do one for professionals on empty chair work and/or inner critic work—or one for the public on inner critic work. I put myself completely in your hands in this regard and am ready to go (or at least to schedule something) at a moment's notice!

I have a fantasy of us leading a group together. Wow! Before us lies the huge continent of our relationship, which we are exploring bit by bit. What a delightful prospect!

I send you wave after wave of my love, to enfold you and your work as your love enfolds me and mine. From my office I know which direction you are, where to beam my feelings and warmth. Be assured that my love is steadfast, will never lessen no matter what, will always be there for you to enjoy and bask in. And I send you waves of strength and power and support in everything you do. I am behind you 100%. I love you,

FEBRUARY 14, 1989 2:30 PM

My dear Jim —

I feel like I need to write you about 3 separate letters: one to process my journey; one to respond to the wonderful loving letters you've sent me; and one to process intellectually re: your articles on imagery etc. and Women's Ways of Knowing. In order to solve this dilemma, I'm going to rely on a path that works for me: follow my energy. (I guess that's a spiritual as well as physical and emotional stance on my part.) My strongest energy drive right now is to process my journey, so here goes…

Physically, I feel off center. That is most disturbing to me. My heart is racing, my blood is racing, and my attempts to meditate are just not relaxing me. I feel some grief here, because I've just spent two years of peace and centeredness in this same chair, same spot in my office. (One explanation that helps me is the Enneagram — have you read about this — a typing according to compulsion as well as gift — Sufi. I fall into the "9" category — compelled to resist anxiety. I hate to feel off center. Yet I feel my task is to be true to my dream; my drive and to include in my experience the anxiety and unrest it necessarily engenders. (It's helping me to write this. I'm already released of some franticness.) In looking at my handwriting, I see how frantic it looks. Eek! I'm frantic, Oh, my God, how terrible, etc. etc. Good grief. Being frantic is part of the human experience. It's okay.

I'm scared to write the next part in case I'd trigger stuff for you. But you've invited me. So, I've had input that makes me scared about my motivation for loving you — 1) One is Bruno Bettelheim (The Uses of Enchantment). I'm reading his work in my fairy tale study, and he being a Freudian, is always harping on the oedipal significance in fairy tales. So, I go off the deep end—oh my God, what if my feelings for Jim are Oedipal. Well, just to process that, we've already spoken of me projecting daddy on to you, and you've already elegantly extricated yourself from that projection. ("Kathy, I am not your daddy. Repeat after me, 'You are not my daddy, Jim.'") I ask you, Jim, can cognitive work, like an affirmation, counteract some unconscious drive? You also told me that when it comes to inner black holes, we just have to do the work and direct it to the person to whom it belongs. So that helps. If there is more unresolved daddy stuff (do we ever fully resolve our parental stuff?), then I just need to work it through. (I have this judgment that I should bring myself to you as the all together person—no unresolved matters to darken the door of our relationship—That's absurd, isn't it?) (2) The other is a conversation with a friend, recently separated, who spoke of not wanting to give away his freedom to a woman again; not to emotionally take care of a woman again. I'm not real clear what this triggered in me—well, maybe I am—tacky inner voice saying, "Kathy, you just want somebody to take care of you." Yuck. I feel regressed, not in my power. Bear with me, please as I work through this junk. I will work through it, I know. And if you have any contribution, I'd appreciate it.

You did a beautiful job of responding to my need for processing. You shared from your own experiences (that has such power for me), didn't rescue me or give me answers, but you did give me reassurance that the turmoil I feel is a good sign of following my growth destiny and you offered me your steadfast friendship and companionship. You encourage me to let my feelings blossom. I feel like I'm in labor, giving birth.

And I guess I am. I went and sat in my office for two years and ended up pregnant! I love your calling me a fellow struggler with you. "We will do battle together side by side, you with your gleaming sword, I with my skill and knowledge, shoulder to shoulder." I love that image, Jim. Thank you. Have you ever coached a woman through labor? Here goes...

Letter 3 (Letter 2 later)—processing intellectually on Women's Ways of Knowing—Actually, I can't just process intellectually, because it touched me too personally, so you'll get some of my heart, some of my mind. First, some questions for you I jotted down while I read. 1) What is your experience of those 5 ways of knowing? (I related to each so intimately. It made me wonder if it's gender related or if you had had similar developmental tasks—when you shared with me about your family of origin, (I loved it, by the way). I heard a time of silence—"go play in your room and invent the atomic bomb" and "every patient wants to be a psychologist." Those seemed to match a silencing experience. I was silenced as a child in subtle ways: the baby—eight years younger than my sister. I learned not to make waves, to keep quiet, to be compliant. Everybody parented me. (Mama; Papa-my maternal grandfather; my sister, and my dad). I became very quiet; very good.

Where are you now in these 5 ways? I hear constructed knowledge (integrating intuitive and external knowledge) in your thinking. But does that cover it for you? For me, I think growing in constructed knowledge is my doctoral task. I am following my heart, my intuition and yet taking in new external knowledge and developing an articulated, rational/ intuitive approach. This was very validating for me.

2) Referring to procedural knowledge, do you use both

separate and connected knowing? I think you do. I feel I rely almost exclusively on connected knowing. So, when you ask me to critique/respond to your work, I come from connected knowing; from seeing your point of view, yet adding my thoughts. Are you satisfied with that? Or were you asking for separate knowing on my part? I've developed connected knowing to a fine art through my counseling experience. I can be with about anything anybody tells me, but not from cool detachment, rather from empathy. I want to process more with you on constructed knowing as I read, and I will.

But I want to share the tear-wrenching insight I had Sunday as I read subjective knowing—I realized as I read that I developed an inner voice of subjective knowing out of failure of male authority, as Belenky, et al., say. Actually a whole string of failures: Daddy died (1980). I had placed so much power in him as the authority I must please. I had not separated from him. I spoke out loud to Cali as I worked through this, "Daddy's death really set me free." I had never said this before, and even though I had acknowledged that healing had come from it. It was a powerful realization for me. Then Steven (the guy I was semi-engaged to at the time of Daddy's death) failed me. He just was not there for me, didn't come around hardly at all. I felt abandoned. Hale and Cali saw me through the funeral. Then the pastor at the church that had nurtured my spiritual rebirthing moved away and the following minister was obnoxious. Then I went to another church that I thought would nurture my spiritual vision. But they ended up concentrating on missionary work and stating that the single person's role was to support married people. (What garbage!) My break from the church was scary (last 2 years). But I think it was the crux of liberation for me; to risk removing myself from that external (mainly male) authority has been so liberating to my inner self and has catapulted me into subjective knowing. It's not that simple, but it gives you the high points. Belenky then says that the person seems to need nurturing for that voice to be strengthened. Prayer group, Cali, Hale, my students, my colleagues, Della, and now you and my colloquium buddies all have nurtured me. Thank you. I would love to hear your thoughts on the book.

Letter 2 — Thank you, my heart, for sharing the evolution of your dream — and the dissolution of the old dream. Yes, I absolutely support you. I am your friend. And yes I source strength to you. (I love that you appropriated my love at the philosopher's speech and were empowered to speak out.) There is so much power between us and radiating out from us. We enable each other to touch our own greatness; to risk our separate possibilities. I have a quote for you again from Rainer Maria Rilke: "Love consists in this: that two solitudes protect and touch and greet each other." As we are doing. And it is so beautiful (as in your oasis with the fine bakery and the French restaurant with rice and brown gravy). And you are relieved to have found it; what a pleasure that is to me.

Thank you for your wisdom on dependency, very helpful. I was so moved by your rhapsody on your feasts of affection. I love your boldness in risking what is in your heart and mind. I love that you are an open channel of love to me, not blocking or halting it or putting a bit in its mouth. I bask in your terms of endearment. Don't stop! As for me, you draw me forth to risk more; to get beyond my old tapes that censure my loving freely; extravagantly. So I surround you and enfold you again in my love; I lubricate you with myself. I wish I could hold you right now. Well, here. I commune with you now.

Thank you so for addressing my questions and for your response typed in bold letters so I wouldn't miss it. You won't go away. You receive what I give. And you want as much as you can get—what a delight! To be so treasured. Thank you too for inferring my question about loving two people. What a challenge! May I be a clear channel. Yes, we are something aren't we? I'm glad you're as big as you are and that I am too.

Thank you, too for continuing to route articles to me. I am amazed at how well you understand my needs and my work. The Progoff article was incredibly contributory. I'll write you more detail on that. You are increasing my vocabulary—new words for me: trenchant and sui generis—But they're mine now! Tee hee.

Your tender precious expressions of love for me melt me, enfold me, empower me. My womanness is blossoming. Strange men and old men friends are being very attentive. (I just take it in.) I think I am letting my Self shine. And you empower that. My intellect is deepening. (It is helping so much to process with you. You are my peer and could well be my adjunct. Thank you.) Am I helping you enough? I feel like I do so much personal work, that you may not be receiving enough. If you have specifics that I am neglecting please place your dear beautiful hand (I memorized them at colloquium) on my arm and let me know.

I want to come to do a workshop with you. You've got me very excited on that. Are you open to doing a UGS seminar with me sometime? I would love it. So perhaps we can be on the alert for common interest ones. (I don't want either of us to compromise on content.)

Anyway, I must get this in the mail. Darn. I'm never quite through. I could talk to you for hours and hours and days and years. Well, I guess we will, won't we! That's my agenda.

For now, receive my deep love, admiration, and affection for you. I treasure you, dear one.

& I love you deeply,

Kathy

WEDNESDAY, FEBRUARY 15, 1989 2:25 PM

My beloved Jim,

I'm working on my workshop which begins tomorrow night and am loving the preparation. It's been flowing well. I'm incorporating your article on the Dream and on Daniel Levinson. Thank you. You'll be quoted as one of my experts. There is a centeredness, a trust in myself today. It's an experience of power and wisdom in myself. I feel I am starting it right. Here's my plan for the first night:

I.   Introduce myself, what brings me here to do this (my own inquiry into callings and my doctoral study) — Create rapport with the group. Ten people have preregistered, which is a good size for what I'll be doing — lots of group/ individual work

II. Introduce themselves — who they are, what they do now, what brings them here

III. Define/expand the title of the workshop "Vocational Choice-Making: An Inner Journey" (I'll take each word and explain, set tone)

IV. (Develop idea of Journey) — Preparation for the journey

V. (Legitimacy of your own journey)

a.   Some ground rules — (Experience, respect for self and others, openness, inner freedom, take what you get)

b.   Knowing our starting point — initial experience of locating where we are now (If your current vocational spot were a season of the year, what would it be? (Represent this through drawing, acting, words, song, image or craft)

    c.   *Dropping of unneeded baggage for the trip —*

        i. Sloughing of names/images re: ourselves that weigh us down (Exercise)

        ii. Healing wounded trust in the inner Voice (I'll use voice of authority — Belenky, Levinson, Jung, Progoff (thanks to you) and your own words (Elliott) and Joseph Campbell

        iii.Healing the wounded Listening Function & the Wounded Voice (whole course will address this, but I'll introduce them to it); processing ways they've been silenced; locate their developmental stage in having & using inner listening/voice — where did our dreams go?

    d.   *Packing for the trip*

        i. Language of Inner World — dreams, fantasies, images, heroes, etc.

        ii. Clothing — protective and symbolic costume

        iii.Diary

VI. Setting Out on the Journey (if time, if not, next week)

    a.   *Energy as Source of Vocational Guidance*

        i. Chakra System as source of personal information

        ii. Archetypal Energy

I love it. I can't wait to see what comes of it. I don't have the next 3 weeks planned, but I will let what happens tomorrow night suggest the next step to me.

As I was going through my notes, I came across a fairy tale of my life I wrote at a workshop in November, and I want to share it with you: "Once upon a time a little girl lived in a great oak forest. She especially loved to sit at sunset on three little steps at the front of her house. It was at that time that she could be at peace, watching the golden sunset colors through the dark, heavy branches of the sheltering trees. She very much needed this time to be alone — to tap into her greatness; her solitary specialness. This special time was the one time she could stand on her own and connect with some deep spiritual place that only she knew was sure to wait and welcome her under the trees, to remind her that it lived within her even when she forgot or when no one else noticed. And she longed for them to notice and to honor that specialness. Yet only the trees lifted their welcoming arms in salute to her. So she returned time and again to her little steps…And when she grew up, she set out on a journey not quite clear to her. On this journey she met a cowboy who saw her specialness and bowed to honor her. But both he and she knew they could not journey together and so parted with a blessing. Her journey took her many places, and in each stopping place she appeared, she waited and hoped for the salute…"

So, as I processed at the workshop, I got that I have longed all my life to be seen for who I am. Special, spiritual, solitary, and with my own greatness. The leader had us declare an affirmation that emerged out of our fairy tale. Mine was "I deserve to be honored for who I am." Well, needless to say, the colloquium experience and my relationship with you have catapulted me into a living fruition of that affirmation. Can you see why I am so incredibly empowered? I see a — new as I reread this fairy tale.

What books are you reading? I'd love to know. You seem to be a fast and voracious reader. I am too. But I am taking notes on much of my reading, so it's slowing me down. I just got a new book through interlibrary loan, *On Writing Well* by Zinsser (?). Have you read it? Thanks for sharing your IQ scores. I love your intelligence and am glad you've come to own it for yourself.

Thanks and thanks again for Progoff. It's really contributing e.g., p. 14 building atmosphere that supports and strengthens inner work (yes, for me too); p. 78 inherent capacity for inward perception (good justification for my work); p. 79 beholding our inner work (I like it); p. 83 inner correlation) p. 179 (Ch. 13) wonderful for my work & p. 181 too & 182 & 184. So I'll be using all this. I'm finding the task imagery (Shorr) material for possible use, I see it as useful for remediating work, and I can imagine that I'll get into this along the way. We'll see.

I have some notes on Belenky et al., I'm going to copy and share with you. They're fresh from my reading.

I want to mail this, so I'll stop for now.

I love you from the depths of me. In my body I can even locate it — my head (right upper near surface), my heart (the whole breastbone area); and my vagina (what can I say?).

Till we speak again —

Kathy

WEDNESDAY, FEBRUARY 15, 1989 11:40 AM LETTER 1

My precious treasure,

When I look in my post office box and there is a letter from you, I begin to feel a glow that starts in my chest and spreads throughout my body, and I sit out on the ledge in front of the library near the steps and read it, and the whole world of Berkeley with its panhandlers and weirdos falls away, and I am intensely with you for a few minutes as you speak to me through your letter, and I have a vivid sense of your sweet presence.

Once in a while something you write touches me so deeply and gives me such a strong sense of you that your essence leaps out of the page at me, and it's much more than a presence, it's as though you were really here full of life and love and strongly connected to me. Such a sentence was: "sometimes I think you are shy about saying anything directly to me."

Oh, yes, I am! And then you miss out on the good things I have for you, and it's not fair, and you are right to complain, and I want you to continue to complain whenever I do not give you the fullest contact, with no punches pulled, from my heart. Please keep reminding me; please teach me how to give to you. I will learn quickly, I promise.

Now, about content. Yes, I want to bestow on you as much of my male energy as you want to take in. I can go on endlessly about it, so let me know when you've had enough, or want more. You know I am a strong powerful male; as a little boy I learned to play with trucks and guns, not dolls. In eighth grade, we boys played a game called flinch. You made a fist as though to hit someone on the arm but stopped short of touching his arm, and it seemed to the other boy you'd hit him (but you didn't), and so if he flinched, then you got to hit his arm really, as hard as you could, while he stood there and took it. But then you had to "wipe it off"; that is, brush the place you hit with your fingers, and if you didn't do that, he got to hit you as hard as he could on the arm, while you stood there and took it.

So we males learned to endure pain without flinching, a lesson that stood us in good stead, because in our rough and tumble world, we were exposed to a lot of knocks and hits, in schoolyard fights, in football, and so on. So we learned to be strong. (Unfortunately, we learned to cover up our feelings too; that is, they did; not me, as you can see.)

So I bestow on you the male strength I have learned throughout my life. My strength and my power; my thrusting-forth; my fighting spirit. That's the animus I give you, my precious Kathy, my darling. As much of it as you want. I give it freely. Let me know if you want more; I have more to write.

Now, on Women's Ways of Knowing. When I first read it, I got very little from it; now that I have a chance to discuss it with you, and in the context of your journey, it has become alive for me. I was not fully aware of how much women defer to men (authorities), nor did I know that subjective knowing (p. 54) was actually a reaction to that, a move away from it. I just thought, well, women have this funny thing where they have difficulty reasoning.

I like BGG&T's concept of procedural knowledge. "Intuitions may deceive" p. 93. "Gut reactions can be irresponsible." "You cannot 'just know.'" (p. 94). It's necessary to "generate a series of ideas instead of stopping with one" (p. 97). And "a variety of perspectives." And subjectivists profess to be open-minded but are "stubbornly immune to other people's ideas." (p. 98). And "the inner voices sometimes lies" (p. 99).

I like the concept of separate v. connected knowing. "Presented with a proposition, separate knowers immediately look for something wrong—a loophole, a factual error, a logical contradiction, the omission of contrary evidence." P. 104

I think in the field of spirituality, there is much subjectivism, much connected knowing—which is crucial but which needs to be balanced by separate knowing.

I am becoming dimly aware at how women have been battered by men's reasoning, which leads them strictly logically to conclusions that don't feel right and that really aren't right. The animus, unless balanced by the anima, can be a grotesque simulacrum of human beingness. And destructive.

There is so much in this book I need to read again; it's a source on giving voice to the truth with which one is pregnant. Delivering oneself of it. Any thoughts about the above points?

And now a change of topic. I need to tell you more about myself, what I like and don't like.

Here are some dislikes: camping, opera (except Wagner); ballet; concerts, especially chamber music (except that I like classical music if it's emotional); poetry readings; swimming; dancing; art museums (though I like art); sports of all kinds, either participating or watching; politics (mostly); superficial chit-chat; most movies.

What I like: going to lectures, conferences, conventions, etc. in my field; being in a group; giving lectures; leading groups and workshops; writing; reading fiction; watching really good TV shows on PBS and also comics like Johnny Carson and Tim Conway; ice creams of all kinds; French pastries; going to libraries and bookstores; good food — especially French, Mexican, Creole, and Hungarian. Meat pies, foods with rich sauces, I like to cook, too. I like the ocean.

My idea of a perfect event happened at Asilomar. Before UGS, I thought some day (when my book comes out and I have money), I'd like to meet with colleagues for a weekend at some resort by the ocean, eat good food. I thought this would happen in the distant future; much to my surprise, along came Asilomar — exactly what I wanted! My only wish was that it could have been warmer, say, in Laguna Beach or La Jolla.

Ever since leaving Detroit, I have wondered where I wanted to live. New York? Too many jangly people; too much crime. Vancouver and Toronto are nice places with good people but not good enough libraries. California, I think is the state for me. Berkeley has too many weird people and too much crime, but the libraries are superb. Palo Alto has a good library and is close enough to Berkeley, so it's an excellent prospect. Low crime, no deranged people. Good restaurants. One hour closer to

Pacific Grove, Carmel, etc. But still a bit cold. Los Angeles is warmer but smoggy, except that Santa Monica is less smoggy or not at all. The libraries there are also good, but the traffic is fierce. Carmel itself would be nice but distant from good libraries. La Jolla is a place I need to visit; close to the UC San Diego library, a train to Los Angeles (from Oceanside), warm, low crime. I like warm weather, the ocean, good Libraries, good restaurants, but most of all—people I enjoy being with. (Well, Jim, what about Lafayette? There's a person there who is my soul mate. Don't think I haven't been thinking about this. Or New Orleans, with better libraries, good food, and the gulf. Well, these are some of the fantasies I've been having.)

Your letters are so chock full of juicy and meaty things, and there are so many things to respond to, that I feel like a kid on Christmas morning, with too many presents, too much excitement, too many things to play with, I can't tell which to address next. I love this, Dear Heart. You are a bountiful giver. I can no longer respond completely to each letter as it arrives, but I promise a full response in time to every item you bring up.

I love your encouraging me (and us) to present my (and our) soul(s) to each other (that sentence is getting a bit unwieldy), and I want to say there is lots I could write about, most of which is sexual, and which I am deliberately (at least for now) restraining myself from doing.

I played your cassette (What a lovely Valentine present!) and while listening to the first two instrumental numbers was transported by ecstasy; like nothing before.

Kathy's music! Her gift to me of herself! You are such a treasure.

But then the vocal stuff I found a bit jangly, and I thought, oh my god, I can never tell her that! I just won't say anything. No, I can't do that; I've got to tell her. What if she feels dismay! Oy! And then you wrote: "I'm really okay if you don't like the same music." And I felt suddenly released; how sensitive you are! So now I can comfortably write the above. (Yes, I would like more music.)

Then at the end of the tape came "The Same Stars", and I got melted down right into a little puddle of love. Oh my! I've played it over and over. It's so powerful, I'm afraid to play it sometimes.

Yes, I will pray for you on Thursday; my time, 3:30pm, and I'll be thinking of you and praying off and on till your workshop is over, just being with you in my heart, and also talking to God about what a wonderful precious treasure you are for me.

Oh, I love you so!

FRIDAY, FEBRUARY 17, 1989 5:10 PM

Dear Kathy Jo—

I sent you a long handwritten letter today, and now in the afternoon mail is your letter of the 14th, and it's so full of exciting and connectedizing things I've got to respond to it right away, and I wonder if we would ever run out of things to say if we lived near each other, and I guess we would never be like those long-married couples who go out to dinner and eat silently; anyway, I am reminded of some time in my childhood when some friends must have visited and slept over (or was it a cousin?) and we talked late into the night, sleeping in the same bedroom, until Mom or someone came up and scolded us, telling us to go to sleep. And things keep getting better and better, always in new ways I never thought of, and I wonder how long this can keep up, and what tests our relationship may undergo, and if I will have the courage to tell you if things might not be so good between us, although I can't imagine at this point that that will happen, but there is something of a cynic in me that wonders if it might.

I applaud the way you're dealing with your feelings of being off-center and your anxiety and feelings of unrest; I want to assure you again that these are signs of impending growth, and you are accepting and integrating them instead of making them go away. I am with you in this task. "Being frantic" is indeed "part of the human experience"—part of your growth experience right now, no matter what your inner critic might say. So keep encouraging your jangly feelings to bubble up;

they will inevitably lead to growth. If you ever need to talk about them, please call me any time. I mean that. As I mentioned before, even in the middle of the night.

Okay, about oedipal stuff. Why sure, your feelings toward me are Oedipal; as are mine toward you. So what else is new? All we need to do is keep that in mind, to keep reminding ourselves: "Jim you are not Daddy; Kathy, you are not Mom." Otherwise, we'll begin forming expectations of perfection from each other—perfect love, perfect caring, and so on that can't possibly be met. The reminder is that each of us is an imperfect peer. But let's enjoy those Oedipal feelings anyway, as long as we don't give them the power to drive our expectations. What I mean is that if we do give them such power, we might begin to feel hurt at the other's not being a perfect giver of love—then become angry. But if we feel hurt and angry, that's okay, too—just be aware that oedipal stuff is getting in the way.

You ask, "Can cognitive work counteract an unconscious drive?" Why, sure, my love. The drive (or strong feeling) will be there no matter what, given that we had parents. Most people just act it out. But it's important to know what "counteract" means. It means, to me, that knowing what a thing is will disengage us from its power to drive our behavior automatically. We retain the strong feeling but now have a new relationship to it; we no longer "grab on" to it, no longer let it hook us into unrealistic expectations. We are aware, my sweet one, and that's why we can navigate these rough waters (that swamp so many boats). So cognitive work can indeed counteract, but in the sense of leading us to understand, disengage from, no longer be driven by (Anthetic inner freedom) all those parts of what I call our machinery that would make us into robots acting out destructive scripts.

And yes there will be more unresolved Daddy stuff (and Mom stuff, for me), for as long as we live, and it will be an interesting and growthful project to chew away on, but you and I know how to do it, and we will help each other, and we know the kind of work that needs to be done, and while we may not always be immediately successful, we know which direction to move in.

So yes, you just need to work it through, to process it, to feel the pain and express it toward Daddy, so you won't attribute it to Jim (and me, too, mutatis mutandis).

You say you have a judgment that you should bring yourself to me (Oh, what a felicitous phrase; how it set my heart leaping!) as an all-together person, "no unresolved matters to darken the door of our relationship." First, that seems better called a "should" then a judgment (it comes from the i.c.); and second, let me say unequivocally that if you had no unresolved stuff, first of all, I wouldn't believe you, but if you somehow should have no unresolved stuff, I would not find you much of a partner in growth; that is, perfect you and imperfect I would have little to share. Let me tell you that your unresolved stuff-plus your willingness to work so diligently on it — is one of the major attractions for me in you; that is, I wouldn't have it any other way. The more stuff-plus-work, the better I like it. This is a topic in my groups now: "What's the main requirement for a possible life partner?" Lou, from Boston, put it this well, when he said: "She's gotta be willing to work on her stuff. And Ah'm willing to work on mah stuff." And that goes for me, too. And let me tell you, it's rare. So I'm so lucky to have found you. If you ever need reassurance about this issue, let me know, and I'll be happy to say it over and over again. Every time you reveal what seems to you to be an imperfection is not that to me at all; it's what makes our relationship worthwhile; it's that, without which our relationship would be quite banal. Well, at least not as exciting. And you did not trigger my stuff, but if you did, I would welcome it, and I honor and respect your feeling of fear at such triggering, and I cheer you on, and it's okay to be scared, too. I will not leave you, I will not abandon you.

Okay, now I've got to talk to you like a Dutch uncle: you write: "Kathy, you just want somebody to take care of you. Yuck." (The yuck comes from your i.c.) (So does the word "just.") First of all, it's not "just." That's not all you want from me, but suppose it were, or suppose it's a big part; I'll be glad to take care of you. But not rescue you. My caring is Anthetic — encouraging you to get deep into your pain, if it's there, or any sadness, anger, rage, embarrassment, fear, and so on. My care-taking is different from that of others. (Well, I will comfort you if you want me to, also.) But it's okay to want someone to take care of you (I do, too). It's just important to deal with that with a cognitive (Anthetic) affirmation: "Just because my black hole wants to be filled by someone's taking care of me, that doesn't mean I'm going to pretzelize myself to get it and give up my autonomy. So, black hole, you can cry for Daddy (and Mom) as much as you want; hurt child, you can cry your little eyes out; I'm here to listen and care for you and comfort you; but I won't let you run my life the way you'd like; I'll just acknowledge you and give you care myself, so you don't sell out to others for it."

Now, dear Kathy, have you read Karen Horney? Or the Cinderella Complex?

Yes, you are indeed in labor, giving birth—and to what you do not know, nor do I—but I will be here to give you whatever help you wish and to hold your dear hand when it gets painful, as it will indeed, and encourage you to bear down, although I have never coached a woman in labor. But I have always seen my therapy as maieutic, in a sense more than that of Socrates (who said "I am here to help people give birth to the truth with which they are pregnant"). I am here to help them give birth to themselves. Their new selves, whatever that may be. New parts of themselves. Remember that whatever pain exists is of two forms: inner critic oppression, which needs to be challenged; and grief, which needs to be cried out, as fully as possible.

I love your metaphor of one's voice—which can be silenced. It's new for me. I think I am a lot like a woman. If there were such a thing, I would like to be made an honorary woman. I would be proud to be one. (I missed that metaphor when I first read the book!)

Okay, silence. Yes, I was silenced. Be a good little boy, and shut up. I was always quiet. And then those bastards would ask, "What's the matter? Cat got your tongue?" The experience was one of being blocked, just having a mental blank. Yet I saw other people speak articulately about ideas, and I said to myself (somewhere about the age of 17), if they can do it, I can learn it. Even though I didn't know how. I think the gender difference here is that men think that way: I can do anything (or learn) that someone else can do. But I had an extra problem: I had read a lot and from my reading had developed ideas that were so idiosyncratic that they didn't fit anywhere into the public framework. I thought about galaxies when I was 11 and read science fiction and wondered if I could invent a universal language and thought (when I was 16) that if world leaders just got together and talked rationally, they could organize everything so people would have enough to eat—all idealistic stuff that was unconnected with the realities of the world. But my mind was fertile, always coming up with new ideas just not geared in the right directions—just spinning fantasies. When I did try to talk of these ideas, I got silenced all right (Mom said, "you're just out to get me!"), so I stopped talking, but the ideas continued to proliferate, and I couldn't stop them. I did not learn to distrust words. I was just puzzled by the isolation I felt; I even blamed other people for being too dumb or stodgy to understand me. I never doubted that I was able to think well.

I never had those things so many other people reported having: an understanding teacher, a mentor, a guide of some sort. I was on my own from the beginning. That was bad, because it took me longer to figure out how the world worked; but it was good, too, because I was able to come up with some novel approaches. (One issue in my group people is the same: "I never got any goddamn guidance as a kid." I think that's partly why I want to give people guidance now — something I wanted so desperately and felt so keenly the pain of not having. Other therapists have reported something similar.) It's called a magic gesture — giving someone something you wanted for yourself as a kid. (Edmund Bergler coined the term.)

Nobody encouraged me to get a college education. In fact, my best friend, at the age (me) of 27, told me, "Education is for the dumb" and suggested I could be self-taught. I had quit high school in the 10th grade, wanting to be a writer like Hemingway, thinking I didn't need all this education.

So between the ages of 13 and 16 I felt quite alienated, doing some reading in philosophy and psychology, moving from one job to another (at age 16 and 17), quitting by just not showing up, wondering if I were going crazy, not having friends (not being enfolded in any pleroma) but not knowing that that was my major problem, than finally, a stroke of genius: I joined the Navy. Suddenly I was in a pleroma! I had dozens of ready-made friends, and all the structure I needed. I spent two years having the fun I was denied before, getting plenty of guidance, putting my career goals (such as they were) on hold. I was happy as a clam in my cute sailor suit.

Then college, where I got depressed (no friends again), and was recalled to active duty and spent another two years having fun in the Navy again (this time at Pensacola, from which I visited New Orleans and loved it). Still, my main journey was on hold, while I had fun. I needed these four years of fun. I wasn't concerned with my "voice." I just wanted to fit in, and I did beautifully.

After my second hitch, I got a job as an editor, finished

my degree in psychology with a minor in journalism. Got married. Had a son. Then came to California. That was a big thing for me. Then followed about three years of limbo, which a lot of my clients have reported, too. I was a clerk-typist in a San Francisco chemical company. Read psychology books and journals. Began publishing a psychology magazine.

At this point I began following the voices of others. Trying to discover the rules so I could follow them. Deferred to all the psychological authorities; they were PhDs; they must know what they're talking about. Took seriously what turned out later to be a lot of garbage. Couldn't tell the good stuff from the bad. Thought I wanted to be a reporter of other people's ideas.

Then, out of the sheer need to make money, I began leading groups. Began trusting myself, following some guidance received form a woman who led the T-group I had been in. Terrified during my first session, but had a good rule to follow: Don't say much. Deflected requests for structure. And it worked. Kept leading groups.

As I led groups, I began trusting subjective knowledge. I knew what should be done, subjectively, and I did it. Followed my intuition. There were no training programs at this time in what I was doing.

But there had always been a strong drive in me to formalize my subjective knowledge; that is, to put it into words, principles, theories, etc. I went through a period when I thought I must be wrong, there were so many authorities who said the opposite of what I was learning from my groups. Then I misinterpreted them egregiously; when I read their books, all I could see was myself, I was so self-centered. I made a few mistakes in my lectures, in presenting other people's ideas. (I shudder to think about what I said; i.c. stuff, of course.) Then I got inflated; I thought I had the true Truth and everyone else was wrong. (I'm still overcritical of others' theories.)

Finally, my pendulum swung back to where I could learn from others again, and realize that they were wrong in many cases (and not read my own theories into what they said so as to make them right). I prefer the term integrated knowing to constructive knowledge, because I think all knowledge (even subjective and procedural) has a constructive aspect. (Kant was the man who showed that so clearly that it's now difficult to dispute by any philosopher.)

As I got loose from silence, from reliance on authorities, from rejection of all authorities, from reading myself into authorities—I developed a way of knowing that did include connected and separate knowing. Fusion and disengagement. Immerse oneself in the experience, feel the Truth, then back off and take a close look at it. Then formalize it: put it into words; try first one thing, then another, until something clicks.

I have trained some entity in my subconscious mind to do this formalizing work; if I run into an organizational problem in my book (of which there are many), I just stop work, turn the problem over to this entity, and do something physical like washing dishes or cooking or cleaning. I check from time to time: How are you doing? Got a possible answer yet? But gently. So I don't pressure it. Then, suddenly, when I'm least expecting it—when I'm sitting down to a meal, the perfect answer pops into my mind. My entity has provided it, and I've come to trust it.

I like it when you say that growing in constructed knowledge is your doctoral task. (Oh, Kathy, what a fine person you are! How intelligent! What a good match for me!) Yes, that's right. But few people are aware of that goal; most settle for going by the rules of external authority, or sink into fuzzy-minded subjectivity.

In answer to your question, I am satisfied with your response to my ideas—but I do want more separate knowing. More challenges, criticism, even cynicism. Cool detachment.

I hope this (above) has responded to your requests. Let me know if you want more.

(Oh, God, I love you so!)

Okay, failure of male authorities. Daddy, Steven. The pastor who moved away. The obnoxious minister who replaced him. The other church that you also left. Yes, sweet Kathy—all painful failures of external supports, and so necessary so that you could find your own voice. I have not had such failures, although I have tried to find male figures who would accept me and whom I could support: Eric Berne, for example. Each rejected me, and I felt the pain, and was later grateful that I had not crystallized out into some rigid ideological position. (I've seen so many people who had, so I thank my rejecters for liberating me, painful though it was.)

About Belenky's book: A fine thing. I'm appalled at how little of it I understood until you and I had discussed it. Look, Kathy Jo, the dialogues we have are not luxuries to me, not things I can do without very well.

As you know, my work is my life, and my discussions with you are crucial to my work. You enrich me.

(God, you are so precious!)

Ah, what good things you say:

"I absolutely support you."

"We enable each other to touch our greatness."

About UGS Seminars: remember, I'm going to the one at Pawling, NY, in March. Stories, Versions, Conversations: Ways of Knowing. I think you'd get a lot out of it. March 15-19. Can you join me? (If not, or even if so, let's plan others.) (Issues there are yours!)

About my receiving enough from you: How sensitive, how dear, of you to ask! No one asks things like that! Yes, enough. If I'm helping you more than you're helping me, I'm more than happy with that. You give me so much that if I hadn't met you, my life would have been bleak indeed — a fact which, of course, I would never have known, just thinking, well, this is the way it is; there is no one in the world like you, Jim, and you just have to accept that, and enjoy whatever else there is.

I am overflowing with such joy that I can't give it words! To know you! To not have missed out on you during my life! How lucky I am. (Do you know that we are doing the equivalent of one peer day per letter, almost?) (Or me, anyway.)

How can I tell you how much you mean to me; words are so inadequate, I just want to cry out a great wild cry —

FEBRUARY 17, 1989

Beloved One,

I received two envelopes from you yesterday. What joy! Your valentine came. That was precious. Thank you. It took 5 days to get here, but as it turned out, it was perfect timing. Yesterday was, as you know, the first day of my workshop. I especially wanted to be centered and on top of things. Unfortunately, I was greeted at school with the news of the suicide of one of the psychology graduate students whom I knew casually. It was very upsetting to me, and I had a hard time shaking off the shock and grief. I looked terrible. Even my hair looked limp; my complexion was rough; and my eyes were weak looking. I decided I'd better go home early and rejuvenate. Well, there in the mailbox was your letter. My chakra information says that jasmine is a heart chakra healer. So, I took a shower, a ritualistic one; washing off the grief and shock. I used your soap and received the healing, love and blessing that I knew you intended toward me. I washed my hair and blessed myself. That led into "pleasuring" myself to the max! I stepped out of the shower a new woman. Then I drank a tall glass of ice water in a yellow glass (the color for the solar plexus chakra –the seat of personal power). I listened to a meditation tape and then the theme music from Epcot Center. Taking such good care of myself was a gift I gave myself, and it worked. I looked great and felt great to take authority over the material and to set the tone for the workshop.

I'm sure you'll want to know how it went. Well, it was a great first session. There are three men and seven women participating. They are a really diverse group; from farmers to chemical engineers to counselors to hospital administrators to mommies. I was a little shocked by the diversity. I guess I expected a more homogeneous group. Isn't it wonderful to know that my approach appeals or calls to a wide range of people? I am going to learn so much from them. I took you with me as an enfolding blanket, sort of an Indian style blanket, as I entered the room. I enfolded myself in your love, because I knew you were beaming your love to me, as you say, and I was totally secure in that. Another neat thing was that I was totally myself. I thought about kything you body to body, but that was unsatisfactory, because it felt invasive, like I would have to do the workshop your way. So I adjusted my image to the Indian blanket, and that was wonderful, intimate and appropriately empowering. It feels very good to be so intimate with you and yet have such healthy boundaries for myself. As a final note on the valentine, YES, of course I am your valentine. Bask in that. And thank you for sending Cali your love. I gave it to her, and she was surprised and touched.

Now, for your second letter, which got to me in 2 days (!). I am so glad that you were able to move from your closed, cold place into love and warmth by writing to me. I could feel your transitioning as you wrote. Thank you too so much for the copies. Just keep all the money, as I may have others to ask you to copy, and as postage can get costly. Thank you too for delighting in serving me. Do you know how you bless me? Also you notice the little things I do! What an honor to who I am. Even the seat belts. I'm lovingly amused at our connectedness, because unhooking the seat belts was significant inside of me, even though I hadn't thought about it a lot. I do remember unhooking yours at the same time. It felt intimate to me. I love your description of my voice. I guess I hadn't thought about it. And, yes, I am so willing to be a soothing, gentling *influence on your harsh edges. I really haven't seen harshness in you, but you know how you experience yourself, and I honor that. I await your response to my comments on your booklet. I love the interchange with you. Do you know how enlivening our intellectual and emotional and spiritual interchange is to me? I think that was a rhetorical question, because I get how enriched you are too. I love Leonard Bacon's poem. "For something that they never could have proved compelled them and possessed them and obsessed" was especially meaningful to me. I would love to do a peer day on spirituality with you. Would you like that? I have some suggestions for reading for you: Stages of Faith by James Fowler; Modern Man in Search of a Soul by C.G. Jung; A Stone for a Pillow and And It was Good by Madeleine L'Engle; and Wheels of Life by Anodea Judith. My spiritual reading is quite eclectic, as you'll see. Mostly I base my spirituality on experience, so your idea of creating a personal religion resonates with your spiritual teacher! I am pretty much in awe that you have given me that title, but I have no desire to escape from it. I am like Belenky et al., as they explain teaching as a midwifing task. I've even used that image for a couple of years with my students. So I will midwife your emerging spirituality, if you like.*

So, in that vein, my beloved learner, I want to share with you some ways in which I conceive spirituality. Spirituality to me is absolutely and foremost about relatedness. And that relatedness is on several levels: self to self, self to others, self to the world, and self to the transcendent. It is a dynamic relationship, involving and requiring ongoing communication on all those levels. Communication is a developmental process and requires both listening to the other as well as speaking our minds and hearts. Give and take (mutuality) is necessitated in each sector. Boundaries are necessary, and this must be negotiated. I am beginning to dare to believe that I can relate spirituality in all these areas with all of them. (I had an experience at the Ashram where I had a physical interchange with a tree, and it was amazing. I gave the tree a blessing as I held it, and I swear that I felt loving energy and a blessing pass from the tree to me.) In relation to others, since colloquium, I have a reemerging sexuality/sensuality in my relationship to others. I feel it as an enlivened interchange, and yet with good boundaries. Then in the relationship between me and God, I feel an incredible shift, and I think that this may be where the biggest change is happening for me. For one thing, I am bringing my intellect to the relationship more and more (in response to the invitation, "Come, let us reason together," from the Bible). I am daring to go tete-a-tete on issues that puzzle me. I am also looking inward for my god. And I am daring to let sexual images emerge as a way of understanding the intensity of my relationship with God. That's got a lot of power for me, but it still scares and scandalizes some stuffy part of me. My concept of God is in great flux right now. I am including the feminine more, and that is a weird shift, since I have conceptualized God in masculine terms.

Your notes on spirituality (thank you for revealing those to me) go so much farther back to origins than my thoughts do. In many ways, I see that I confine myself so much to personal experience, concrete lived experience. Your abstractions teach me. I want to give you some quality time on this so I will do a separate letter on your notes. Now, I need to get this in the mail. I am impelled to communicate with you, and that is a bit surprising to me. I am so glad you are verbal. That is a real treat for me. Daddy (sorry, he keeps cropping up!) was the silent, introspective type. Andy was verbal, bright, but we did not discuss a really wide range of topics. Hale talks a lot, so that has been really good for me, and you can see how I would value my relationship with him. Yet, you are a gem of communication. We talk about everything, and I love it. I get to talk, and I love that. You value what I say, and I am lifted into my own humanity and greatness. I just want to gush right now with love for you; with gratitude for your being in my life, for honoring me with this incredibly intimate relationship. I image myself close to you, looking you in the eye, meeting soul to soul, and I am moved to the depths, as I was at Asilomar. My communion with you is psycho/spiritual/sexual, and it fertilizes all those places in me. I am blossoming in response. Very Anthetic of us, isn't it? I have this sense (fantasy?) that seeing you again, looking each other in the eye, and your holding my face in your hands would be enough to bring me to orgasm (no genital touching necessary). It's scary for me to risk that with you. Nevertheless, that's how deeply you touch me. And that's a tribute to you and the quality with which you relate to me that I could be moved so deeply by the emotional/spiritual interchange with you.

I leave you with that image. I pour out my love and support and warmth to you for your good days and for those bad days. I am with you, and I enfold you.

I love you,

Kathy

FRIDAY, FEBRUARY 17, 1989 11:15 AM LETTER #2

My Darling,

(Okay, I'll try a handwritten letter. Let me know what you think. I'm new at this letter-writing thing.)

Now—you write something that thrilled me so much I had to shut it off as soon as I felt it, it was so powerful! You wrote: "You love me as I would hold the ideal of how I would want to be loved by a man." Oh, Kathy! ("She can't mean that! She's just being nice. She doesn't even know me, really.") Well, I know you did mean it, and I guess you know enough about me to mean it. (Oh, but what if we find that we disagree about some really fundamental thing! Well, I guess we'll just have to go on loving each other anyway.)

And yet I feel an urge to warn you of some of my flaws. I'm sometimes coarse. I curse and swear like the ex-Navy man that I am. I say crude things. I have a terrible memory; I must constantly make notes and lists, and even so, I'm apt to forget important things (mostly because I'm inundated with things to do). I'm relatively poor—for now (just wait till my book is set!). I'm often inarticulate; my words come out jerkily instead of in the smooth polished way I'd prefer. My handwriting is terrible. If I get angry and desperate I sometimes express it by being very very logical and highly focused. I can't stand it if someone I'm close to refuses to talk about an issue in our relationship or work though an argument. I mean I go crazy with enormous pain if someone says "I don't want to talk about it!"

Like the black hole I lecture about, I sometimes

need huge amounts of reassurance that I am loved. I get impatient if someone doesn't understand what I'm saying. My paranoia leads me to think they really do understand but are playing dumb just to make me feel bad.

I often get lost in an intellectual argument, driven to prove my point at all costs, while I ignore any feelings involved, and I forget that the point may not be very important anyway. I try to please people and get them to like me, twisting myself out of shape like a pretzel and pretending to like things I don't like and dislike things that I really like.

I hate it when someone crunches on an apple in a quiet room.

I can't quite believe that anyone could be really interested in me; I think they're just being nice.

I sometimes try to change people so they are more like me; I have trouble knowing where they are.

Well this is all my stuff, I know. And there must be more. ("Why did you tell her those things? She won't like you anymore!")

But on the other hand, I'm a good man basically. Honest. Playful. Nice sense of humor. Intelligent. Like to talk about ideas a whole lot. An original thinker. Warm and loving for the right woman (someone with the initials K.V.) Hard-working. Caring. Sensitive. Know how to help someone with a problem. Like to snuggle. Open to spiritual realities (but want to use critical thinking skills). Willing to change. Know how to talk about very deep feelings. Feel comfortable with rage and deep pain. Will always answer if my woman

(K.V., again) asks "What are you thinking about?" Will always deal with relationship issues, no matter what. Always. Willing to negotiate and compromise. Strong and courageous. Willing to take risks. Willing to experiment. Like to, that is. (Sounds like a singles ad. Maybe that's what it is — addressed to one person.) (See how indirect I am? Well, if you did not already have a relationship, I would want you for my — what? — wife? Not exactly. Woman? Life partner? Yes, Life partner. Dare I say this? Too late.)

Well, I love you, precious Kathy. I think one of the reasons I dived in so deep with you so quickly is because you do have a relationship, if that makes sense. I am free to love you quickly. If I were to think of a traditional relationship with you — marriage, for example — I would be much more apprehensive. But I would still do and say all the things I have done and said. But more slowly.

I did pray for you while you were having your workshop. I asked God to be with you and support you. I sensed your triumph and good feelings — and the good feelings of your participants. Thank you for asking me.

Now — about your comments on my booklet. As you can imagine, this is important to me, since my work is central to my whole life.

— Primary and secondary self are my terms, but they come directly from Freud's concepts of primary and secondary process and are almost identical.

— Your suggestion for marketing my idea to alcoholic/ACA/recovery audiences warmed the cockles of my heart. I feel really understood. It's a good idea, and I'll think about it. I also liked your comparison with the physical discomfort of unfolding from crampedness.

—I like your "stack attack."

—Yes, depth communication is what we do. It hadn't occurred to me that this was the reason for the aliveness and power in our relationship. You're right. (Oh how fine it is to dialogue with you about my ideas!)

—Yes, please feel free to feminize and Kathyize my work. There are times when my methods are too brusque. For some people, this is not a problem, but for others it would be. I accept your gentling. And I accept your suggestion, which I will now show as an option.

—About reactive caring, you wrote: "I guess that's what scared me—when I touched the reactive part of myself toward you." Can you say more about that?

—Orthogonal simply means "at right angles to." Once a person has spoken to the empty chair, she/he is moved to a third position to observe.

Yes, I would like to sit with you and talk about ideas. And put them into practice. More and more I'm coming to feel the strong need to be with you in person. Letters are all well and good, and can be re-read, but I need immediate interaction. So let's explore more the idea of doing groups in each other's area.

What about your beginning with a vocational group here? I'm enclosing some ads. I'm not clear enough about what you might present at a spirituality group. Can you say more? Then, too, there are lots of spirituality groups here and none that feature vocation plus visualization/ archetypes. Moreover, I'd have no place you could stay at the present. I'll be getting an apartment later.

But I could do an inner critic workshop in Lafayette

any time. I've been running them since 1970—both for professionals and the general public. Let me know what you think.

About your music—I didn't tell you but I felt chills and shivers when I heard it—up and down my back and along my shoulders and arms.

I can't believe this is happening to me—this relationship with you! ("God, you knew what you were doing when you led me away from the Seattle, Denver, and Chicago colloquia and to the one in Asilomar! You brought Kathy and me together, and we did the rest. Thank you!")

Do not ever doubt that I love and support you, my precious treasure. If there is a day without a letter from me, it does not mean I have abandoned you—just that I'm working hard on my book. I keep you in my thoughts and in my heart. I seem to be thinking of you constantly—when I wake up, my first thought is of you. You come to my mind unbidden, your sweet presence infuses my thinking and feeling without my asking. When I go to bed at night, my last thoughts are of you. You still live in my head, looking out through my eyes at my world—not quite as strongly as before, but still there. I have never before felt this way about anyone. My heart is full.

Let me say again this scary thing, more directly now: I want somehow to share my life with you. To be with you in person more. To hug you and touch you. To talk about ideas with you. To argue with you about ideas. To experience your spirituality even more—and your fine challenges to my thinking. In person. In the flesh. To go to lectures with you and talk about them afterward. To give lectures with you and talk about them afterward. To browse through libraries with you. And book stores. To sit with you, each of us reading, and from time to time, to have one of us look up and share an idea, discussing it, then returning to our reading. To cook for you. To wander through a shopping mall with you. To walk by the ocean again at Asilomar with you. To find the places where we had those conversations, those life-transforming communions. To look in the window of Curlew, where we sat. To ride on the merry-go-round this time.

Is this direct enough? No, but it's as direct as I dare be. I guess I just mean that I love you a lot and want our lives to be intermingled more. Will you intermingle with me? Will you be closer to me than a sister, closer than a twin, as close as I am to myself? I want to be that to you. So familiar to each other that anything we say or do would be acceptable. Merging but still being autonomous. Being able to say anything and ask anything. Being alter egos for each other — but still separate. Does any of this make sense?

I yearn for you. Life is so short.

I love you, Kathy,

TUESDAY, FEBRUARY 20, 1989 11:30 AM

My beloved,

How many ways are there to express my love for you? I am trying them all. I notice that you are too. And maybe we're afraid of being trite, but expressions of love are never trite. Let's dare to be as trite as we want, because the love we have for each other will overcome all inner critic stuff about triteness; I love your idea of extravagance. Let's blossom profusely and to hell with conventionality, with whatever voice inside tells us, "You can't do that!" We can do that. We are doing that. We will do that—whatever we want; we will go wherever this relationship takes us. I am willing to let us indeed be extravagant with each other with our expressions of love. Oh, Kathy!

I feel like a puppydog about going with you to New York, wagging my tail about the chance to be with you on the plane and share experiences at the seminar. ("But, Jim, suppose you run out of things to talk about? Suppose she finds out what you're really like? Suppose you come on too strong?" Shut up, i.c.)

Our discussion of Belenky has stimulated me; I'm a fireworks explosion –with ideas popping off almost constantly as my inner entity works and reworks B's ideas. Here's the latest:

I share with women the fact that I have been oppressed by male logic and "knowledge." All these years (up until about 15 years ago), I have been intimidated by so-called experts in the field of psychology and philosophy. I hadn't known it so clearly until I had discussed it with you. I've had enough of this oppression. I see now that I have been working my way out of it.

Connected knowledge to me is the same as subjective knowledge. But I'd rather call it empathic knowledge — or, better yet, tacit knowledge. Knowledge at a gut level, that has not been formalized (put into words) yet.

Instead of "separate knowledge," I want to say "critiqued knowledge." Tacit knowledge needs to be formalized, then critiqued — via critical thinking. Uncritiqued knowledge is what leads to oppression by the knowledge-givers; we just swallow whatever they feed us without even reflecting on it.

Uncritiqued knowledge (i.e., my lack of critical thinking) has always been a problem for me. When faced with erudition, I become a pleaser — kow-towing to apparent profundity, especially when the "expert" has good credentials and a convoluted prose. I did this with Freud, Heidegger, and Husserl. They seemed so profound, and everyone seemed to agree. So I bought what they had to say without thinking. And I thought I must be wrong to disagree. (I couldn't even let myself think of disagreeing!) I pedestalized the experts.

But in recent years, I've learned to critique — to think about others' ideas critically. This helps remove me from the victim position. I now distance myself from the information and examine it carefully. I automatically wonder how it could be wrong. I ask how it checks out with my experience; what it entails in practical options and consequences. I check for any gut reactions that the information doesn't feel right.

And I need to say: this writer is just a human being,

like me. Not automatically smarter than I am; maybe even not as smart; maybe even someone who has introduced a few mistakes or infelicities in her or is work. Not some PERFSAT: Perfect Source of Absolute Truth.

So I have the right to reshape Belenky. I say "not connected, but tacit." "Connected vs. separate" is a pejorative dichotomy; the former term carries with it a load of emotional baggage of goodness; the latter has some badness. And I ask, "Didn't these people read Polanyi or Heidegger? Are they, as is so often the case in psychological writings, rein-venting the wheel?"

So now it feels okay. I have appropriated the ideas in Belenky and made them my own, reshaping them to a closer fit (as I see it) to reality.

Well, there are many ideas I have that were sparked by our dialogue, but I think I'll reserve them for the trip.

Now about how you might help me. Well, you have given me so much—your spirituality, your love, your support, your precious self itself, the many treasures of your responsiveness; I made a very long list of the things I get from you, and I want to assure you that I don't get them from anyone else. And I just want to stick this in here: you are so precious to me—I will never abandon you, I will never leave you, never go away from you, never withdraw from you; I will stick to you like glue, through thick and thin, through whatever comes; I will be loyal to you, Darling Kathy, my love is steadfast; it still shines forth even when you don't get a letter from me. Okay.

Now—what more I would like from you.

First, more challenges. More personal questions. Pushy ones, prying questions, intrusive ones. As many as you can bring yourself to ask. Questions that might trigger my discomfort. I would find these very valuable. (It might be a bit scary for you to ask.)

Second, I have some concerns about how to make money with my work. There's my book, the one I'm working on on self-sabotage. My groups and workshops, too. I guess I would like you to ask me questions about these things, but I'm not sure what the questions would be. Certainly not, "How's the book going?" But maybe, "Any blocks to making money?" Or "Are you holding yourself back from projecting your power into the world?" Or something like that. Helping me discuss those issues. I have so many ideas, I have trouble narrowing them down and shaping them correctly so they result in people paying money to come to the events I might offer. Advice or suggestions along these lines (like your suggestions about a book for ACAs) would be helpful.

Third, reassurance that you love me. How chagrined I feel to ask for this! So needy! You are already giving me this in just about the right amount. I'm just saying again here what I need, maybe to desensitize myself to it. My hurt child needs comforting from you from time to time. ("Will she find this burdensome? Will she feel smothered by it?")

Just the fact that you have asked how you might help me is a big thing itself. (Who asks questions like that? Nobody. The world is full of takers. Oh, wonderful, wonderful Kathy! How lucky I am to know you!)

You mention the various parts of your body from

which your love comes. Me, too, but it's all of my body. My arms want to hold you close. My mouth wants to taste all parts of you. The front of me wants to press its naked self against your soft flesh. My legs want to twine themselves about you. And my penis; well, it wants to enter you so deep, so deep — to explode inside you. (Dare I write this? Have I really written this?) I want to thrust my maleness into you, to heal your wounds with my masculine balm. To bathe you in strong male acceptance of all parts of you. To affirm and confirm you with my masculine energy; to assure you of your female goodness, to confirm it with my maleness.

Oh, I love you Kathy Jo,

TUESDAY, FEBRUARY 21, 1989 12:10 PM

Jim, my love —

I am full of love, excitement, and anticipation to see you in three weeks. I can barely believe it's true. I wasn't expecting to see you for a good while. (So now you see my impetuous side.) Yet everything is opened up beautifully for this to happen. Your getting to fly to Dallas and for us to fly together. (I am ecstatic! Then to get to talk and talk, be together, be close will be glorious.) I have my ticket already, so that makes it a reality. I cleared my schedule with no hassle, and I got approval from my department head for leave. So everything is in order. Every door is open. Thank you, universe!

I have so much to tell you, but I have been too busy to sit down and write. Today I have been at the hospital with my precious friends, Emily & Cam. Emily is in labor right now, and we'll have a baby soon. I haven't been through labor with anyone I was so close and bonded with. It is exciting, scary, nerve wracking; a feeling of powerlessness. I find myself getting angry at things I have no control over, like monitors, inducing through drugs, how they treat the babies in the nursery. The feminist in me is roaring. I want women to take their power back. Medicine just wrests power from our hands. ("We know best." "Fuck", I say.) Anyway, I also feel elation and joy that my friends are having this experience and that I can be part of it. (It doesn't make me want one, though.) Although the intense shared experience is very attractive. (Now I'm being shy.)

Anyway, it's now 3:40. Emily had an epidural (the pain got too bad) and we're still waiting. I'm on my way to teach class at 5:00. I just wanted to have a connection with you, so no content in this letter. I will write you a content letter asap. Thank you for the incredible experience of honoring me by rearranging your flight to fly with me and for taking charge of getting seat assignments. (It thrilled me to look at my ticket, see my seat assignment, and to realize you'll be sitting next to me.) You wanted to know what you're doing that is new for me. This is new — that you go out of your way to be with me and then taking charge was also new — for a man in my life. Thank you, dear heart.

I love you so I want to cry.

Till we speak again —

Kathy

P.S. Would you please send me your flight number from San Francisco to Dallas — Thanks, K.

WEDNESDAY, FEBRUARY 22, 1989 10:05 PM

Dear Kathy Jo,

I was so thrilled to hear you speak of your jasmine soap ritual. I felt so close to you. I wanted to hear it again and again. When I bought it, I selected it from several kinds, and I thought: Kathy is an olfactory person; this is an exquisite scent; it will anoint her body with my love; but I had no idea you would receive it and use it so spiritually; and this is one of the things I love about you — that nothing you do is ordinary; it is charged with meaning, and I am sensitive to all those charges of meaning, and I merge with them, from the jasmine soap to the unbuckling of seat belts! — and Oh, Kathy Jo, what a rich life we have here, with so many things full of significance; it's like a rich and exotic feast.

You asked me once about my calling. I date my life not only before and after UGS (and before and after you, dear Kathy), but also before and after a three-year period of limbo I went through when I came out to California from Detroit, and to which I think I have referred. This was 1961–1963. Before limbo, many options were open to me, and I considered them on the basis of how well they fit my interests and abilities: advertising man, association executive, editor, publisher, owner of a printing business. I couldn't decide, but almost any of those would do. During the limbo I was in, as I mentioned, I worked as a clerk-typist and in my free time, found myself reading psychology journals and books. Then in 1964 I decided to combine two interests: (or more than two) advertising, publishing, and psychology. I began publishing a little magazine about psychology called Explorations. At that point I realized I was riding a tiger: I couldn't get off, or the tiger would eat me up. I was committed to something that I had to continue no matter what. I asked myself: Is this what you want to commit to? I answered yes; I want to do this no matter what else I do. That was the beginning of the calling. At this point I felt trapped but by a trap I liked. Then I began leading groups. Then workshops for professionals. I realized there was a very narrow market for the kind of groups I was leading, but an enthusiastic one. I was good at what I was doing, and at that point I really felt called to do this — but in the sense of a talented parson being called to exercise his talents. There was no turning back now; I was firmly committed to leading groups. I published two books. Then there was a change. I wanted more than being a practitioner — a leader of groups — even an author. I wanted to create a body of knowledge that was unique. This became Anthetics. At this point, I felt called by destiny, not merely by the exercise of my talents. My work began having a world-historical significance; I could make a contribution to the ideas that support our culture. And then I met you, Precious One. Now I am called to a work of spiritual significance, but I don't know what it will be yet. In each case of more "advanced" calling, I felt doors opening — doors that I hadn't even seen before. Whereas before I had chosen what I wanted to do; now, the thing has chosen me. It has me in its grip and it won't let go, nor do I want it to. I am just going along for the ride wherever it takes me. I'm more trusting now, too, that it will provide whatever I need to get to where I'm going. And I don't even have to succeed; just the journey, the attempt, is enough. And now I have a sweet companion to share this journey with. You, of course (let me be very direct).

And now I would do this work no matter what. If I couldn't make money doing it, I would work as a temporary secretary (as I have before) just so I could do it in my spare time.

It is so good to have you to talk to about this, to have you to ask me about this. To share this with you; to have you share our journey with me.

I drink in your words about spirituality. I'm aware of an inner "thing" that I call God and that feels very stable and fine (and that has an air of amusement about it; that is it's a person who is faintly amused) and I wonder if this is an aspect of God or a god, or what, but it feels good to be in touch with it; it seems to be like a good friend who loves me. But it never created the world, or so it says. Nor does it talk to me about sin, Thank God.

I think there is some connection between spirituality and sexuality, but I can't see it clearly, so I am fascinated by your statement, "I am daring to let sexual images emerge as a way of understanding the intensity of my relationship with God." That rings true, but I want to know more. God does seem to encompass both male and femaleness but how I can't see. Anyway, that would include male and female sexuality; is God the source of sexuality as it is of love? Are we channels for spiritual sexuality? Are our feelings of sexuality essentially spiritual? And physical too? I'm not sure whether these are rhetorical questions or questions addressed to you.

At this point I want to say something about bisexuality, just for the record. I think we are all bisexual, at birth, with perhaps some genetic predisposition either way, but then culture brainwashes us into monosexuality and our inner critic condemns the opposite of whichever tendency we have overdeveloped, so we develop either homophobia or heterophobia, and I am happy that I can accept my own homosexual feelings, although I am indeed genetically predisposed toward women. And fascinated by the secret mysteries of their lovely flesh—oh just fascinated! Your lovely flesh (being more direct). And all the intricate and secret places of your body, Kathy darling.

Now, about my verbality and your reference to Daddy as silent and introspective and your apologetic statement, "Sorry, he keeps cropping up." Please don't apologize; there's just nothing to apologize about. It's not insult or offense to me whatever; quite the opposite. I want you to mention him whenever you want. He will indeed keep cropping up and rightly so. Let him show himself here in our relationship and be exorcised, but let him have his place openly, or he will take it subterraneanly. Please speak of him whenever you wish.

And I love the comparisons you drew between me and Daddy, Andy, and Hale. I don't know where I'm at with the people who are and have been significant in your life and remember I need to know where my position is. I think this may be a subject you don't like to talk about, though, so I will respect any reluctance you may feel. (I hope all that is clear.)

Finally, your statement at the end of your letter. I remember holding your face in my hands and looking deeply into your eyes, and it was a powerful moment for me, and I wanted to ask you what it was for you, and now I guess I'm beginning to know, and I feel so elated and yes, honored, partly by your trust in me and my full awareness of the precious parts of yourself that you are trusting to put in my care, risking, and perhaps wondering, "Is he going to treat these things with care?" And I am, of course, as you are slowly finding out, because in the past I have trusted others with vulnerable parts of myself and they have shall we say not been perfectly accepting of them, so I know what it means, the importance of it, to have someone as tender and delicately loving and a bit shy even (as I am), yet who values love so highly she is willing to take a risk with this man she has known for less than two months (and who wondered at the beginning of our relationship, Hey, is he a rapist maybe or something?). This woman, Kathy trusts me with these tender parts of herself, and I know how to receive them, a knowledge that comes from my own pain and wounded parts—and I am so glad that I can welcome them and know them for the precious treasures that they are. And cherish them. And I want you to know, my beloved, that you can say or write ANYTHING to me, anything at all, the most vulnerable and scary things, and I will receive them with awe and love and perfect acceptance, because of the person I have become.

Beloved, be wrapped in the warm blanket of my

love, feel all cozy there, warmed by my love for you, my strong arms holding you close. Oh, Kathy, I love you!

(8:30am the next day) But I see as I re-read the above that I have been so powerfully affected by what you have written that I have totally evaded it—you have such feminine power! You wrote about your fantasy that just looking would bring you to orgasm (there I've said it!)—and that blew me away (Shut up, i.c. It's ok to be trite; it did blow me away, dammit)—and I'm still incoherent from thinking about it (and I see your warm smile as you read this). Oh, such power you have over me, and I welcome it.

I truly love you,

WEDNESDAY, FEBRUARY, 22, 1989 9:50 AM

Beloved Jim—

I am so hungry to respond to content in your letters. So I'm diving in now. Thank you for the two glorious letters (even one handwritten!). I did fine with your handwriting, by the way. I'd love to receive handwritten or typed letters from you, so go with whatever you have grace for. You are amazingly able to make a typewritten letter warm and alive and personal, so it doesn't offend me. So letter writing is new for you? Well, let me assure you, beloved, that you are a beautiful communicator in letters.

For content, in interaction with your letter of Friday (responding to mine). I love your image of sleeping over with a friend. I long to stay up late talking and talking with you. My Peace Time friends feel that way too, and do you know that we actually had a slumber party (all women that time) at one of our homes. It was wonderful. We ate gourmet shrimp spaghetti, drank a little bit of Zinfandel wine, shared wonderful stories of developing as a female, and ended up skinny dipping together in her pool at midnight! Then all of the group (men and women) go off together to a state park once or twice a year and stay up late talking and talking; get up and have coffee in the early morning quiet. It is glorious. So, I don't think your desire to do something like that together is strange. It is so natural.

Yes, things in our relationship keep getting better and better. So your inner cynic can't quite trust it huh? I don't think I have much of an inner cynic; instead I have a little fearful person with a history of various hurts who also can't quite totally relax. Thank you for the offer to call you any time. I hear you and will follow through if I need to.

Jim, you've given me a gift. As you've talked on the phone and in your letter re: Oedipal stuff, you have really helped me. It is inevitably breakthrough for me when I'll just not panic and try to make my experience go away. If I'll just include and work with stuff, it always integrates and enriches my life. I love your boundary about not letting the oedipal material shape expectations of perfection from each other. That is so helpful to me. Again you provide specific info that clarifies and equips me to deal with my stuff. You surprised me with the info on your own "mom stuff." I didn't know you were feeling that. You hadn't discussed details with me on that. (And you don't have to.)

Thank you for the reassurance about my imperfections being a gift to our relationship. I keep learning that. Perfection is not human. I am human. Our greatest gift to another is often our weakness. That's the genius of A.A. Your story of your own trials, brokenness is actually the greatest thing you give to another. I know when I'm struggling with some part of myself which I consider shameful, I call the person/s who have revealed that "flaw" to me before, not a person who projects all-perfection or no problems with that issue.

Dear Dutch uncle, thank you for your words re: my statement on wanting to be taken care of. I keep expecting you to be shocked or repelled by my stuff, and you keep responding in a way that affirms, gives life, and is so balanced. Anthetic caring. I'll take it! You mentioned speaking to the black hole or inner child. It made me wonder something. Cali asked me about you, "Does Jim have an inner child?" We know and are getting better acquainted with the parts of ourselves that consist of memories, experiences, and a still-living entity we call our little child. That's where Joey is (my little black boy) and where Kaffy is (my precious, vulnerable 2-year old). Have you ever done this kind of work? You say you are playful. Does some of that playfulness come from a child place within? Do you ever act it out? We do. It's fun/enriching.

Thank you for being willing to coach me in labor. I know you will and are.

I was touched by your ability to say you are a lot like a woman and would be an honorary one — What an honoring of the feminine. You have such a nice blend of the masculine and feminine. I really like that. I really have trouble getting close to men who are not in touch are unwilling to be in touch with the feminine (except as a "lay" an object to spill their seed into. And yes, I operate from metaphor a lot, so I would pick up on the voice metaphor in the book. Metaphors are intensely powerful for me; life blood in fact. Gee, even in talking about them, I use metaphor!)

I am so glad you had a fertile creative childhood. I take issue with your judgment that you were not geared in the right directions — just spinning fantasies. My thoughts are that a child's fantasies are necessary, not just as seeds for future sprouting in adult life, but just in themselves, as a work, a legitimate one, for that time of your life. Please don't put young Jim's mental/fantasy life into a negative category.

Thank you for mapping out your own development in ways of knowing. That could be part of your paper for the March seminar! I also had not heard of Bergler's "magic gesture." I think I would have a negative judgment on that. But I immediately counteracted that thought with a sense of goodness in giving what you did not receive. I would come to that gesture on an individual/contextual basis, because sometimes it may be appropriate for the action to be outward-directed (e.g. if the person/receiver wanted what you had to give and if you were willing to let go of their response and have your own inner satisfaction just for having done it). But other times I think it's more appropriate and powerful to give that missing something to yourself, as a symbolic/spiritual/ritualistic act of self healing (e.g. when the person really would be offended, wounded, burdened by the gift).

I really wanted to know your journey, so thanks for sharing details. I am so grateful your journey has taken you through intuitive/subjective knowledge. It enriches you in my eyes and it reassures me that you can understand me. I like your idea of "fusion and disengagement." I still like connection and disengagement. (Fusion is scary for me. I might get lost in it.) "Immerse oneself in the experience, feel the truth, back off and take a close look at it." I love that. I do the first two very well. The backing off is sometimes difficult for me. Separate knowing-a real challenge for me. I wonder if I can do it. Or even want to. Perhaps there is a happy medium. I think that's another issue I'll be clarifying through the seminar. (Oh fast heartbeat, I'm really going. I'll be with you. It will be a banquet!)

I adore your process of letting your inner entity work on problem areas. That is beautiful, so appealing to me and makes me love you even more. I do something similar to this which I call following my energy. Don't force the answer. Back off. Inner guidance comes when least expected and from surprising sources.

I am enriched that you say that our dialogues are not luxuries; that they are life blood (my metaphor) to your work. What an honor to me. Yes, our letters/conversations are like peer days, so rich in learning and interchange. I am learning so much by our interchanges. Thank you, Jim. Thank you, God, for giving him to me. You are a gift, my heart.

I am so blessed that you want to share seminars with me. Yes, you are right, the March seminar is for me. I started reading "Diving Deep and Surfacing" by Carol Christ night before last. And as I read all manner of new insight surfaced. I wrote pages on my development—perfect info for the seminar paper, wept, healed, and entered into awe again. The book was calling to me, but without the seminar and the questions it has placed before me, I would not have had the structure to unravel what came up. I'll share more details later. Maybe on the plane. (Oh, God, on the plane! We're actually going to be together, sharing, loving. I am in expectant ecstasy!)

I love your salutation—a wild cry to God. I hear it. I am on my face before God, before your cry.

Now, to your wonderful handwritten letter… Yes, I was sincere that you love me as I would want to be loved by a man. That gushed forth from my soul. And yes, I believe that our fundamental disagreements can be included in our love. Absolutely. And I have 10 years of experience of this in Peace Time. Getting to know each other's dark side; seeing each other's jerkiness; showing our ass. My inclusion in love muscle is strong.

Then you list your flaws (some). How dear of you! I like that you're capable of being coarse. I curse too, mostly when I'm angry. You say crude things. Well, I fart! Ask Cali, it's one of the things I do best! Love me; love my flatulence (tee hee). I'm glad you compensate for your poor memory by writing notes. I actually have felt so honored (like at Asilomar) when you wrote things down you wanted to say to me. So you are poor for now. I struggle financially too. Although, I am a "nester" and love to have pretty things around me and to wear pretty clothes. I struggle for words too and am blessed that you're not so articulate that you can't understand my struggle for expression. When you get angry and desperate you can be logical/highly focused. Sometime when I get angry and desperate I turn cold. (Andy said I could be cold and take myself away.) So if I ever do that to you, call me on it, okay? I'm so glad you want to talk through problems instead of taking the "I don't want to talk about it" route. I have a low threshold for staying stuck in interpersonal conflict. I must resolve it. I'm so glad you need huge amounts of reassurance. I do too. Please, if ever you feel I'm not understanding you and your paranoia arises, let me know. I want to understand you. Always. I love fiercely, intensely. I have a people pleasing part too. But, I'm less driven by it now. Much less. I don't eat apples, so you don't have to worry about crunching from me! (I actually don't care for normal fruit—apples and oranges. I like fresh figs and bananas though.) I am really interested in you. I am not just being nice. Believe me I am long past putting this much energy into a relationship where I am not vitally interested in the person. So thank you for sharing your flaws with me. On the contrary, I like you even more, knowing them.

Some of my flaws are: I give up my power too easily (power to believe in myself and my work). I can crumple into a little ball when plunged through with someone's scorn or disdain for my work. I can be passive, but I'm also capable of being quite assertive. I'm cowed by disapproval. I still feel like a little child sometimes, waiting for someone outside of myself to give me the go-ahead. I can get myself into trouble by not letting my head serve my gut. (But it's always turned out alright in the end which is why I take issue with Belenky's position that "You cannot just know" and "the inner voice sometimes lies." I from my own experience, find that that inner voice always has a core of truth to give me. What my mind and emotions do with that may lead me astray. But not the intuition.) I have some shame about my sexuality I have not worked through yet. I don't always trust that my personal journey is valid and worth honoring. (Yet I follow it anyway. I'd just like to be more comfortable.) I still need to grow in expressing anger. Anger in my family was either cold rage or cursing frightening rage. (Oh, so your cursing would only bother me if it was turned on me. That would be awful.) And to risk with you one of my crudities, I have this gross habit of picking my nose. (God, now he'll go away for sure. You've grossed him out.)

I love your "good" list: I see and am experiencing with ecstasy your goodness; intelligence; originality; sensitivity; caring; hard-workingness; openness to spirituality (would you put on your 'burner' talking to me sometime about your idea of God?); comfortableness with strong emotion; strength; courage; willingness to negotiate; warmth and lovingness. I want to experience your snuggling side. So, I respond to your singles ad with "warm, loving, sensitive woman would like to get to know you much better, to experience you fully, to share life with you." KV Yes, my being in a relationship already takes the "automatic mating game" out of the picture and frees us to love fully and to create something new. Although my mind keeps mating gaming me. I'm glad we don't have to approach our relationship that way. It has a gaminess I don't like.

Thank you for the prayers so much. I'm glad you felt my triumph. Isn't that remarkable?

In further dialogue re: your booklet…you wanted me to speak more re: the reactive part of myself. Let me see if I can remember…I believe I meant the part that comes from the black hole and wants you to fill it up. That part is desperate; not in touch with my autonomy and personal power and my connectedness and grounding in God/in the universe.

About possible groups/workshops we could do together. I thought of this and it holds a lot of energy/attraction for me: How about a workshop (1 day) on "Healing the Wounded Listening Function: Triumphing over the Inner Critic"? I could talk more on wounded listening and do that half, or we could do it together. And you could get nitty gritty on the Inner Critic on the second half. We could market it in Lafayette to the people who are on workshop lists for the Serenity Center (a counseling center here). I'm just now developing a relationship with them.

Thank you for the ads for vocational workshops. I saw two that used inner work (hypnotherapy/visualization). So that's affirming that a market exists. I think my perspective is new though.

I'm so glad my music gave you chills; it does that to me too. I was hoping it would touch and bless you. The jangly stuff is for the passionate part of me; the part that loves to dance and to sing. I love to sing and dance. They restore my soul. I dance and sing like other people do exercise: to relax, to let go, to renew. Music is so important to me. (I hate opera — don't understand it; I love romantic, powerful classical; Cajun music, and I dearly love rock and roll. Cali hates to ride in my car when I have my music on. But that's me; I do try to respect others and turn the music down if it's too offensive.)

Yes, there is disbelief/awe in me too that you and I have come together. Not an accident to my way of thinking; rather a Gift. I love your calling me your precious treasure. I read those words over and over. They go straight to my heart and to my solar plexus, loving and at the same time, strengthening me. I too think of you all the time, during the day, when I go to bed, when I wake up. (Deep sigh.)

I love your desire to share your life with me. I want that too. I want you to hold me, touch me. To talk about ideas. To be quiet together. To sit with my head on your shoulder. I want you to cook for me (what a pure delight). I want to cook for you. To share our spirituality. To browse bookstores and libraries and malls with you. To ride the merry go round with you. To commune with you, my beloved. Yes, I will intermingle with you. Let us be our greatest (in the human sense), our most creative, our most loving in fleshing out this intermingling. Yes, your words of closer than twinning, siblings, make sense to me, bless me, give life to me. Our yearning is mutual, powerful. I am overcome with love for you. But I will stand in this experience and glory in it.

I love you, Jim,

Kathy

P.S. I am not ready to speak to your spirituality notes yet. It's coming though.

164

FRIDAY, FEBRUARY, 24, 1989 4:45 PM

Beloved Soulmate —

I've been sitting/walking with some resistance in myself to responding to your notes on spirituality, and I've come to this insight: I think you and I may approach spirituality from very different perspectives. It seems very important, in fact vital, to you to have an understanding of spirituality; in other words to use your mind to come to it. I, on the other hand, come to it from the heart and from experience — a kinesthetic approach. And for me that is just as vital as mental understanding is to you. I don't see these different perspectives as a problem, but rather as more richness we have to share. You invite me to talk about, expand on, explain my experience/ understanding of spirituality. I invite you (I think right now may be the first time I've done so) to tell me, expand upon the personal experiences that have led you to your understanding of spirituality. So, given that, I think I can dive in. Oh, and I would love to hear what you think of what I just said.

You first imply that you see spirituality as a personal growth process — not an arriving but a becoming, am I right? I like that. Yes, I agree. That's what leaves me angry/cold about "born-again Christians" and other absolutist spiritual stances. The position of "I have arrived" is to me a spiritual blockade. You can easily get stymied in that stance. I like your idea of inclusive transcendence, and I find it very important. However, I disagree that it is the basic process. For me, and from what I have observed, the basic process is relationship or relatedness — to the self, to others, to the transcendent. Don't skip relationship as a first step, because I think you're implying relationship when you speak of inclusive transcendence. (How can we disengage from something with which we are not in relationship?) I think it is life-givingly, literally vital that we see spirituality from a framework of relationship. (I think that's what you experienced for the first time so strongly when you spoke of the Navy as pleroma.) But you must understand my bias. And my bias is in my personal experience: Spiritual life to me has been an unfolding of the "Word become flesh and dwelling among us." When the transcendent (Word, that which is source, beginning) appears in my life as a nature connection, self-connection (being present to my Self), interpersonal connection, or Higher Power connection, then I come alive, my life deepens, enriches. And it has powerfully time and again, and still is. God, my whole doctoral work process is a spiritual experience — the transcendent connecting with me through the books I am reading, the colloquium big bang, the appearance of Della, the relationship with you, the appearance of Ben, my adjunct). I know that there are many religious paths that don't touch on relationship, but to me they fall short, leave out a gigantic chunk of truth. And perhaps this is what I can give to you; what I want to give to you — a living proof of spirituality as relationship. Will you have that from me?

I like that you address the "I" as that which does the transcending, knowing, deciding, observing, etc. (very cognitive terms you've used, of course, since you come from that approach). So I would add that which does the seeking, longing, connecting, and relating. (Thank you so much, my heart for giving me the opportunity to put all this in words. I feel the passion in me about this—and it is so freeing to put this into words.) Still, you have such a fertile idea in inclusive transcendence. That process could be applied to all the relationships I speak of.

Well, I must wrestle with you on the next issue too! The idea of the physical and spiritual (noetic) being separate and being kept separate — oh no, no, no — please no! (Only separate them for explanation or for searching.) But for a more holistic approach, I experience that the two are intertwined. I cannot separate spirit from physical. Yes there is hunger for oneness. The physical and spiritual must intermingle, giving each other life and substance. They were intended for each other. But as I read on, I may be misunderstanding you. I see, you're explaining a physicalist viewpoint. Yet even in that world-as-physicalist, the noetic is infused — from atoms to galaxies, the awe, the evidence of the transcendent is there. (The physicists say so too.) Also, coming from experience as basic (that's my way of course) I have experienced time and again the noetic touching on the physical (physical healings in mine and others' bodies; financial provision from unexpected sources; and many other miraculous manifestations of the noetic on the physical plane). I wish we could be talking through this face to face, because I feel that I might be missing your point and might be off on a tangent. So, let's do talk about this when we're together (very soon!).

You speak of micro in the noetic realm as the "purified self." Could that correlate to Jung's idea of Self? And could macro relate to collective unconscious? Oh, wait, scratch that. I see you're addressing that specifically. Thanks.

Well, I disagree with Ellwood that "this unobstructed contact can be established only when man is no longer subject to the attachments and fascinations of the lower worlds of sense perceptions, emotions, and analytical reason." My experience (again) has been that I have experienced the transcendent through my senses (a beautiful sunset, walking hand in hand along the Asilomar beach, being held and comforted); through my emotions (tears, awe, raucous joy, and laughter, and even rage); and through analytical reason (reading the books I've been reading, interacting with you). You say that bracketing the physical world view and looking within can access contact with the pleroma. Yes, I agree. But don't limit contact to an inward look. Sometimes the pleroma is contacted in a Navy camaraderie!

Your speaking of pulling oneself out of the pleroma as one grows up is interesting. I think again of James Fowler's Stages of Faith. Has that beckoned to you yet? And your explanation of relying totally on the physicalist and detaching from the pleroma is meaningful to me.

Your speaking of the evolution from embeddedness in the pleroma to being enfolded by it is so interesting. It suggests a possible new interpretation on "You must be born again." And, of course, I love your examples of enfoldment. I relate to each and would like to talk to you about how I've experienced them and hear how you have.

You say the noeticists and physicalists are at odds, each claiming the Truth and each having some part of the truth. Yet there must be a third position of which you are not clear. Does not the Transcendent enfold them both? Issue them both?

I like your idea of inner critic work as a good clearance-maker for experiencing the pleroma. Perhaps we could include that in a spirituality workshop!

Ok you suggest an experiential foundation for a fresh personal religion. You know that that is my base, so I agree. Perhaps that's part of your attraction to me spiritually. May

I share more with you re: experiences? I would love to. And I would love to hear yours. We have so much to talk about.

I like your Anthetic approach to religion — caring, critical thinking, and inner freedom. Yes. I have taken comfort from "Come, let us reason together," the Biblical invitation. And you say we must adopt an empirical approach to the Transcendent — well, I would say, only to the point that you would adopt an empirical approach to a relationship! Once relationship enters the picture, love and attraction, compassion, and caring must walk side by side with reason. What is this? How does it fit into my living? Yes, certainty of theory must be set aside in favor of experience's revelation.

I like your willingness to question maybe God's not responsible for evil; maybe there are many presences; manifestations of the transcendent, maybe God is indulgent. I too am walking with these questions. Joseph Campbell helps me in this. Have you sat at his feet?

Then you conclude with "Religion is the study of relating to the Transcendent, letting it descend" (or I say blossom — pretty Anthetic of me what?) "and pour into and through one's life as love and caring." I love that. And it affirms what I've come to know. I'm glad you have space for that.

Well, as I read over this I feel a mixture of awe and fear. Awe at my own expression of inner work that I had not "given voice to" before. (I have been in such a subjective, individuating spiritual journey that was filled with diffuse awareness and gut guidance.) I like what I wrote! It has passion and reason for me. Fear because I'm afraid of your activation of feeling that I came on too strong; gave too many corrections, etc. I think that's probably my old "silenced" pattern and my old sense of loyalty (don't upset the man; don't speak like you know as much or more than him). This is very healing for me, I'll have you know. Thank you, thank you for your invitation for me to voice my spiritual self. I want to take a deep breath (I just did) and stretch (I am) and eagerly await your reply. Oh, I wish we could discuss it right now, here at my table (with stewed chicken — good brown gravy!) cooking on the stove (as it is right now). Oh, I'm so glad I finally faced this and wrote to you about it. You are a gift to me, beloved. I celebrate you. I love you with my heart, soul, body and mind.

Kathy

P.S. I've read your wonderful letters over and over. They feed me with love and with the experience of being treasured.

MONDAY, FEBRUARY 27, 1989 6:15 PM

Dear Kathy,

My group will start in a few minutes, and I want to say a few things to you before it does. I'm glad I got that letter off to you this afternoon. I need to figure out some basic things about relationships, and I'm having a hard time. Loving you is not a simple thing (but it sure is rewarding—so much so that I will give anything, pay any price to continue).

I don't know why I want to say what I'm about to say; partly for me, partly for you. But here's a list of things I treasure about you, things I value you for, things you give me that are such that I would never leave you. (Would I leave my work? Never. And you are on that level.)

First, your spirituality. That which first attracted me to you. I need this; it fills a gap in my life—just experiencing you. And you haven't crystallized out into some ideology. Your spirituality is raw and pure— experiential and powerful. It is your own. I like the fact that you come from a strong tradition of Christianity and not, for example, Eastern Philosophy, too. That seems more human to me, more personal. So if it were just your spirituality that would be enough for me to have our relationship.

But you are in my field. No need to explain things. And you give me input. And we can work together. We're both working on books. We have a professional rapport. That too in itself would be enough, at least for me to be your friend.

But on top of that, you have an ability to handle ideas and an interest in them. Most people in the field are technicians; you are an original thinker. That's a great delight to me. You take thinking seriously. You give me high quality intellectual dialoguing. That's extremely rare; you don't get that very often. And you quote me Rilke! Not once but twice! Nobody does that. Nobody has even heard of Rilke. My God, woman, you are superb!

You are willing to work on your stuff. Some people are, so this is not as rare as #3 above. But I've been in relationships with women who weren't and it's so comforting (I think that's the right word) to know that you will. If I can bring myself to trust it. (It's my stuff; I can't believe you are so perfect for me!)

Moreover, you are emotionally literate. You can talk about feelings. You like to talk. You are not saying, "I don't want to talk about it!" (As you know, my fear.) How safe that feels — that you will always talk with me about any problems we might have. I can risk a deep connection, given that.

You are so loving and caring. So vulnerable. So in touch with your own pain and dark places, so knowledgeable about how important it is to love, to make contact, to be close. Freely expressive of your love. Not stingy. (Oh, Kathy! How I love you!) (This free expressiveness of yours is extremely rare.)

And on top of that, you are so accepting of me (and of yourself). We've both been risking saying things to each other, and we both stand in awe of how well the other accepts what we think of as our darker sides. For me, that's easy; but I've never found another person as accepting as you. That's very rare.

Then there's the fact that you take the initiative. You call me. You make of my gift of soap your own ritual. You suggest things. I can't tell you how wonderful that is.

There's another, more subtle thing. You are assertive but not rigid. Many people are passive and flexible; that is, their flexibility comes from (I think) being passive. Many other people are assertive, even aggressive, but are rigid. This is hard to explain. They get locked in to some position, which is what gives them the strength, I guess, to be assertive. But you combine flexibility with assertiveness. You hardly ever find that.

You are a vibrantly sexual woman. Wow! You are supercharged with sexual energy. Lushness, voluptuousness, tenderness, fierceness—all combined. This is a real delight.

You inspire my creativity. When we talk, when I read your letters, when I write to you, it triggers ideas in me and catalyzes my writing, my work on my book, the flow of ideas. I wouldn't dream of giving this up.

I love your femaleness; it is so different for me. Mysterious, as I've said, secret, fascinating, of the earth, infused with exquisite niceness.

You are someone who wants to receive what I have to give. My givingness is not wasted.

Well, these are the reasons I am so devoted to you. And why I would never leave you, abandon, you, reject you, etc. I think I'm writing them so you can look at them whenever you want, whenever you need reassurance.

Remember when I asked you at Asilomar why you like me? Many people like me, but not all of them for the right reasons. I loved your reasons. I need to know why people do like me, and I think you might also.

(11:30am the next day). Now, I've been grappling with a problem and not knowing even what it was. But late last night Ann C. called, and we had a long conversation, and exchanged some warm feelings, and now I'm beginning to know what my problem is.

Let me begin by talking about some feelings I've been having and which I thought were so despicable I couldn't tell you. Let's see; how to say this. When I met you at Asilomar, you presented yourself to me as immersed in a circle of friends in Lafayette, chief among them, Cali and Hale. And I thought, OH, she has so many friends, she doesn't need another one. Dismay. And then as we got closer (and after Asilomar), and you wrote about this or that person, I felt twinges of jealousy. Desperateness. Will she really go on loving me? Who is this Hale that she's close to? And Evan? And here she's going to a Jungian workshop; will she meet someone there she likes better than she likes me?

So that's my problem: possessiveness. I didn't know it before. I don't want to be possessive; I want you to be free; I want to work on my stuff. (I keep thinking: Do I have enough to offer her? What am I giving her that other people aren't? Does she love Cali more than she loves me?) (My inner critic says don't tell her that; pretend to be mature!) These feelings seem very ugly to me; maybe I can say them partly because you spoke also of your jealousy.

But I know you are a loving person, and you will love people other than me. It's just your nature. (And I guess I will feel love and express it for others, too, but I feel guilty about it.) Oh, Kathy, there's my problem. Is there anything you can say to me? I mean more than reassurance, which I know you're ready to give. I need to work on my stuff here, and I don't know how. Yet. This is the biggest whirlpool/sandbar/rock of all, and I don't want to founder on it. I think I'll call and ask you about this. (Well, I feel relieved now that I've said it.)

I smile as I think of you (but now I think more of your body, so precious to me), and I feel an aura of your love enfolding me. Once in a while I say your name out loud, and it comforts me. Once in a while I write it on a piece of paper: "Kathy." It triggers chains of memories.

I recall to myself the things you've said to me; the latest one about putting your arm and leg over me to wake me up gently. Oh, sigh! I love you, Kathy Jo, so much. Only two weeks and we'll be together! I can't believe it. (Will you still love me? Yes, I'm beginning to believe that you will!) (I'm such a—what?—I guess what I want to say is sometimes my needy child takes over so much.) Anyway, I send you my love, wave after wave of it. It touches all parts of you: Your dear mind, your fine breasts, your secret place between your legs, every inch of your skin, your feelings, your essence.

Oh joy!

FEBRUARY 27, 1989 9:35 AM

My love,

I have had people tell me about growing up on a farm where daily milking of the cows brought fresh milk in an earthen jug to the table. This non-homogenized milk was special, because rich cream would rise to the top. It was a lucky child who got the first glass, because he got that delicious cream. Well, I have some rich cream that keeps rising to the top, and you are the lucky one who gets to have it poured out to! Today that cream is in the form of a fantasy.

I woke up at 6:30 a.m. this morning even though my alarm wasn't due to go off until 7:00 a.m. Even in my still sleepy state, you came to my mind and with you this picture: you and I in your room in New York loving, greeting each other. Then lying in each other's arms on the bed and moving, moving, and melting into each other. All the while speaking into each other's ears, intimate words of love. "I love you, Jim. I love you, my darling Kathy. I want you, Jim all of you. Imprint yourself upon me and melt into me." Then I see you lift my sweater and touch my bare back with your wonderful hands. And hold me and stroke me. And I moan with pleasure and feel myself creaming. I reach within and give you a taste of that cream off my finger. Now you moan and bury your face in my breasts. You move up to my ear and speak to me of your delight and affirmation of me as woman, as feminine, as your girl. And I delight in it and move more into you...

I love this fantasy. I've never written anything like it before, but you make me feel so safe and welcomed that I can dare to risk it. And to delight in it. And know you will welcome it. Will you tell me how you liked it? I know you will, and I want to hear it. Oh, I have so much love for you. It is fuller and bolder and firmer this morning than ever. I am so ready to risk this love with you; to lavish it upon you. I was so touched by your call last night and by your sharing of shame. And by your courage in addressing and putting words on the age difference and your dying and abandonment issues. Because I had thought of that but had not had the courage to speak of it. You help me so much. Thank you, my darling. If you would die before me, I want to see your going forth. I want to hold you and lay you in God's arms. (Do you think I am morbid?) Sorry, but I just must risk every thought with you, every expression of love Oh, I love you so. Meanwhile, I want to enjoy life with you, growth with you, being with you. You are a gift to me. Loving you so boldly and being cushioned in the blanket of your love, I had the courage this morning to set up an appointment to speak with my dean re: my doctoral program. He told my department head that he had questions about it, and she said I should talk with him. I have no qualms about doing UGS or about my path; I just want him to get its awe and wonder and to get the awe and wonder of me and my journey. But with me bathed in the light of your love, how could he help but get it? Oh, I want to reassure you of how precious you are to me, how life-giving. How much I love you. Let my love soak into adult Jim and seep down onto little Jim, comforting him and cradling him. Let him lie in my breasts. Let him nurse nourishment/strength from my love.

Well, I will write intellectually connecting content later. I want this to be your love letter. Your fantasy letter.

God, I love you so, Jim—

Kathy

MONDAY, FEBRUARY 27, 1989 3:30 PM

Dearest Soul Mate,

I'm in the middle of preparing for my lecture tomorrow evening at the Eric Berne Society ("Achieving Greater Depth in Personal Relationships") and putting together copies of my booklet in case anyone wants to buy them then, but I want to take time for a brief letter to make contact with you.

You called this morning; I had turned off my telephone because I woke up in the middle of the night and couldn't get back to sleep and wanted to make sure I'd sleep, and I was so sorry to miss your call, but there it is now on my answering machine, and I can replay it whenever I want, but I still wanted the real you in person; anyway, I won't do that anymore. (You're so thoughtful and considerate; it's a powerful experience for me — to call me, wondering if I'd need your support and reassurance. You not only give it when asked but offer it when I don't ask! What a treasure you are!)

It feels like now I'm on that raft zipping along only it's now rougher than ever, and before I could handle it okay, but now I've got to exert every ounce of skill and ingenuity to avoid the rocks and whirlpools and sandbars, and I wonder if I can; well, I know I can. But it will not be easy. Your support and patience and understanding help so much.

I've got to say something about a workshop in Lafayette. At first I thought, well, I know how to do an inner critic workshop; what sort of place would Kathy have in that? Why doesn't she just attend? And then

I saw your idea (which you said holds a lot of energy for you—thank you parenthetically for calibrating your wants) about "Healing the Wounded Listening Functioning: Triumphing Over the Inner Critic," and it suddenly occurred to me where my work has a gaping hole—once the inner critic work is done, what then? No focus on healing and self-love after that work. So I propose the following title: "Disarming Your Inner Critic and Healing the Wounded Child," with me presenting first, followed by you with your loving and healing presence and methods. How does that sound? I think the order is correct: first IC work, then WC work. Let me know your thoughts on this.

Oh, Kathy, thank you for helping me; please-I don't know what—please something or other. Give me support and reassurance? No. That you are already doing. Maybe just be there to listen. Maybe something else I can't get in touch with yet. (Tacit knowledge.)

Be assured that I will never abandon or reject you; I'm working on another letter listing all the reasons why you are so important to me. I'll write again tomorrow, so you'll get another letter in your tomorrow.

Oh, so much love! So much tenderness for you!

Oh—I'm inarticulate, but my heart wells up—

FEBRUARY 28, 1989 10:50 AM

My love,

I have a hundred things to say to you! First, did I tell you how powerful to me your statement, "I want to cook for you" was for me? No, I didn't, so I am now. That holds deep power for me, and I'm not real clear why. Some inklings: (Daddy cooked and I loved his cooking and his bigness in not being afraid to do a traditionally feminine task.) Also, I love the bigness in you. As a matter of fact, I love how huge you are to include so much of me and my complexity (bisexuality, brokenness, awesomeness, etc.). How did you get to be so big? Many people your age (and my age, for that matter) remain so little and so narrow. I'm so glad I met you. You are a heart's desire fulfilled for me. (I think that just melted you. Right?)

Second, I told Mama about you yesterday while we had lunch, and she said, "You love his maturity. You need that. I did too." And you know, I had forgotten but Daddy was 16 years older than Mama. So my model was of a mature man totally devoted to this younger, feisty woman. (Sound familiar?) Do you know my feisty side? It's there. Like my rage at the medical establishment in Emily's birth process. So, I assure you that your age is not a problem for me. It is in-stead the thing I love. We keep surprising each other, don't we? I love you so.

Third, I am elated. Donna N. agreed to be my 2nd core reader, so my committee is complete. I am so excited to have that all in place.

Fourth, have you read Imagining Argentina yet? I'm anxious to have you read of Carlos and Cecelia's love (I think I have their names right). It was so solid, so powerful, such a thing of faith, that it kept them both alive, literally. I sense that you and I have that and will grow in that.

I'm anxious to hear your response to my fantasy letter. (I should have warned you not to read it on the steps of the library!) I am so pleased with myself for risking that with you. Especially after your wonderful letter assuring me I can say anything, ANYTHING, to you. I am taking you at your word.

I love going home and finding a letter from you in my mailbox. It thrills me, warms me. And you are such a wonderful communicator, my love. I want you to risk with me too. Dare to speak. I welcome you. I love how you remembered that I am an olfactory person. (I didn't even remember saying that to you.) And that you notice details and "charges of meaning" and that you merge with them. Oh, Jim, what an extraordinary person you are — you delight me to the core. Yes, we are at the banquet table. I anointed myself with your soap and your love again this morning. I needed the blessing in order to go to the doctor and have an ulcer on my tongue cauterized with silver nitrate. The doctor and his staff kept saying, "Oh this is going to hurt you." (They're my friends.) But I didn't feel anything but the slightest burn. (I was enfolded in the blanket of your love.) I am so infatuated and obsessed with you. You are always on my mind. I pray for you and love you and think about you. I read your letters again and again. Part of me says, "Is this okay?" Another part says, "Enjoy the hell (heaven) out of this. It's a rarity."

Thank you, my love, for the recounting of your calling journey. Thank you especially for the distinction re: "being at choice" initially but moving into "being chosen." That is a beautiful distinction. And I think very important. And I keep being surprised that my coming into your life has made a vocational significance to you. I'd like to hear more about that, although I hear you still don't know the details, just an intuition.

I love your "amused" inner being. My Inner One has a sense of humor too. And is a gentle revealer. I have an image that when it's time for me to learn something new about myself, he (I think "he") gently turns over a card (like a playing card) on the table. (One card amidst others that are face down, some face up, like in a solitaire game.) And it is always gentle, often amusing, always enlightening and life-giving. Revelations for personal growth have come to me in that pattern.

You want to know more about my sexual images re: God. Well, I am blessed and captivated by the Bible verses that have given me life. I want to share them with you: "I found you in your blood and said, 'Live.'" (Ezekiel 16) (I really need to give you more detail — more in person — in person — oh, glory just 2 weeks from today!) Also, I have an image of God putting his mouth over mine and breathing life into me. That has deep sensual/sexual significance for me — like a lover's kiss of life. Also, "I have called you by name. You are mine." (Jeremiah, I think.) "Your husband is your Maker." (Isaiah) And the Song of Solomon I take as God's description of His love, lovemaking to- ward us. He is so much more at risk than we. Always initiating. Holding out his arms. Walking beside. Holding my hand. Simon and Garfunkel's song "Bridge over Troubled Waters" is a hymn for me that I take as God's love song to me. "Like a bridge over troubled waters; I will lay me down." "Sail on, Silver Girl, your time has come to shine. All your dreams are on their way. I'm sailing right behind. Like a bridge over troubled waters, I will lay me down." I also had a meditation once on Mary, and that insight was that she is an archetype of how God wants to impregnate all of us (and *me specifically) with Himself so that I may give birth to him in the world, as Mary did to Jesus. So these are a few of my spiritual/sexual images.*

I was thinking of your knee problems and had the warmest feeling come over me. It's a new (?) interpretation for you. Perhaps you may see it as I see it—you bear a love wound. I thought, "What a precious thing that you would take the brunt of the fall yourself, even to the point of causing chronic problems, rather than have your daughter hurt." That was a redemptive act, an act of love; an act in the heart of God (as I know him)—to take the pain yourself rather than have your child hurt—a Jesus act. You are beautiful, Jim. And then I thought—I want to honor your love wound by kissing your knees and breathing (as in God-breath) a blessing on them. "I know what you have done, and I honor you." (I can imagine that this is hard for you to take right now. But I want you to be with that idea and to be open to receiving this sacrament (sacred act) from me. Thank you, my love, for drawing forth the goddess, the god-like in me and for honoring it and for giving it a place to be lived out. I do believe you are big enough for me. Please don't sell out to a thought that you could not bear such things from me. I long to give them to you. Jesus said as he wept, "Oh, Jerusalem, I long to take you under my wings as a mother hen would her brood, but you would not" (Now my inner critic is saying, "Don't get so inflated, girl.") Yet, I sense that I can risk the greatness of my spirituality with you. And now I need reassurance. That my spiritual power won't scare you away. That you will receive it and hold it. I was so blessed that you saw your evasion of facing my feminine power/my orgasm-just-looking image. And that you chose to face me, to speak it, to hold it. Oh, you are big enough for me. I long for a man to face me head on on all levels—emotional (you do), physical (you do), intellectual (you do), and spiritual (ah, you do). Thank you, Jim.

I shared the Maslow article with Mama, and she said a very interesting thing that made me step back in awe at her greatness (and have some knowledge/recognition of my origins). She said, "I disagree that some emotions/experiences may be too big for us, may tear us apart. We have to watch the power of the Word—if we say, 'Ah this is too much for me' it often is. But if we say, 'I am big enough to contain this, we can.'" Isn't that powerful? And you are saying, time and again, "to hell with conventionalities. We can do this; we are doing this." And I am right with you.

You ask me to speak of your position in my life. Oh, god, I am giving birth to that reality. I am risking the birthing of you, Jim, into primary position. I am scared. Because I think, what does this mean to all my other relationships? What changes? My heart is clutching right now. And so, would you go easy with me on this? All of my relationships were in place when I met you. They're all being rearranged, and I want to give them time for natural and divine order to order them accordingly. For now, know that you are so consuming to my mind, heart, and spirit. This scares me. Please hold me. Reach out to me in this. Well, in balance, I say I can grow into this too. I am big enough to have a mature/powerful/transcendent relationship with a man (with you, Jim). That is a new thought to me. Bear with me as I give it time to blossom and come to full fruit. It is budding now, fragile, yet with the strength and tenacity of new growth.

I love you so.   *Kathy*

WEDNESDAY, MARCH 1, 1989 3:45 PM

Kathy Darling,

I was so glad to be here for your phone call earlier today and then to go to the post office and get your letter about my comments on spirituality! Two connectednesses in one day. (I was worried about what your responses might be to my comments; I was hoping we would not disagree about fundamentals — and we don't! Whatever disagreements we have will only sharpen our ideas, as they have begun to do already. You are my treasure, my precious girl, my joy!)

Oh, you female, you!

More on this later when I've had a chance to think about your letter.

For now I want to reassure you again that I will never leave you. Look, Dear One: YOU ARE IMPORTANT TO MY WORK! You make it creative and fertile; you inspire me; you help my work grow. If that were all, it would be enough. But there's so much more — everything you give me that makes me feel like a kid on Christmas morning.

Now, I want to say again how important it is that we revolve around the sun of each other at the right distance — close enough to be warmed and heated through and through by the blazing love that pours forth; far enough away so we don't fall in and lose ourselves in the other. That kind of thing has destroyed many relationships of lesser intensity than ours. We have a responsibility to the greatness of our identities. We are indeed navigating very swift and troublesome currents right now, skimming past many hazards. Let us continue to help each other; with patience and love, with the ability to accept any mistakes either of us might make; remember that any such mistake is always correctable. We don't have to do this perfectly; all we have to do is learn as we go. And we are just the right people for this relationship! (Well, I guess that's a double entendre.) I mean few others could handle it so well. Take my hand, Dear One, and we will move through these dangerous waters together; I have a map.

Here are some things you may want to say to yourself:

Just because I love this man, it does not mean…

—that I must give up my identity

—that I must give up my likes and dislikes

—that I must give up my work

—that I must do whatever I think he expects of me

—that I must give up my friends and relationships

—that I cannot challenge him, even bluntly and firmly

—that I must lose myself in him and his goals and dreams

I need you, Dear Heart, as a complement, not a duplicate. I do not want you to sit at my feet (or at anyone's for that matter; something I mean to take up with you later, in my Dutch uncle mode). I need you to be free, creative, your own person, mentally powerful, able to challenge me—even when you're not sure of the adequacy of the grounds for your challenge. I need a full human being. I will encourage you at all times to maintain your own identity in the blazing power of our love for each other. I know you can do it. I care about you so much that I want you as you are, not a pretzelized Kathyoid. And I will not leave you just because you continue to be yourself. I will go on being charmed and pleased by your otherness.

I have never loved like this before.

FRIDAY, MARCH 3, 1989 10:00 AM

Oh, my lovely Kathy—

Here are two letters, a jangly one, and an ecstatic one. I wanted to separate them. The jangly one is not really so bad, but it doesn't belong on the same page with the ecstatic one. I am also enclosing (how formal!) a copy of my workshop announcement, for your comments and feedback. I handed these out at the lecture I gave at the Eric Berne Society in San Francisco last Tuesday—a triumphant lecture. You were there with me in kythe, but how nice it would be for you to be there in person, so I could say (not only at the lecture but at the workshop), "And now I'd like to introduce Kathy Vermillion, who will talk about...." And have them experience your lovely spirituality and your precious love. Jim and Kathy. Kathy and Jim. Oh, my!

As I was coming from the dentist's yesterday, I ran into Kerry, my favorite school comrade at Cal State Hayward, my master's program. She's in her 30s or early 40s, I guess, cute, happily married, lively and aware, playful; I'd like you two to meet. We talked over hot chocolates, and I noticed the change in myself that I had wondered about; I hadn't seen her since before the Colloquium. I was more open, more loving, much more boldly emotional. It felt so nice to watch myself enjoying the fruits of our precious relationship (yours and mine, that is), to see the change in me because of you. Your femaleness is so damned good for me! I'll have more to say about anima and animus, but for now, here are the two letters… I love you Kathy Jo Vermillion,

THURSDAY, MARCH 2, 1989 9:30 AM
THE JANGLY LETTER

Darling Kathy (My own girl),

I want to say quickly that this letter is about projecting the anima (and animus) and the feelings triggered in me by your distress at reading Sanford. I need some reassurance, and I know you'll be willing to give it, and then I'll feel okay again so everything will be all right—but there are some things I've got to say.

What Sanford writes (p.161) seems to fit me: the woman will seem "highly desirable. She will fascinate him. He will be drawn to her." And so on. That certainly is me. But Sanford writes: my longing is only my "unconscious longing for union with my own soul." I will be "demanding and possessive" (p. 162) and not want you to become yourself.

Well, I wouldn't place much faith in Sanford. If you look at his ideas critically, you'll find them vague and loosely presented. They don't intermesh with other theories. He is not one of the better Jungian therapists. For example, he does not say clearly enough that anima projection occurs ONLY to the extent that the man is out of touch with his anima, his own feelings. Someone like Jack. So take a look at me. Am I out of touch with my feelings? With my feminine side? (In fact, I can respond so positively to your mysterious and fascinating femaleness because I am in touch with my anima!)

Now, here are the apprehensive feelings I'm having: I know you're going to a Jungian conference in May. Jungian psychology, it seems to me, has some very good ideas, but it has a great many partial and flashy half-truths. And some outright mistakes. It can be like a swamp: easy to sink into and become fascinated with.

I guess I'm afraid that in your reading or listening to lectures at the conference, you'll say, "Oh, now I see that my Jungian type is not compatible with Jim's. I thought we were in love, but it's only superficial—and even pathological." Well, that's it. That's my fear.

Oh, Kathy dear, please reassure me that you will, as you so wisely said, not give away your power to books or to "expert" lecturers. I have a horror that some person, unknown to me, will have some negative influence on our precious relationship that I will not be able to address. (I do know of course, that you will tell me of any negative feelings that come up for you. I trust that. Without that, I would really feel insecure!)

Let's talk about this some more; on the plane. I guess I'll call you about it too. My guess is that you get scared of losing yourself in our closeness and then are vulnerable to something you read that might lend itself to saying there's something wrong with our relationship.

I value our closeness so much, I'm going to fight for it as hard as I can. So, please, darling Kathy, sharpen your critical thinking skills (your gleaming sword?) so you can do battle with anything that might threaten what we have created. I love you so much. I feel like a Daddy Tiger whose mate and cubs are threatened by outside forces and who will fight to the death to defend them.

Oh, Kathy! I hold you so close, hug you so tight!

THURSDAY, MARCH 2, 1989 12:50 PM

My dear soulmate,

Your fantasy letter came today. I thought, as I took it from the post office box, it would be easy to read it on the ledge by the library steps. I thought I wouldn't heed your warning. So I began reading it. When POW! I got overwhelmed and had to stop. You were right. It was high-level stuff. (Your letter felt hot in my pocket as I walked to my office.)

Oh, such bliss when I read it! Such charges of sexual energy through my body! And it wasn't nearly enough; just a brief section; I wanted more and more. (And I didn't even ask you for it! You just offered it!)

How can I begin to respond? First of all, the word cream—what a sexy word. I used to live on a farm with my cousins Norma and Shirley; I was 11, they were 8 and 10. I didn't know it until later, but I had strong sexual feelings toward them at the time. They were prototypes for me, and I often have fantasies about them, completing unfulfilled impulses.

And we did buy milk from a neighboring farm, and one day I didn't shake the bottle the way I was supposed to, and poured myself a glass of what turned out to be almost pure cream, and felt guilty as I tasted it and went ahead and drank it; I was too embarrassed to say anything, and I'm sure they noticed but no one said a word. So ordinary cream has sexual connotations for me. But sexual "cream" does too—not only your cream (sigh! How tasty it would be!) but mine. Oh, me!

How bold and courageous you are to write that

fantasy! How I admire you! I loved it. I want to know two things: One, how much of your fantasy was erotically aimed at my needs and wishes, and how much was it for your own arousal? Second, how could you possibly have known what would arouse me? Did you guess? Or did you have a good idea? There are more things I want to ask you, but I'm too damned shy at this time. Hell!

Well, that's all about that for now. Yes, for now…

How to write about this next part! When you write of death, you write of my concerns, my fears, my issues! In thinking about spirituality, I've been wondering: Well, what about dying? How does that fit in? Is there life after death, and so on? And by your statements, you have cut through this Gordian know (with your gleaming sword!), and you have given voice to some powerful words that have touched me to the core — no, deeper yet, deeper than the core — so deep I didn't know it was there. "If you would die before me," you wrote, "I want to see your going forth." (How felicitous a phrase!) "I want to hold you and lay you in God's arms."

Well, I want to cry, I am so touched. I am so embraced by (your love? — no, something much more profound that, something beyond love but including it, something unnameable). Death is such a powerful thing, and you will be there with me, the power of the Transcendent (of God) flowing through your sweet soul, so what do I ever have to fear?

How safe I would feel with you then! How comforted! So what are all these questions about death? What does it matter? Here is Kathy, who says that relationships are the essence of spirituality, and she offers me her very self to be enfolded in!

What can we know of mysterious things beyond the life we perceive except that they are mysterious indeed, but here is my lovely Kathy, my life and my darling girl, my soul mate—to be with me—I am all choked up; I can't write a coherent word about this. That she will be with me if I face this—Oh, my God! That she will be with me if I face this strange and powerful thing, Death! Oh, my! Oh!

The word love is not strong enough to express what I am feeling for you—

FRIDAY, MARCH 3, 1989 2:30 PM

Darling Kathy,

I can't seem to stop writing to you. That's a backlog of ideas you gave me that I want to respond to. So here's another non-rhapsodic letter. I want to address the ideas in Bruce's newsletter.

First, why do men fear marriage? I think a distinction must be made between men's fear of marriage and their fear of femaleness. Men fear marriage it seems to me, because they feel trapped by it. Only one sexual partner! For the rest of one's life!

But men fear femaleness—right—because they fear being pulled into the vortex of the womb. Or rather the vortex of the female pleroma. Losing their hard-won identity. In order to grow up, men must differentiate from the mother; must disengage from softness, tenderness, gentleness. Must become tough, hard, strong, independent—like Dad (who shows them the way out of Mother's femaleness). They must condemn their anima, submerge it. So they fear falling back in. But to the extent that they have repressed the anima, they marry women who embody it, whereupon (and this Jung does not say; this Elliott says) they will have something to criticize. Because they had to condemn their own anima, they criticize it as embodied (not projected on) by the woman. So men criticize their wives for being unassertive, wishy-washy, soft, emotional, illogical, and so on. And are indeed fascinated by the dark emotionality they find in women, but so fearful that they cannot partake of it or merge with it or appreciate it. So that's why men fear femaleness, it seems to me.

Moreover, men try to "own" it by marrying it; they think they can control it once they capture it. They're fighting their own inner conflict, objectified in the relationship with a woman. Wanting to subdue her (as they subdued their own femininity, in order to "grow up and be a man").

Women, when they grow up, do not have to differentiate from their basic care-giver but must be more like her. So they're closer to the pleroma, more comfortable with falling back into it.

Are women drawn to chaos? Not really. Only the mysterious and seductive darkness of the pleroma. It just seems like chaos to a man. To a woman it's earthy, gut-level, intuitive, magical, but with its own inner logic.

What about women's resistance to men? I think it is, as Bruce says, through a fear of losing a sense of themselves—but as connected to earthiness, to tacit knowing. Oppressed by male logic, they distrust it and fall back on tacitness. Having submerged their rationality (or not yet developed it), they may express it as animus—in which case Jung may be right, that they adopt and present pseudo logical opinions, overvaluing logic even, but not able to maintain an open mind—a kind of simulacrum of male reasoning.

As long as women feel unassertive and helpless, they will distrust and resist male reasoning and logic; what they need to do, it seems to me, is learn to reason, to balance their tacit and intuitive knowing. Learn to think critically, as I keep saying, and realize that this skill will not eliminate their pleromatic knowing but will enhance and balance it. Then they will no longer be oppressed by male authorities. They will have weapons to resist. And need not fear maleness.

But there's another fear of maleness that I think women have: fear of being put down for being emotional, intuitive, and pleromatic. (I have this fear too.) I guess it's not so much a fear of maleness as fear of having those sensitive tenuous, but really important pleromatic things made fun of. Women can be critics, too. Here the solution seems to me to be developing crisp, clear boundaries. "Oh, you feel critical and judgmental of my intuitions? You've got some stuff to work on!"

About women's love of made-up beds and straightened pictures. Of course, not all do. But those who do — let's say, to an extreme degree (and that includes men who do, also), do so, I think, because they are enmeshed with their environment. Hyperpermeable boundaries. They let in too much stuff from the outside; can't close it off and have a clear sense of "myself" vs. "the external world." So crooked pictures, unmade beds, fish held captive in the Monterey aquarium, someone's pain, someone's anger — all that stuff seeps in through the permeability and they are at its mercy. Most men learn to have good boundaries. For women it's harder, partly because to have good boundaries with the external world means shutting it out — and also shutting out one's inner world, too. Men with rigid boundaries can do this — and they become insensitive clods. When they hear the word "teddy bear," they think of those 50,000 teddy bears they need for a Christmas promotion — not a cute little stuffed animal that can make someone cry just to look at it. So the trick is to have boundaries that are flexible: permeable when they need to be (to let love flow out — and to let it in from others), impervious when they need to be (to keep out the effects of someone's anger, for example).

So I think there are a lot of intriguing ideas in this newsletter, but somewhat in need of coherence.

SATURDAY, 9:00 AM

Oh, Kathy, I guess I love you a whole lot. Isn't it nice that we love each other equally? That we are equally infatuated and obsessed with each other? How painful it would be if the other were not there to match the love that is given! (Well, the infatuation means that we are probably over idealizing each other, and maybe we'll be in for some dis-appointments if the other doesn't measure up, which will inevitably happen. But in the meantime, let's enjoy the lovely power of our feelings — but give our work and our other relationships enough time, too.)

Yes, I am big — big enough for you. I got that way by doing lots of work on myself over the years. Self-acceptance has been very important to me, and acceptance of others. Love is a pleasure to give and always has been- but not many are willing to receive it (as you, dearest, are). Many people like me for my acceptance of them but are not willing to reciprocate — are instead, judgmental. I will include all of you dear one, every last jot and tittle of you (tee hee, as you would say): I can't say it, because I'm a man, and we men don't say tee hee). You have so far experienced about one tenth of one percent of my ability to be accepting. There is nothing you can say or do that I would not embrace, lovingly.

When you write "you are a heart's desire fulfilled for me," no, that does not melt me down to my toes — but it does melt me — but lately every word you write practically melts me somewhat. But what does melt me so much I am overwhelmed by it is what your dear

Mama said: "You love his maturity. You need that. I did too."

Oh, Kathy! I read those words over and over—to get your Mama's imprimatur! (For some reason, that's important, she approves! I guess). She understands us! She is a great woman—especially re: her comments on Maslow, with which I agree.

Your feisty side? No I don't know it well. But I'm looking forward to meeting it and cherishing it. (Oh, I love you!)

You are like a great mansion, and you have invited me into you, and at first I stood in the hall while we shyly got to know each other, and then you invited me into an inner room, wondering what my reaction would be—and I loved it—and so we are now exploring this mansion, with you opening one door after another (not that quickly, of course) and showing me those rooms, as we explore hand in hand, as you look at my face to see my reaction. And I love this house of you, and we are wondering whether to open the door to the bedroom…

I might say again that I enjoy sexy lingerie. When I was five, my parents took me to a radio station transmitting tower in Chicago (we lived nearby), and there was a little girl there about my age, and she did cartwheels for me, and I was overwhelmed with pleasure to see her pink panties as she did cartwheel after cartwheel, and so I was imprinted on brief pink panties. And so I like girls who wear skirts, too, from time to time. (I guess this is as close as I can come to saying I would like you to wear a skirt once in a while so I can look at your dear legs, my darling.)

Yes, we do keep surprising each other. The above was scary for me to write, too. It was my risking with you, at your invitation. Another metaphor occurs to me — one I tell my groups about from time to time. We each hold a hand of cards, and we play them one at a time, to see what the reaction will be — first deuces and treys, then higher-value cards, and finally kings and queens. We play a card and wait. If it is accepted we play another, higher one. That's what I've been doing with you, and Little Jim is fearful, but I reassure him: "Look. This is Kathy! We love her, and she loves us, and she's not going to reject us! So let's risk our vulnerability." And he smiles shyly and says okay.

Now, about your comments on my knees. You wonder if they are hard for me to take. Oh, quite the contrary, darling Kathy! My reactions are indescribable because they are so profound, but all overwhelmingly positive. Before, I thought: well, no big deal, it was just a matter of course that I would avoid any injury to Carol. So what? But now you say I bear a love wound, and I am ennobled and transfigured by your statement. Why, of course, I think; that's exactly what it is! Before, it was a physicalist disorder of torn ligament and sprained muscle. Now it has acquired pleromatic significance by your Word given to me — your precious voice, seeing me and transforming me, and this is one of the things I deeply cherish about you. You give my life significance, by speaking of your deeper Truth to me. OH, Kathy!

You are my priestess, my intermediary between me and the Transcendent, my celebrant of secret mysteries that are moving my soul in a way that Biblical writers never knew. Yes, you are the water of life for me, the channel of God.

I feel like a little child, trusting and good. Innocent and loving. Facing you.

Ah, you are risking the birthing of me in you! Why, of course! — that's what you asked me to help you with by coaching you in labor — one of the things. Oh, I will be glad to help this germinate in you. This insemination of you I have performed (at your sweet request on the beach by the crashing surf and the big rocks and little birds!), and feel your tummy from time to time to sense the quickening within you of me. And get you special foods if you want them, and let this wondrous pregnancy take its time. I will be there with you, there for you.

OH Kathy! My God! Oh I love you!

FRIDAY, MARCH 3, 1989 10:30 AM

My darling Jim,

I'm rereading your letter of Feb 20 in my office. And I want to respond. First, to your wonderful bold last paragraph — the parts of your body that long to love me. I love everything you said, everything you risked. Thank you, my love, for your boldness. I have yearned for masculine strength tempered with sensitivity and gentleness toward me. And you give me that. One of the feminist authors I read recently said, "As women we have too often mistaken passivity for gentleness in men." That was my inventory! Because I thought Steven was gentle (and he was) but he also had some major weakness and passivity that translated to non-support, abandonment, and isolation toward me when I needed support at Daddy's death. You, on the other hand, are gentle yet strong. You don't abandon me. You see me through my dark times — side by side — being strong enough to bear your own pain and to help me to bear mine.

So about your body's yearnings. I want your arms to hold me close. I want your mouth to taste all parts of me. I want your warm flesh against mine. I want to entwine legs with you. I want your penis to enter me — so deep. Oh, and your final words were beautiful, were balm to me — "I want to assure you of your female goodness, to confirm it with my maleness." I don't know if I can convey to you how powerful these words are to me. They take my breath away. I am in awe of your willingness, of your love for me, of the core understanding you have of my need. Oh, Jim, my turn to be incoherent.

I'm scared to say the next things to you — Oh, God, my stomach is churning. Anyway, I would be inauthentic to myself and to you if I didn't say that I am open to a sexual consummation with you in New York. I'm not saying, "Let's do it." I'm more saying I want to discuss that option. Well, there are some realities: 1) I am still of a fertile age. 2) I have not been sexually active in a long time. 3) I am not using any birth control measures. (I used to take "the pill" when I was active 10-12 years ago.) 4) I don't know any details about you, like have you had a vasectomy? 5) If not, would you be willing to use condoms; and if so, would you take responsibility for that? 6) Since you have been sexually active, can you give me some reassurance re: AIDS? There, I feel much better having communicated that. Also, on an emotional level I am so scared of changes and colorings that occur in a relationship when sex enters the relationship. Do we want those colorings? (For example, even more longing when apart? Fear of abandonment — "once a man gets what he wants, he'll go away." Isn't that gross, but it is an old tape in me.) Chemistry abounding (how would I keep equilibrium at the seminar and in our work together). If you have any thoughts, let me know. I have never been this transparent in communicating about the outworking of a relationship before. You and I are incredible together!

Now, different subject. I am more in equilibrium than when I called you this week. More in myself. Which is good. But I also have had some dizziness, and my mind's in a whirl!

Thank you, dear heart, for taking time to write me a quick letter in the midst of your lecture preparations. (And I want to celebrate more fully with you. I'm so glad that you were in your power and that the audience honored it and was touched. After I reached equilibrium I grieved that I hadn't been able to talk more deeply about your experience, because I was so into my pain.) Well, I want to hear some content from that lecture. I laughed delightedly at your topic: "Achieving Greater Depth in Personal Relationships" — nothing like speaking from what you know and are experiencing.

Now, about a workshop in Lafayette. I am so blessed by your process of looking at an area of competence/experience in your professional life and then being big enough to see a gap. You are incredible. I love your openness, your bigness. Then I am thrilled that you see a way for me to fill the gap. Yes, I do bring healing, self-love to my workshop participants. But I'd have a hard time doing inner critic stuff (as in leading it). That's your province. I love your idea of doing a one day workshop for the general public (I agree; not geared to professionals) with IC content first with you equipping them to clear the path for healing. Then, yes I can do a healing portion. But I don't think I want to entitle it "Healing the Wounded Child." (Yes, what I do is that.) But a couple of reservations are that it's a little too broad and diffuse for me. I'd need to narrow it down. I still like "Healing the Wounded Listening Function." But I'm not happy calling it that. Help! I need your good thinking skills. (My other reservation is that there's a guy in town who does these "healing the inner child" workshops regularly and does a good job at it. I don't want to duplicate; want to offer something fresh and wholly me.) How about (& this is brainstorming; I'm not really satisfied with it, just with the concept) "The Voices Within — Disarming the Inner Critic: Reclaiming the Inner Affirmer." (I don't like term — help!) First order of the day, I think would be an introduction to inner listening to frame the whole day. And yes, we wouldn't do it unless we could get your air fare. But at $35, it would only take 10 or 12. Hopefully, we could get *enough to each make a little money too. Let's not sell ourselves short.*

Now, I am here to receive you, to hold you, to walk by your side as you frame and concretize your "please…" to me.

Oh, I really liked that you moved from "Why doesn't Kathy just attend my workshop" to, "She could contribute a whole area I don't touch." It's really important for me to not lose myself in you professionally — to be honored by you as professionally gifted and to not expend all this energy in getting together a workshop you could give, but I wouldn't get to exercise my gift. I'd take a back seat. No, I think that would be self-negating at this point. Something I don't want to do, and I don't want you to do. I love your salutation of love, tenderness, and inarticulateness with your heart welling up. You are beautiful. I want you as my man. You are man enough for me. Glory!

I wrote some journaling stuff after we hung up, and I want to share it with you. "Jim had to take a step back; about to fall into me. I'm glad he did. I'm glad he possesses himself. I love that. And I want to do that too. Possess myself. Be myself fully — retain myself. In my family, my loving others was held in some contempt, so there is a part of me that holds myself in contempt for loving too strongly. So I give this part love and reassurance. You are beloved, dear part of me that loves so strongly. You are beautiful. I take you in my arms and assure you. You are good. You are of God. You are not to be despised. You may express yourself. You may have life. We will work together in this. I won't abandon you. Won't shut you in a closet again. You give me life. A dimension I wouldn't have without you. Without you I am incomplete. So we will do this together. But I will be firm with you sometimes. You may not overtake me or command me. You are a gift to me, and you have your place."

Oh, another concern I have, dear heart. When we are together at the seminar, I fear that I will overwhelm you with wanting to be with you too much. I know that I do want to make the most of our being together in the flesh — won't want to miss a second with you. I just needed to say that. To tell the truth. Yet, you may have some need to be alone or with others without me, so let me know if you do. Just reassure me of your love and I'll be okay. Let's just communicate real clearly. I'll be fine. I'll tell you too. But as much as possible can we be together there? That's my heart's desire. Eek, I'm still scared to speak so truthfully and transparently to you. Will he go away, scared, smothered? You keep reassuring me and your reassurance invites me into more risking.

So for now, I love you so. I have more and more to say to you. But I want to mail this on my way out of town. (I'm going to Baton Rouge to see Bruce.) Oh, I'm enclosing stuff to share. See notes on copies.

I love you.

Kathy

MARCH 5, 1989

Dear Cali,

The more Kathy talks about you, the more I am coming to love you. This may sound strange, since we haven't met, but it's what's in my heart.

I have the need to make contact with you, and I don't know exactly what to say. I feel awkward and shy.

I want to say as firmly as I can that I honor and respect your relationship with Kathy. That relationship is very important to me, and I don't want to do anything to jeopardize it.

I think you and I will like each other when we meet, but let us resist any pressure to do so. There's a lot at stake here for both of us, but we must be true to ourselves first and foremost. If we should find that we don't like each other, that needs to be okay, too (I say this to release us from any "shoulds" we might have. Incidentally, would you like a copy of my book on shoulds and inner critic work?)

I feel that what I have written above is totally inadequate and unclear (that's my inner critic), but I've got to make a beginning some place.

Well, I reach out my hand to you, and if we were together, I would offer you a warm hug.

Love,

SUNDAY, MARCH 5, 1989 8:20 PM

My Beloved Kathy.

I felt so close to you this morning while talking on the telephone with you. I hope you don't mind my crying out (and crying) from time to time when you say highly charged things to me. I think they must sound quite loud over the phone. I love to hear you say those things, and my cries are cries of joy, even the painful ones, strangely enough. I think you know about that sort of thing; we are so much alike! Anyway, I expect that when we see each other next week and talk, you will go on saying those charged things (I hope), and even more of my joy/pain will get triggered, and I might make very loud sounds indeed. Have no fear; I'm not going berserk. That's just my expressiveness needing to be voiced.

In thinking about our relationship and where it's going (so rapidly!), I am trying to fantasize (i.e., brainstorm) a way I can live in Lafayette full-time. I would sorely miss my libraries. And lectures. Lafayette would be quite isolated and painfully so, for me. I would get books through ILL, but not journals, I think.

I'm thinking somewhat seriously of moving to Los Angeles. There are libraries and lectures there. And plenty of colleagues. Could I commute frequently to Lafayette?

I'm stumped by this. My interior problem-solver has not yet come up with his usual solution. "You're forgetting," he tells me, "that you don't have to do this alone. Your dear Kathy has some input to give." (He loves you too, you see.)

"How could I help it?" he replies.

A thought struck me today: I have been in training all my life for this relationship with you.

My love grows and deepens each day. Every letter you send me brings surprising new delights — new doors are opened onto new vistas. Your love is like flowers encircling my heart.

Oh, Kathy dear! Oh, sweetheart! My treasure!

Let us remember that other people might come from their own stuff when they perceive us and will, perhaps through envy or spite or narrow-mindedness, say jangly and judgmental things. I can imagine some of them (I say them here so we can be desensitized to them):

"Why, Kathy! He's old enough to be your father!"

"You've only known each other two months? Sounds pretty immature to me!"

"Oh, is he one of those crazy people in Berkeley?"

"You're going to continue your relationship with Cali? Things like that never work."

"You think you're in love with him, but it's just: (check one)

Dependency

Animus projection

Oedipal stuff

Pre-oedipal stuff

Puppylove

"He's got children? You'll have problems with them." (Not true; my kids will love you!)

"You're not married? That's living in sin."

Each of these things has power ONLY TO THE EXTENT THAT IT TRIGGERS YOUR INNER CRITIC.

The proper response, I want to suggest, is not to defend and try to get acquitted, but simply to smile and make a releasing statement, either mentally or out loud. (I'll tell you more about this when I see you.) And tell the person that when you need their advice you'll rattle their cage.

New topic. Because our love is so powerful, each of us will have an ongoing struggle throughout the rest of our lives with, on the one hand, wanting to merge and fuse with the other — giving up our identity — and on the other hand, disengaging and recovering our self. This will be a continual refrain in our loving. We must be prepared for it and recognize it when it happens.

The danger is that if one person is disengaging (or even just off on her or his own), the other person may feel painfully abandoned. One way of dealing with this is to delay gratification and just feel (and express) the pain, connecting it up with the past, and crying about that. And trusting that the other will return.

But we may not always be able to do that. We may need the other to quickly soothe the seemingly abandoned inner child. Maybe all this will take will be a smile across the room. Or a brief touch or hug or kiss. Or a reassuring note. (If one of us, for example, goes to a Jungian conference, perhaps a note that says, "I may make new friends, but I will never leave you, because you are so precious to me and will always be special.")

But maybe it will take more. Maybe one of us will need to discontinue what we are doing and attend to the other. (Perhaps until we feel more secure.) As far as I'm concerned it is ALWAYS okay to ask for reassurance at any time, and we are quite skilled at doing that, I think.

We need to signal our need to the other as quickly as possible. If we have some procedures in place, we can take even greater risks of surrendering even deeper to this love we have opened ourselves to. I'm suggesting maybe some nonverbal signal when we're with others—one that says, "I need to talk to you alone"—along with a calibration of the strength of the need. I am willing to go a very long way to safeguard our relationship's depth, to brace it with tactical measures that give it a supportive context within which it can flourish and blossom—and within which each of us can learn to be autonomous, too.

My God, Kathy!—isn't this relationship a great learning experience?

Just think—tomorrow there will almost certainly be a letter for you. It is 9pm now; you must be just going to bed. I see you crawling under the covers, your body all lush and voluptuous. As you lie in bed, you are thinking of me, feeling all warm about our meeting in a week. You think about our telephone conversation, of this morning, and you smile. Oh, my love!

(8:45am Monday). I've just said goodbye to you on the phone. I was so glad to be with you in your pain. You seemed so clear about the issues, somewhat confused about what to do, but knowing what needed to be honored, and aware that no perfect solution (maybe) is to be found. There will be pain from time to time for us in the future, and it's nice to know that we can be there for each other when it happens.

Now—about some of my own pain. I'm still feeling discomfort about that thing Bruce said to you. It seemed gratuitous and insensitive, and the only way I can understand it is that it comes from some of his own pathology—possessiveness, perhaps. I don't know exactly why it bothers me so much maybe we can talk about this on the plane.

I have such tender and affectionate feelings toward you; they are growing day by day. We are such good matches for each other.

I love you dearest—

MONDAY, MARCH 6, 3:00 PM

My precious soulmate,

God, I love you. I thank you so for your beautiful, competent, supportive walk with me through my pain this morning. I felt you enter my pain early in the conversation and take on your own, then struggle with me to work with it to some relief; then to victory. You are incredible. You are worthy of my love – what a glorious discovery. And I want you to know how core-touching and depth-healing your Litany of Expectation was for me. It was a sacrament for me, I want you to know. As you took me chronologically and geographically through your life, searching for me, longing for me, I was so touched and healed. Oh, I don't want you to doubt your loving extravagance to me – your verbal outpourings. I am hungry for them; I welcome them. I never tire of hearing your warm, loving voice saying, "I love you." Your pearls are safe with me, treasured by me, my darling. You call forth from me love and extravagance I have never risked before. And that is because I have been brought to a point of readiness for you; I am in possession of myself, and I sense and know your trustworthiness and your readiness for me. This is so glorious.

I shared with Cali after I hung up with you. That was good. She's still scared and disbelieving that you could search for me your whole life and find me; then not want to take me all to yourself. But she says if we are able to negotiate this, we'll go in the Guinness Book of Records. I told her of your letter and your love for her and of the kiss on the cheek you had for her. She offered both cheeks! Then she ended our conversation by saying "I would love to see Jim and Laura (her therapist) write books on this." (Meaning, it will be so marvelous a passage that it will have to be written for others to learn from.)

Mama and I talked about you a lot at lunch. She senses your greatness, your specialness — partly from what she hears of you, partly from her own intuition and spiritual sight. I told her, "Mama, I am so in love with this man." Dear One, I have never declared that to my parents before about anyone. We celebrated you all through lunch.

Thank you so for your frequent letters. I long for that contact with you, that connection. And you are being so generous. I honor and thank you for spending time with me this way.

I am in a faith place now. Thank you, God. I know we will do fine at the seminar about balancing separateness and togetherness. Your assurance to me was perfect, that I could signal my need to you. Oh, thank you, Jim, for letting me in to you in that way. I also have more faith that we will enjoy each other's company in the flesh to the fullest and have wisdom about choices on how we act out that intimacy. You know, I think it's not so much sex that I want as it is a desire for a consummation with you — a sense of completion, fulfillment. Can you understand me? And yes, sex would be wonderful if there were no other considerations.

I have read and reread your list of things you treasure about me. And they ring so true. You do see and value me for who I am. Thank you, my heart. And the way you write — like a free outpouring of your mind and heart. You are the most special man! I am so grateful that God gave you to me. How can I tell you how your words touch me? "Look, Dear One, you are important to my work." I know what your work means to you. It is your life; your calling. It has you in its grip. And for me to be able to inspire, enrich and deepen it is a huge honor. And then to know that I am on the level of your work! Oh, my… I love that you say, "Take my hand, Dear One, and we will move through these dangerous waters together. I have a map." Oh, melt.

You want me as a full human being. (I laughed at your "pretzelized Kathyoid" — I love your sense of humor.) Well, as you said that you weren't ready for me before, I declare to you that I have been ripening for you and for our relationship too. I am more a full me than I have ever been. I think, "How strange that this man so perfectly mated to me should come into my life when my life is most full." Then I think, "of course, how perfect that this man has come when my life and my self is most full." Otherwise the danger of losing myself in you would be so much greater. It is perfect timing, divine order. And we will work out our "in the flesh" needs for each other. We will be and are creative enough for this task.

You are my treasure. How can I affirm you enough for who you are.

I love you, My Jim.

Kathy

TUESDAY, MARCH 7, 1989 7:30 PM

Dearest Kathy,

Yes, "Dearest." You are my dearest. My darling; my treasure. I have so many things to say to you; whatever made me think I wouldn't have anything to talk about on the plane!

I think about you constantly (I mean every single minute, except when I'm with a client) and hope you are bearing up well under whatever pain you might be experiencing. I am with you in this at all times.

When I cross the street now, I am much more careful. I am taking better care of myself, for you (if this makes sense).

When I called you back the other day, and you asked me to put it on my bill, it felt so intimate — that you could presume to say that and take it for granted that I would accede. We are indeed becoming one thing; (and each of us is struggling to preserve identity in this merging.) I love it when you ask me for things.

Yes, I am both gentle and strong. Strength is an issue I'm grappling with right now; does it mean being aggressive and dominating, as my male tapes say? You have introduced me to a new idea when you compared me with Steven, maybe strength is being able to confront conflict and deep feelings; listening to the other's pain; not abandoning the one you love when the going gets rough.

Yes, I am strong; my male strength is here for you whenever you want it. My maleness has surveyed (and will survey) your female qualities, traits, characteristics, feelings, thoughts — will look over all of them — and will pronounce them (and does pronounce them) exquisitely good and wholesome. Just the way you're supposed to be. I will stamp your femaleness with my male warm approval, I will cherish and caress the delicate tissues and joinings of your splendid female body, worshiping all its parts, kneeling reverently and lustfully before it, celebrating it with my masculinity. Over all parts of you, physical and mental, I will cast my strong male look of deep satisfaction and approval. You are my choice, among all women; you are the way a woman ought to be.

And I will never abandon you. I will be there whenever you need me, as you are gradually finding out. I will be careful to ensure that your slightest fear, your tiniest qualm will get my full care and attention. It will be an act of love to do this, a deep pleasure for me.

Oh, my darling Kathy! How sweet it is to have someone who will accept and enjoy these words of endearment that I am bursting with! What a good fit we are!

Now, about sex. We absolutely do not have to have intercourse when we are together in New York. Or ever. There must be no pressure driving what we do. If we do not have sex, I will not abandon you.

And if we ever do have sex, in whatever creative style you and I will be sure to invent, I want you to know that it will be a sacrament for me. A holy event charged with meaning. Sigh!

Oh, Kathy — you wrote: "I want you to be my man." And "You are man enough for me." Oh! How thrilled I was to read that! Need I say that you are my woman? And that you are woman enough for me? Yes, I need to say that: You are indeed my woman. You are indeed woman enough (at last!) for me. (Thank you, God, for sending her to me, and vice versa.)

About the technical details with regard to sex. How courageous of you to bring them up! I applaud you, and I am getting used to your strength, not so much being surprised by it. I am warmed and delighted by it. I will talk to you on the phone about this. No, I don't have AIDS or herpes or any venereal disease.

You will never overwhelm me with wanting to be with me. For I want to be with you as much as you want to be with me. (Isn't it so nice that it works out that way?) I welcome being overwhelmed by your sweet presence. Come on full blast, girl. (Girl. How I love to call you that; how sexually exciting that simple word is for me!) My heart's desire is the same as yours: to be together as much as possible. To sit next to each other like a married couple. If we happen to get assigned to different subgroups to meet afterward quickly and share experiences.

I understand quite well your fear of saying that you want so much of me that you will scare me away, but I will not go away. Never. I will be even more attracted to you (if that's possible) because of it.

Right now we're in a very intense phase of our relationship, an obsessive phase, and rightly so. We are two very intensely feeling, very sensitive, very responsive people. What we are doing now is building our relationship, letting our neediness show (risking it:

Can I really let the other see how strongly I feel); actually, checking each other out to see if the other can stand the power of our emotions. We are not wishy-washy, phlegmatic people. We love fiercely, extravagantly (I love your word), deeply. (Will the other be burned to a cinder by this love?) But each of us is quite strong, each of us can confront great intensities of feeling; as we test this acceptance in the other, we will begin to feel more and more secure. I expect the combination of fear-and-obsessiveness will, in a year or two (or less) die down somewhat, and evolve in to a steady glow as we feel more secure about each other's love and acceptance. A deep, steady, powerful glow. It will warm us as we go about our daily affairs, as it does now, but it won't be as frantic.

Oh, Kathy Jo, how nice to have found my dream girl! (I thought I never would.)

This letter should get to you by Saturday. It may be the last one I'll write before I see you. The closer it gets to Tuesday, the more excited I feel. (I have a couple of olfactory surprises for you.) (And a tactile one; well, several tactile ones.) And now my sexual fantasies rise up in me. I want to hold you tightly in my arms, stroke all the soft and exquisite surfaces of your womanly body, to investigate and explore its secret places, to kiss your soft and tender lips, to whisper little love words in your delicate ear. I am enflamed with passion! I burn for you! How can I last till Tuesday? I am inarticulate with love for you —

MARCH 7, 1989 10:45 AM

I want to lavish every love name I know on you: My beloved, precious one, dear heart, baby, darling one, soul mate (okay. Now I can begin!)

I've just come from the Dean's office, explaining my doctoral work at UGS to him. If you think I didn't need to appropriate your inseminating of grace, strength, and focused consciousness, then know that his first words to me were, "We were concerned about your being in a program that would leave you with nothing. This isn't a diploma mill, is it?" So I presented myself, my study, the UGS process, accreditation information, faculty info, etc., and when I left, he said, "Well, you know when new non-traditional things appear we approach with caution; this doesn't mean we already have our minds made up that this is not valuable." So I inferred (since he was speaking at a distance from his personal self) that he was more open, concession giving, and even interested in UGS and my program. So I left satisfied that I had presented myself and the program adequately. (All this was by way of decompressing so I can enter a full communication with you.)

I got your wonderful dual letter (jangly and ecstatic) yesterday and want to respond to it all, it was so wonderful to me. First, your cover letter was so dear. Do you know how to melt me? Oh, yes. That I was with you in your triumphant lecture; that you want me to be there to present with you (that is not a fantasy to me — I want to experience it in reality); that you try out Jim and Kathy, Kathy and Jim — Oh, you are beloved. And your self-study over your meeting with Kerry. I de- lighted in the fruits you see from our relationship. Your freeing up to love, to be open, to be emotional. I know that feeling so well. I love the fierceness that I see in you — "your femaleness is so damned good for me."

Fierceness too as I see your Daddy Tiger side — Yes, fight for me, oh thank you. Please don't go passive on me. Fight to the death for me. And fiercely take on the demons that torment and rip at our love. So, for your need for reassurance re: my not giving up power to a lecturer/book. Oh, I have a deep reassurance to give you, my Jim, that this is a primary area of focused, intentional growth work for me. (Oh, Jim, one of my former students just knocked on my door and said with a glowing face, "18 months yesterday" meaning sobriety time. Then he said, "Thank you." I am on my face — He declared that he got into sobriety out of my chemical dependency class.) Okay, back to former topic…You may witness my affirmation of declaration of intention. I shall grow and am growing in critical thinking and will do so through all of these experiences. Yes, I will keep communicating to you. (I've already through my past years learned not to isolate when in pain.) My struggles — you can count on that. And I want to thank you for teaching me and giving me instructions on how to think critically. And in the sweetest way. (You do have a gentle way about you.) In a former letter you said to me exactly how you go about the process of critical thinking: "I now distance myself from the information and examine it carefully. I automatically wonder how it could be wrong. I ask how it checks out with my experience; what it entails in practical options and consequences. I check for any gut reactions that the information doesn't feel right."

Oh, dear Teacher, this is a beautiful guide to me. No one ever taught me this and I didn't learn it.

My problem is Step 1: I distance myself from the

information – that's the rub for me – how do I accomplish that distancing – well, just a moment, I have a thought – I don't have problems distancing if I don't get into a one-down relationship with the author/speaker. I think I must need to not put myself in that position to begin with. This feels right. Can you help me with this? I think it's vitally important. I make relationships as my way of being and doing in life – even with authors. I automatically think, "Oh I'm wrong to make relationships like this; oh I should be able to learn without relating." But I also know that's my genius and my gift. I am a relater when I teach, when I counsel, when I live. Any help for me here? It's a morass in my mind. How do I extricate from these sticky spider webs? Another plane conversation? You said something that struck me as a healing revelation: "My guess is that you get scared of losing yourself in our closeness and then get vulnerable to something you read." Yes, this rings very true.

I'm rather pleased with myself that I can agree with you re: Sanford's loose writing. The whole first part of the book to me was poor. I got some good content from his vocational section. Then I hit the anima stuff and got hocked. I don't know what happened, but I sure would like to know. And I agree with you that you have made friends with your inner feminine and are integrating anima beautifully. You are so whole – masculine/ feminine; fierceness/gentleness; vulnerable/defended; intellectual/emotional; spiritual/physical. Oh Lord, now I enter ecstasy over you! Oh, wait, one thing, you protest that Sanford says your animus is only an unconscious longing for your own soul – well, didn't you tell me I connect you to spirit? I have something you want – my spirituality? How do we distinguish this? Can you speak to this? Is it a matter of blanket statements? Judging the whole by its parts? Or something else? Oh, I love you so.

Now, letter 2-Your response to my fantasy letter – I loved that you have had a personal experience with farm milk. To tell you the truth, I'm rather in awe that an image came to me that would have a historical image for you. And this was a creative writing piece for me – I have never written so boldly before, and although I have participated in oral sex, I have never so poetically(?) offered my juices as cream on my finger before. That is new; that is creative; that is for you and for me. And I do glory in what is coming forth in me by being in relationship with you, and your reception of my offering was so honoring. Thank you. And I am so happy that little Jim is unfolding! Thank you, too, my lover, for telling me the details of your masturbation image – I love it – I'm reading it now as I write, and my cunt clutches for you. Now, as to your questions, how much of the fantasy was for you, how much for me? Hmm, interesting. I don't know for sure. I just know I needed to express that to you for my own sake – to declare myself and speak myself about this – it was an act of growth; of declaring my womanness, my wholeness. Then it was also an act of love that flowed out of me, not premeditated, just spontaneous. And knowing my feminine power, I had a good idea that you would be blessed! As for the specifics, that was a risk; I didn't know what would arouse you – it's not an act I've ever done before and that would have some personal history for me. I am in awe how connected we are – in our intuitions and unconscious material toward each other.

Now, your response to my words on death. Ah, I think I didn't even dare to touch how powerful that was. You draw forth the goddess in me – and when I touch that female spiritual power, I am taken up by it and in awe/reverent of it. My humanness doesn't want to touch that subject — it's too painful. But, once again, you draw forth my greatness. God is with us! I was so moved by your response. OH, thank you, you marvelous man, for speaking to me your heart.

This is such a combination of ecstasy/pain for me. Ecstasy as our beautiful, powerful loving relationship unfolds — pain as I see Cali so hurting and scared. I have pain over that. I have an image of Emily in labor with Cam (her husband) coaching her. I feel like Emily — I go through moments of ease, when I can talk and laugh and relax — then the contractions come — and I need your help (just as Cam stroked Emily's hair and pressed her back for support, held her hand and spoke to her of how much longer it would be — you're halfway there — just 30 more seconds). I am giving birth to myself, cannot back down from birthing into full life the part of me that loves you fully and makes place for that in my life. So although I'd like for this to be totally idyllic — just "falling in love," it's not that. I birth something in myself that has been repressed; has not been allowed out into the air, to breathe, to live, to run barefoot and joyous! Stick with me, please, through this birthing. I need your help; your encouragement; your strength. Cali knows I must do this, and that is part of her pain. It's not anything she can fight or stop. The fullness of time has come. And you are here. Welcome, my love.

Oh, just one week from now (12 noon) I'll be flying into your arms. Oh, ecstasy —

Oh wait, let me not miss telling you of your workshop flyer — I liked it! (Very personal. I like 2nd person for this) very to the point. Oh, it's missing something — my name(!). Why haven't I seen your works yet (Personal Growth and the Selves)? I'm glad you're not underselling yourself. Your prices are comparable to Lafayette events. You invite with your words. Good!

I long for you. I merge with you.

Kathy

FRIDAY, MARCH 10 10:10 AM

My strong, loving man —

I have a story to tell you when I see you — it's about what it's like to be a woman coming alive — fully — as she is loved totally, selflessly by an incredible, special man. I realized I was living it and that I wanted to tell you about it as I walked on campus this spring-like sunny morning and felt myself and the growth of presence I felt inside. More when we are together--

Yes, together. I so hope you get this Monday. I want you to know how flowing with love, expectation, and warmth I am to get to see you Tuesday. When I read your letters I fall in love with you. When I hear your voice on the phone, I fall deeper into you; into ecstasy. What will it be like to be with you again? Oh, glory! You are my heart — my love — my life — you give my life even more power. I do well on my own — you know that. Yet there is a dimension that being loved by you has added — more than added-birthed — created new life for — I am without words. Oh, Jim. I love you so.

I want to hear more and more about you — your graduate school experience, for example. How you do your workshops. What your 1-1 counseling style is like. I want to tell you mine. I love you.

I must get work done so I can BE WITH YOU!

I am, in your perfect description, incoherent.

Oh, you are my man, and I glory in that.

Till we are in each other's arms...

You remain in my thoughts and heart and prayers. I have never loved like this before.

Part 3

PAWLING

On March 14, Jim and I flew to Dallas; he from San Francisco; I from Lafayette. We would be attending a 5-day seminar for our doctoral work titled, "Stories, Versions, Conversations: Ways of Knowing." As I walked onto the main concourse of the Dallas/Fort Worth terminal, Jim was waiting. I went directly toward him. He didn't recognize me. After all, we had only been together in person once. That had been our 10-day colloquium where we had met. Despite that initial lack of recognition, we immediately began connecting. As our 747 jet took off, I felt fear, and Jim comforted me. Our flight was blissful. We sat with our heads close together, talking and talking. We were in a secluded world of our own; a bulkhead area of the plane with no other passengers. The flight attendants left us undisturbed. We shared food and hearts on that 3-hour flight. I left a portion of lunch on my plate, and Jim finished it off. After lunch, I ordered coffee. I remember Jim saying, "I love the smell of coffee on your breath."

By the time we arrived at our Pawling, New York, conference center, it was dark. Although we were assigned to separate rooms, I went to meet Jim in his. That's when we opened the door to the bedroom...

We wrote no letters during the Pawling seminar. We were together in the flesh. Our letters pick up on the last day of our seminar.

SUNDAY, MARCH 19 7:50 AM

My love —

I want you to have this for your flight and return home. I want you to see in writing the celebration I feel for the wonderful, incredibly loving time we have had together this week. It has been glorious for me, my beloved. I am a well-satisfied woman. Your well satisfied woman. You have done this for me. You are man enough for me. You are all my desire. I love you so much. It has grown tremendously this week into a firmly rooted love — rooted in knowing how well we move and live together. I will ache to be with you again. I will ache for your warm skin next to mine; for your laughing eyes; for your tender touch; for your caressing words; for your luscious tongue; for your hard, shy cock.

Know that this week has been more than, better than I even expected. To be with you, to sit next to you, to struggle together, to process together, to brush arms, to look across the room, to lie under you is…oh, I can't find words.

You are my love, my heart. I, as your priestess, invoke God's blessing upon you — a blessing of safekeeping, of inspiration, of empowerment, of going forth enfolded and of returning to me speedily.

I spill myself out to you, Jim.

Kathy

I claim our emblem — the rose!

SUNDAY, MARCH 19 10:15 PM

Oh, my love,

Rhapsody fills me for you as I fly back to Lafayette. I have been dozing in your arms, feeling your naked flesh surround me. What beautiful memories I have. What warming kything we have now. Oh, I want to see you again already. I will be checking my schedule and letting you know when in May I can come to you. I will write as soon as I see a date. May 10th is my beloved's birthday. I wish I could be with you for that. What would you like for your birthday? I want to give you just what you want. So be thinking.

I felt in shock when we parted and didn't cry until I sat in my seat on the plane. Then I thought of you taking off and sent my blessing of safekeeping to you. Goodbyes are never enough for me. I'm so grateful we had the extra hour together. Surely we have an indulgent God, who smiles on us, surrounds our lovemaking, then says, "My children, have an extra hour together. I give it to you freely." It was a bit disorienting seeing Chad and Katarina right during our last minutes together. I would have wanted to have you two talk together. I wanted to introduce you with some title of relationship to me and didn't know quite what to say. (How absurd when I've called you a thousand love names!) It made me think how pleased and proud I will be to introduce you to all my friends in Lafayette. "This is my beloved Jim." Sigh. (It's a good flight, by the way. Not so bumpy.) I am exhausted now. And as I watched you walk away, I saw fatigue and shock in your body too. I wanted to hold you in my arms and comfort you (all night, of course).

May I tell you again how much I love your body? Yes,

I think so. How I love the thickness and strength of it — the special place that flares out beneath your underarms. (You know what I mean.) Your beautiful erotic hands. (I love them even more now.) Your wonderful beard and gorgeous hair. Your loving blue eyes. Your warm, wet tongue. Your strong chest. Your solid stomach. Your incredible desirable cock. Your warm fun balls. Your muscular legs. Your warm feet. Every inch of you is desirable to me. I love what your fine mind and creative spirit do toward me. What bliss you have given me. I am yours forever. I keep my vow to you. Oh, and your boldness in speaking of our married life together. Sigh again. You are my heart's desire. And we are so fun — playful together. I love our totem pole! And now we're flying in for a landing in Lafayette. And I think, ah, my Jim will be doing this as he comes to meet me soon. What will he think of it? I hope he loves it as I do. OH —

Mon. a.m. — I want this in the mail to you — I love you, I love you, I love you, I love you —

Kathy

MONDAY, MARCH 20, 1989 8:00 AM

My dearest treasure…

I am feeling such sweet pain this morning—more painful than ever, sweeter than ever. I am possessed by it, by you, by images of our week together. Yes, your word is correct: glorious! Oh, Kathy! (I hear you say so thrillingly, "Yes, my love.") What ecstasy! A whole week of it. And there's more to come. This is just the goddam beginning!

Yes: Man and Wife. Wife. Oh, Kathy! Husband. That'll be me. Wife, that'll be you. Married. Wedding. Honeymoon (number two, I guess). All these sweet words that make my heart ache with longing. How powerful words can be!

Now a thought: have you heard the Hawaiian Wedding Song? Please let me know.

And the Piccadilly Cafeteria! I smack my lips over the foods you describe.

I must mention this: It was so late when I got to San Francisco last night. I was beside myself with fatigue (you saw some of it in Dallas). I thought: Well, here I am, at last, home. Then I thought: But it doesn't feel like home any more. What is this? Home is now some place I have never been to. How strange! Well, what is home? I asked. And the sweet answer came quickly: Home is wherever my darling Kathy is.

On the bus to San Francisco, from the airport, I sat with my flight bag on the seat next to me, finding my hand draped over it caressing the soft leather, and the kinesthetic image came to me of feeling the hollow of your dear back. Oh, Kathy!

How delirious I am with love! How much in love I am!

As I think back, the images rush into my mind: You exhibiting your sweet panties to me.

Your fear of analyzing that fantasy. My insistence. Your submission. (I'll help you with any intellectuophobia you might have.) Your fear of flying; I hope my reassuring words helped. (That's one emotion I will not help someone get deeper in; except in a very interesting way I'll tell you about some time.)

Remember waking up in the night and hugging each other as we lay, our naked bodies pressed together, your soft flesh curving into mine, fitting together as though God had made them for that purpose?

Learning where and how to touch each other. Learning so quickly! The smile of a woman who is well loved. The glow that people see: Jana. Warming ourselves by her discovering us. What a dear woman!

Our lovely wordplay 99th %ile! A strawberry on the totem pole! Mr. and Mrs. Tiger! Ready to fight the whole world to defend our love! The two poems and it was not enough that I read them to you, you sweet treasure, you must read them to me. Oh, joy! Bliss! (And this is just the goddam beginning!)

Oh, I love you so damned much!

TUESDAY, MARCH 21, 1989 2:15 PM

My beloved,

I can't stay away from you! I can't stop talking about you to people. A while ago at lunch I ran into Ava (the blond woman in the prayer group Christmas picture you saw). I told you she was my soul sister. We hadn't talked since before Christmas. And the first thing I blurted out was, "Oh, Ava, I'm in love." Then I said, "Do you want to see his picture?" And I showed you to her and we discussed how wonderful mature men are and her friend who was with her sighed longingly!

Oh, I loved talking with you this morning. I love that you are accessible to me and that you welcome my calls so lovingly — and that you and I called each other at the same time yesterday. Wow! We are truly one. And I love that you are boldly talking about our being husband and wife. (Oh my, that's the first time I've written those words — I think the peak in the "s" in husband — I did it again! — is my heart skipping a beat.) And that you are planning our wedding ceremony. I had images of the words we would say as we touched on each figure in our totem group. How we would pick up the little crystal pitcher of cream and speak of it (perhaps of the richness we bring to each other) and then give each other a sip of the cream. Oh my. And how you might read the daddy tiger words from your letter to me as we held a carved (?) tiger in our hands. Do you like these thoughts? I love them. When Andy and I got married, I wanted to write our own vows, but there was nothing to draw from. I see that now. And now, you and I have this incredible fund of love to draw vows from. Oh my.

There is a scripture from Joel I think in the bible that says God's words as a promise: "I will restore to you the years which the locust has eaten." And truly that promise is being fleshed out in my life. All the love and joys and fantasies I held but never saw materialize are now being lived out and given flesh and life through our relationship; through your incredibly loving way with me. And you want to be a morning person! Oh, you are the most fantastic lover anyone could have, Jim. And I love our beach house honeymoon fantasy. Of 2:00 in the afternoon – heat of the day – indoors with the sliding glass doors open, the gulf breeze billowing the sheer curtains voluptuously; the sunshine glowing in; the ceiling fan whirring above our bed, yes our bed; the sound of the waves gushing onto the shore. And best of all the sound of your warm, loving, sexy voice in my ear saying, "Kathy, Kathy, Kathy. You are my wife, my beloved." And "Lift your legs." OH, I yearn for you and for fruition of all our plans. And I am enjoying our making of relationship, our love building, our immersion in each other. I keep having wet images. What could that be?

Oh, my final exam is Tues, May 9 at 5:00. Then I'll have to grade those papers Wednesday and I'll be through. But that wouldn't give us enough time before I go to Georgia on the 14th. The first day of class for summer semester is June 5. So I possibly could go to you on May 24 and stay until the 2nd of June (10 days). Could you handle that? It doesn't look like I could fit any more time in. And I'll talk to Cali about her mom's surgery and let you know.

I have to go now and pay my accident ticket. (My/ our indulgent God has provided the money through medical reimbursements from last year. He takes care of me like that.)

I hope you enjoy the classified ads and get a good sense of Lafayette. More tomorrow on budgets, etc.

I love you, my beloved, my heart, my life.

Your Kathy

TUESDAY, MARCH 21, 1989 1:30 PM

My dearest, precious darling…

I am beside myself with love for you. Intoxicated with it. Wild with it. How can I last? My whole body cries out for you. (I can't keep on in this vein, or I'll cry.)

Okay, how about some practical things. When I come to Lafayette, where will I stay? I don't think I want to stay in your house.

At some time or other I want to spend a few days with Carol, in Houston. Would you like to join me there? I want you to meet her and her family. It will be very comfortable for us to be together there, to sleep together, for our two families to cook for each other.

About trips: I want to visit Los Angeles. In Europe, to visit London, Paris, the French Riviera, and Munich.

Is there a group room in Lafayette I could rent for my groups and clients?

About the things I own: not very much. A biofeedback trainer. Two sled chairs, and some folding chairs. Shelves and a bookcase. Long tables. Group room pillows. A little fridge. Office equipment. Radios.

I have a great many books, which I could begin shipping by 4th class mail. It's cheaper than using a moving company.

I'm going to visit Kevin in Minneapolis, too. Would you like to go with me? I know these visits can run into big money after a while, so I will understand if you decide not to. I'm reorienting my priorities to put a top value on our being together. Until we are permanently together, we'll have to figure out ways to fly to each other.

I would like us to buy a VCR so I can tape late night shows, which I think I'm not going to see many of at the time they are shown.

Oh, Kathy! The above are just practical things. The enclosed envelope contains something of my deep, deep love for you. (I've got to start thinking about paying some bills and sending out announcements.) In the meantime…

Words fail me! I am so in love with you!

P.S. Enclosed also is a note for Mama.

TUESDAY, MARCH 21, 1989 1:00 PM

My darling treasure…

Imagine yourself naked, lying next to me, pressing against my naked body. One of my hands is between your legs. We kiss. Our mouths open…after a while we stop.

I take my hand from between your legs and clasp you tightly to me. Then I tell you the following thoughts about our wedding.

I would like handouts, copies of the poems that will be read. So the people will have something to read while they are waiting. (What about a handout on "How to get the most out of this wedding?" Or "ground rules"? No—just kidding.)

I would like to face the people as we announce our intentions and take our vows. I want them to see our faces, and I want to see theirs.

(Before that, I want short readings from people.) I also want somewhere for us to say "I do" to something. (I give you a tight squeeze now, and your body ripples.)

And then after our vows, I want our clergy person to turn and speak to the people and say the following:

"Do all of you assembled here today to witness this marriage promise to give this new husband and wife your love and support as they begin their marital journey?"

And I want them to say: "We do."

Oh, Kathy…

WEDNESDAY, MARCH 22, 1989 11:00 AM

My dearest soon-to-be wife…

I still walk around saying "Kathy," and I still hear the comforting response, "Yes, my love," and it sustains me, but I still yearn for you and anguish over being with you again. That is, anguish that I am not now with you.

I tell everyone about you—my dentist yesterday, who put in my new crown; a colleague, Susan, who called (we exchanged stories about long distance love, her boyfriend is up in Crescent City, and commiserated with each other).

I'm thinking of places to take you: not only David's but Chinatown, North Beach, the ocean, two libraries: Graduate Theological Union and John F. Kennedy University.

I look at your pictures as often as I can; you are so beautiful, so sweet, so loving, so childlike and playful. Love wells up in me, surges up, and I think I can't get through the day without you. But I will see my client for today and run my group this evening and get through these times which I now see simply as "preparation for moving to Lafayette," so I am beginning to throw things out and wonder what I can sell.

Now I want to talk about an intellectual topic. I'm still chewing away at the spirituality issues I raised. I presented them to you and you gave me a really good challenge—better than any I have previously received (how fine that we can meet on this intellectual level too!). So I have done a lot of thinking and would like to take another crack at explaining what I mean.

The topic is the difference between the physicalist

and pleromatic paradigms. I think there is a difference that needs to be honored, but I'm not clear on what it is. So I'll think out loud, and I would appreciate any feedback or response you care to give. (I am so enriched by your ideas!)

I want to begin by talking about jasmine soap. First, let's take a look at the fact that physicalist science is progressive, and it's progressive in a specific way. Every once in a while a new discovery is made that overturns some old idea. This progress takes place by research studies, usually. Suppose a scientist wants to find out which fragrance is appropriate to the heart chakra. He would (or she would) do some kind of study, perhaps winding up with a table somewhat as follows:

Jasmine	62 times
Rose	10 times
Gardenia	8 times
Violet	4 times

I don't know what "times" means in this table, but you know the kind of thing I mean.

So when the physicalist reports "It's jasmine!" he means, "There are some exceptions, but for the most part, it's jasmine." Perhaps later someone will replicate this experiment and discover that jasmine works only with feeling types. Perhaps someone will replicate it and discover that it's not jasmine at all, but wisteria.

Now, that's the way that physicalist science works, but it's not the way that pleromatic ideas are grounded. You never read a headline, for example, that says, "New Evidence that Jasmine is connected to the Heart Chakra." Or "Jasmine's Connection Disputed by Scientists."

The reason, it seems to me, is this: The idea that jasmine is connected as indicated above is intuitive. For example, it does not feel right to say that the heart chakra is appropriate for skunk essence. But it could have been gardenia, violet, etc., and that would seem okay to me. What I'm contending here is that much pleromatic truth is constructed intuitively. To say that jasmine refers to the heart chakra is to say, "I declare it so." And it is so. The Word creates it. You name my knee noble, and by God it is noble. There's no doubt in my mind, and no need for an empirical study.

And I can add whatever additional meaning that feels intuitively right: that because jasmine is emblematic of our deep love for each other, use of it in a ritual shower armors each of us (as our love does) in any situation we decide to enter. So I have played a part in creating this truth, as you have also. And no one would ever be able to argue me out of it, or to say, "No you've made a mistake; it's not jasmine." I know it is, because you and I have created it so. It might be different for others.

So pleromatic ideas are grounded in the Word, spoken intuitively. At least, some pleromatic ideas. (Incidentally, my dearest one, I continue to experience the immense power of your Word directed to my knees. You are my priestess, my celebrant of feminine mysteries, my channel to God, Oh, Kathy!)

Well, this leads me to a statement something as follows: the physicalist language and pleromatic language must be kept separate for the most part. I would not start a car simply by invoking a Word; I would do so by performing certain physicalist operations. (I might add a prayer that the damn thing would start, but this would be an extra.)

Similarly, I would not do a study of jasmine, although I might do one of people's attitudes toward jasmine. So I think each realm has an appropriate language, and appropriate operations.

Let me know, please what you think of these ideas. (It is what I meant earlier by the need to keep the two realms separate.)

I am so anxious to be with you, my treasure. I'm calculating furiously to find some way of handling the financial end. I think I can. I just need to know about groups there and rent.

Can this really be that we are going to be together? As husband and wife? Isn't it just a dream, from which I will awake, with only a sweet memory, and still the task ahead of searching for you? I've got to keep calling you on the phone to reassure myself that you actually exist.

Yet here are your pictures. You appear to be a real woman. I also have a vivid memory of your body — its lush curves and soft places. Oh, Kathy, I'm wild again with anguished love for you! What will it take to calm the hot fever of my longing for you? It is so painful! And so sweet! God give me the strength to get through this! Is this the power that was planted in us organisms to ensure the propagation of the species? If so, it's no wonder there are so many people! My love for you is so boundless. I ache for you! Oh! Oh! Oh!

WEDNESDAY, MARCH 22, 1989 2:10 PM

My precious man,

My mind is so full of plans and imaginings — right now of a practical nature, so let me talk to you about them right off —

Re: your buying a car…Cali says that if you bring a car into Louisiana, you'll have to pay sales tax and that could be a heavy burden. So it might be better to buy your car here. Also, almost all cars here will have air conditioning, which I again recommend to you. You probably would have a harder time finding air conditioning there. Also Louisiana license plates are $6 per year, and you pay for 2 years at a time. I don't know too many states that are so cheap in that area.

Re: office rent…Cali pays $350 for a beautiful 2 room office (including utilities) and one of our friends rents a house for an office (kitchen, 2 big rooms for group and 3 offices, 1 bath) for $350 plus utilities. They split the rent among 3 counselors — So, you and I could probably find a good place cheap where you could hold your groups, I could do workshops, and we could do things together and see people individually if we needed to — for not very expensive. (Cali pays $9 /sq. ft) She says $9 is pretty much top price — most are cheaper.

Re: furniture I own — nice sofa bed for living room sofa, 2 nice living room chairs, double bed, dresser, night stand, settee, bookcase, coffee table, TV, tape player, amplifier, turntable, speakers (stereo system) — some pots and dishes. My car is an 82 Honda Accord. What would you bring? I also have a great computer with Word Perfect 5.0 word processing for book publishing — except graphic illustrations. You might go to a computer store with your needs delineated and ask if

Word Perfect 5.0 can do those things.

Re: budget…Utilities vary $75 to $170 depending on dead of winter heating costs. Water & sewerage $15/month. Wait, I'll change format.

My monthly:

Utilities	$75-170
(total Cali & I split)	
Water; sewerage	$15
Rent (Cali's house)	$200
Mike's house probably	$350 ($175 each)
Car – gas	$30
Dog – vet	$15
Ins Prem	$35
Disab Prem	$41.14
Bank Service Charge	$7
Food	$200-300

(incl restaurants & groceries)

I also have some medical costs (pharmacy for Iberet (iron) & Minocin) each month, but I get reimbursed 100%.

My income net is $1419 (USL salary gross less $100 savings, $60 computer loan, $35 flex spending acct for med costs, fed and state taxes. Plus I make about $100 per month at Opportunities ½ way house. Then I have various workshops (ca. $150-300 every other month or every third month). I can't think of anything else right now. Oh, yes, I pay about $150-200/month on my Visa/ Mastercards. And I have a guaranteed student loan for UGS and must borrow extra since they didn't give me the full amount to cover all quarters per year.

Now, I feel vulnerable, having looked at all this and having laid it out before you. I need your reassurance that you still love me and honor me; don't think I'm bad, a terrible money manager, etc. OK?

I love you, Jim. On to less practical and more loving matters. I still celebrate our love. It is confirmed in me as a good, wonderful thing. I hear other people describe their relationships, and I get to see how good ours is. I think there is nothing I could say to you that you couldn't relate to in some way. I was musing today over our conversation on pheromones (spelling?) and how you knew what I was talking about. And you knew about color coding for clothes and makeup. You have such a wide range of knowledge — it delights me. One of my friends was lamenting how she didn't get her needs met. Her lover doesn't meet her emotionally. They have great sex, but he holds himself back emotionally — no connection. I love, adore, and am healed by our connections on all levels. I even am in awe of how you meet me spiritually. That is a surprise. And you aren't dogmatic or orthodox. (Thank God! He knew what I needed.)

I say we have an indulgent God, yet I keep being surprised by it (that indulgence). Today I called Chase, my colleague at school, to see if I could borrow his extra car while mine gets fixed. (I couldn't afford to front the money on a rent car, which is how my insurance company works my coverage.) So Chase said, "Sure, but I let my insurance lapse." I called my insurance lady, and she said, "I don't want you driving an uninsured car. Let me call you back." Well, she did, and said, "Your rent car is handled, we'll front the costs for you and you won't have to pay anything." So I am driving an '89 Toyota Camry now. For me, that's just another experience of God's care and indulgence.

He has been so indulgent to me to give you to me. You

are so perfect for me — loving, intelligent, spiritual, sensitive, physical, sexy, affectionate, verbal, Sigh; Hooray!

I talked to Cali re: going to you May 24 to June 2 and she said to go ahead. She'd work with her mother's surgery. So I'd like to firm up those plans. Do those dates work for you? Can you pay half? And when could you give me that money? Again, I don't have lots of cash to work with. I will get a $500 tax refund — should arrive in April so that will help with lodging when I come to visit you.

Little memories keep flitting across my mind — our wonderful meeting at Dallas; the feel of your beard in my hand; your pubic hair to my finger tips; your cream on my thumb; your hand stroking my hair. Oh, my__ I love you so, my darling. You are my heart. Be assured of my love for you. I will never leave you. I will share my mind, my heart, my body, my bed, my soul with you. You are worthy of that gift. You have been groomed for me.

I love you so —

your Kathy

P.S. The Times is a free paper in Lafayette. The Times Picayune is New Orleans

THURSDAY, MARCH 23, 1989 10:00 AM

My beloved treasure…

Your wonderful letter came today, along with the newspaper clippings. It's incredible how low the rents are there! Half of what they are here. So even if you were not there (a possibility I refuse to contemplate), I would want to move to Lafayette. It's a small college town. Isolated from large cities. With good restaurants. As far south as possible, for a warm climate. No earthquakes. Centrally located in the U.S. And of course you are there. All these (especially the last one) are what I desire. Yes, desire. Ah, desire. What a fine word! I desire you, Kathy. What a nice sentence to type! Yes, I desire you. I desire your superb body. Oh, my! How did I get off on this? I thought this letter would be content-oriented, objective, task-oriented. I guess this is what happens when I am head over heels in love. Totally lost. Submerged in our love. Oh, Kathy!

I have been disjointed these past three days, and I think my letters to you reflected it. Somehow a letter from you reconnects me, soothes me, makes me feel secure. Let's write each other little notes after we are married. (What a fine sentence to write!) (My heart leaps upon re-reading it.) Yes, after we are married. Marriage. Wedding. Husband and wife. I love to write those words.

Now about our wedding ceremony. (Again, what thrilling words!) A pitcher of cream — yes. And a bowl of strawberries, what about that? But the cream does not symbolize the richness of our relationship; it symbolizes the richness and exoticness of your cream. Let's keep the symbolism sexual: strawberries symbolizing my cock; and our cream for your vagina's sweet secretion. A rich mixture symbolizing our sexual lusciousness. (And guess what?—we can eat it with a spoon!) (I see and hear your laughter.)

And we can give each other a taste of this sexual confection to show the people how we smack our lips over our rich sexual communion. (Of course, we need not be explicit as to details of this symbolism—except to close friends, perhaps?

As to the tiger: what about a stuffed one? I am already looking.

And of course, roses. Would you like to carry them?

Yes, I love these thoughts; I love making these plans; I love enfolding our actions in the pleroma of powerful meaning.

And yes, we do have an incredible fund of meanings from which to draw. And only in 2½ months! Yes, we are about to live out our most dear and cherished romantic fantasies (and have already lived out some). Mortals are rarely given such gifts.

I must report a peculiar thing: It's hard for me to remember how we were before Pawling. It seems like I have known you and been in love with you and we have been intimate all my life. As though we are an old married couple who know each other through and through. And yet we have not even known each other three months! The solidity of our relationship awes me. What is this thing about thinking we have always been this way?

There was certainly something electric between us the first time you spoke to me, when you asked if you were invading my space. I felt something like a strong magnetic field. All our energy was on the surface of our bodies, ready to commingle. Any comments?

Last night in the group, I talked of love. "That's what this is all about," I said. To be able to say, "I love you" — to let the energies flow freely, unblocked and undistorted by fear, guilt, revenge, anger, etc. I suggested that anyone who wanted could say "I love you" to anyone she or he wanted. Everyone said they couldn't say it, except for one man, who said it, and meant it, to each person. We all felt hushed, we sensed the power of love. All this, dear Kathy, I owe to you. Your influence on me spreads to many others. Oh, I love you so! You enrich my work!

(It occurs to me that you might be wondering if I will still love you and want to be married to you after we have had sex. Oh, yes I do! Even more!) I will not leave you; I will not abandon you; I will be there for you whenever you want; whenever you crook your little finger at me and give me your sweet smile. I will come running! I will stand with you in any crisis, any adversity, any problematic situation. By your side — supporting you with my male strength, being in close communion with you, seeing you through whatever comes. Fighting for you. Defying others for your sake. Battling those who would hurt you. I will be your knight in shining armor, your brave rescuer, your prince charming, the wise magician who casts spells for your safety and happiness. Oh, Kathy, I will slay hundreds of dragons for you!

(Just bring 'em on.) I will spread my cloak on any mud puddle so your dainty feet will not get wet. I will do all the romantic things that men can do for the women they love. You are my treasure!

I love you with such a sweet pain,

FRIDAY, MARCH 24, 1989 10:45 AM

My precious wife-to-be:

I just finished talking to you on the telephone; how sweet that was! How nice that I could say whatever I wanted to you—express my anger, voice my fears—and you can receive that! That is so precious to me. (I think that last sentence sounded like you; I think I am beginning to talk like you, and even think like you. I think we will take the best from each other and make it our own; how nice that there is so much to take!)

You told me you wanted to work with me in Anthetics. What joy I felt! A relief: I think I wanted you to and was afraid you would not want to. I wondered if I would have to do this work on my own, alone, without you by my side. Well, we will be sensational in this project. And please feel free to take as much of it (or as little) as you wish. I want above all for you to not feel any pressure about this. Also: feel free to shape it; to give it your touch, to infuse it with your wisdom and expertise. It has so far benefited from that, and I want it to benefit even more.

I think again and again about our life together as husband and wife. (I love to keep writing those words.)

I want now to go and work some more on my book. See you later.

Oh! I feel disjointed again. It all comes of being so lovesick for you. All I can think of is how much I miss you, how I miss your warm loving body—the special place where your back feels so sexy, the hollow of it, I guess. I am obsessed, a sex maniac. Madly in love with you.

More comments on your submission to me: it is so precious, so tender! I cherish it so much! Yes, my darling: I require that you submit to me. Oh, how loving these words are! And I in my turn will surrender completely to you, will lay myself bare to you, will be putty in your hands; you can do with me what you will, you lovely female. How glad I am to have found someone I trust enough to yield myself to. But I will say this again: you must submit to me!

Oh, my; how powerful our love is,

How many paradoxes it can contain!

GOOD FRIDAY, MARCH 23, 1989 2:40 PM

My precious darling,

I've just finished reading your triad of letters to me – the wonderful first letter after our honeymoon – oh what love and beauty and reassurance you pack on to a page. (You have a gift for saying succinctly what it takes me pages to express. Maybe that's the South in me.) Then I read the "practical" letter with its wonderful intoxicated opening. I echo you. "How can I last?" I want to talk to you every minute – to share every meal with you – to midday nap with you – to lie awake at night in your arms – to come home to you – oh, sigh – I want to shower and bathe with you – I want to submit to you – I want you to make me submit to you – I want to feel you fall into; surrender to me. I want to walk into Girard Hall (my building at USL) with the glow of a well-loved woman. I want to lie naked flesh to flesh with you and let my serenity and languor seep into you and lower your blood pressure and restore well-being to your entire system. I want to wake up in the night and stroke your body in the dark until I find your penis (I just clenched). I want to love him and stroke him and excite him until he wants me insistently. I want to feel you spread my legs with your legs and hear you say, "life your legs." I want to submit to you. I want to feel your hard cock thrust into me. I want to receive your passion with a heated welcome. I want the sweetness and the violence of your passion to break upon me. I long to hear your ecstasy as you climax and lovingly spill your semen into me. Oh, God. I have just melted myself. I can imagine how you are doing reading this. Then I want to pamper you in the morning with orange juice in bed or whatever you want. I want to smile my "totally satisfied woman" smile as the morning sun breaks into the room. And I want you to know that you did that. You, my man, my husband, put that look on my face. Ohh___

So, let me say here, you are my man, my beloved Jim. I want no other. I will have no other. You are all my desire.

Yes, I definitely want to go with you to spend a few days with Carol. And, after thinking through it, I also want to go with you to visit Kevin. It's very important to me to get to know them (they are your beloved children). And I want them to know me. I'd prefer to meet them before we get married, but if that doesn't work, okay. I think I can manage plane fare. Oh my, did I just say "married" like a tacit fact! I think we are going to have a busy next few months. Good! Maybe it will help me survive the waiting until you are here with me.

I talked to Hale about using his offices for groups. He's considering it. There are several places that we could use: the 3 office house I told you about — also Voorhies Auditorium at University Medical Center; also hotel meeting rooms. Also Serenity Center. I will call them this week and get clear on a workshop for us to do as soon as possible. You can stay at a motel in town. I want to be able to be free with you. I don't want to have you at Hale's house, etc.

I like that you said re: our visit with Carol: "for our two families to cook for each other." Oh, melt.

About trips: Los Angeles, yes. San Francisco and points north of it also. In Europe, London, Paris, French Riviera, Munich, yes, yes to all. Also English countryside — Scotland (I've always wanted to go there. Would you go with me?) Also, Bavarian Alps, the Rhine, and French countryside. In U.S.A. again — the Gulf Coast.

Oh, how big is your TV? I have a nice size one, but we can

have both. Did I tell you one of my pet peeves is to have the TV on all the time? I only like it on when I want to specifically watch something. Yes, a VCR. Cali has 2 and will let us use one till we can buy. She told me so today.

On that note, she told me today she is opening to wanting to have a relationship with you. She wants to like you. I told her at one point that you love ice cream (so does she) and she said, really quietly, "Maybe, he can come over and eat ice cream with me." It was really dear. She's really opening. There's been some shift of acceptance or resignation that I am yours, no question. And that we must go on. I am warmed and encouraged and continuing to tell her little by little what you are like and how much you love me. I think she feels better knowing you treasure me and are worthy of me.

I want to keep juices in the fridge for you — and serve them to you ice cold. I want to bring them to you as you work and serve them with an embrace and a kiss — oh, there's your dear tongue on mine. I can't resist you. I don't want to resist you. Can you work with one hand? I want to reach down and hold your penis through your pants. Umm —

Well, will I ever work again? I am useless, hopelessly obsessed with you. I need to grade papers, etc. All I want to do is communicate with you. Well, I guess it takes this kind of driving love to move me out of my complacency and my 10 year abstinence and my 13 years post-divorce. I need to set up a gynecologist's appointment and get some advice on birth control and decide on one method. I feel pretty ignorant on all that.

About our wedding, umm — and a rereading of your power-charged 3rd letter — oh wait, I got caught up in the first paragraph — my mouth is salivating and my vagina is clenching...okay, wedding—glory! Handouts—that's wonderful, yes. My friends are very creative and could probably help with the logistics. No ground rules! I love your idea of facing the people as we "announce our intentions and take our vows." Yes, that's beautiful. You are so romantic, beautiful, thoughtful. And short readings from people—I like that. Can you tell me more about content? Their thoughts re: us? Things we choose? Yes, I want to say, "I do," too. And I like the request for verbal support from the people. And I love the Hawaiian song. Yes, let's have it. Also, I'd like the Pachelbel Canon in D before the wedding ceremony starts. And other loving music during the ceremony. Have you heard, "There Is Love"—it's a popular song based on "Where 2 or more are gathered in my name, there am I in the midst of them." It's a wedding song actually.

Oh, furnishings for home—I like wreaths and flowers and baskets and candles. Can we have those please? And favorite books—things that say, "love," "Welcome," "Peace," "Well-being," "Be embraced," "This is who we are, Jim and Kathy, Kathy & Jim Elliott." Oh, my heart just leapt. This will be the first time I've ever written this: Kathy Elliott—oh my—Mrs. James Elliott—Kathy Elliott—that's nice—Looks good, don't you think?

Did I tell you Mike's house has a bed of about 6 rose bushes? I want you to see his house when you come and let me know what you think. Can you live there? Is it big enough? Does it feel good to you? Can you picture yourself working, living there? Could it enfold you? Can we make it our own?

Thank you, my love, for being so open to my calls and to calling me back. And for writing me every day. Oh, it helps me so much. Thank you for being extravagant in loving me—

in every way.

Well, I want to mail this to you. I want you to hear from me every day — to be reassured of my earth-trembling, incredible love for you.

Oh, my beloved, precious man, I love you so.

Your Kathy

SATURDAY, MARCH 24, 1989 7:00 AM

Good Morning, My love —

It's very early. You're still asleep. I send a blessing of love and enfoldment your way. I'm getting ready to go to the 1/2 way house to do my group. The pups are eating, and I'll be walking them. I wanted to make contact with you. You're always in my thoughts and in my heart. I am at peace this morning. This comes as change, since I've been a bit frantic inside — re: fears of losing you through death (are you getting sick of me saying this?) and a sense of lack of my own power. Well, this morning my devotional reading really helped: "I know the plans I have for you, says the Lord, plans for good and not for evil, to give you a future and a hope." So, you see, I'm on a spiritual journey now. I have fallen totally in love with you and have surrendered to you and to our relationship. That's a vulnerable feeling. I need the assurance of God's protection and the reminder that "underneath all are the Everlasting Arms." And today, I've gotten that. I am powerless over my future predictions (fears). Yet He has us in His arms. He is trustworthy. His plans for me (and for us) are to give us a future and a hope. Well, now I want to crawl into bed beside you — feel my naked flesh next to yours — all warm and thick and solid. (I love your body — and your mind, and your heart, and your spirit. I'm just totally in love with you.) And feel you put your arm over me as I curve into you like a spoon. I feel your semi-hard, semi-ready cock against my butt — a promise for when we awake. Yes, Mama, I have awakened. I love you so, my darling one —

your Kathy

SATURDAY, MARCH 25, 1989 1:10 PM

My dearest one,

Events are moving faster and faster toward our being together. It's still a little scary for me and still exciting. I do so want to be with you, to live with you, to spend the rest of my life with you.

Kathy, I love you so, and I'm so scared. It's such a big change for me, and I don't like changes any more. First, moving to Lafayette. Then marriage. Then all your friends. (My God, what am I getting myself into? And the answer is: my heart's desire — both as to a mate [you] and place to live.) But please be patient with me as I negotiate this passage; I may not be as ecstatic from time to time as you'd like me. It's just culture shock. And marital shock. If you will be kind to me and soothe me, I'll be fine. And listen to any negative thoughts I have without believing them or taking them seriously. Okay? I feel so vulnerable.

I just want you to know that I'm 100% committed to you as your husband. There is no question in my mind at all about that. But I've got a lot of stuff that needs processing. (I swore, for example, that I would never get married again — but now I will, and not only because you like the idea but because it's what I want. I want to be married to you.)

Yes, — about other relationships. I often hear women say they are unhappy with their men. The men watch football or read the paper and maybe are good providers but there is little or no emotional contact. And my men clients complain about their women: too many headaches and not enough sex, or the women are too antilibidinous even when they do have sex, or are too contentious and argumentative, or they are too materialistic, too interested in expensive furniture and not enough in companionship.   Oh, Kathy, I yearn for you so much! I probably won't be able to write any sort of rational letters, or even rhapsodic ones, I am so lovesick for you. Again—please be patient with me. I am so preoccupied with you I can't think straight. I'm going crazy with love of you.

Yes, little memories flit across my mind, too. Many sexual ones. (Will she think I'm a lust-crazed monster?) Thank you so much for saying over and over that you will never leave me. I hope I give you enough. I am there for you when you need my strength. Is that enough? I do know about pheromones and a lot more about other things. I want to do tricks for you, to keep you. Oh, how will I get any writing done? Who wants to get any writing done?

I am at a loss for words. I love you so much I can hardly stand it.

I hold you close and kiss you with open mouth,

SUNDAY (EASTER), MARCH 26, 1989 9:15 AM

My darling soon-to-be Kathy Elliott,

I have been wild with love for you these past few days, absolutely frantic, and last night again I masturbated (with charming fantasies of you that I'm too shy to put in a letter but will tell you over the phone today) and now I feel calmer. You evoke so much sexual energy in me that I've got to marry you, as I mentioned, so I don't burn; with other women, this has not been such a problem, because I have not been as turned on to them, but you drive me wild with sexual longing and desire — not just your superb body but the sexual connectedness I experience with you.

New topic: I want to lay out my rationale for making money, so you can see it and maybe poke holes in it if you can (which I would appreciate; I want it to be workable and welcome criticism). The centerpiece is my first book, How to Stop Sabotaging Your Life. (I think that title is okay; do you?) Once that book is done and published, I can easily sell 200 copies a month via bookstores. That figure is not unusual for the worst possible book — only 2400 copies a year. Income would be $5 a copy, or $1,000 a month. The title would sell forever, with revised editions every few years. Then, as I mentioned, I have another book well on the way to being finished; working title is Anthetics (an expansion of Anthetic Values). This should sell 100 copies, for $500 a month, minimum. Then a third book, to be written: Anthetic Relationships. Another 200 copies a month, for a total of $2500 a month — a figure that will give us a comfortable living in Lafayette with little or no work to be done except process bookstore orders and ship books. Even this can be taken care of by a book jobber, at $1/book. Any additional workshops, seminars, groups, clients, etc., would be gravy. So that's the game plan. It seems viable, in that I have writing ability, the topics seem hot, I have original ideas, I have lots of experience in the field, I do thoroughgoing library research (which hardly anyone does), my ideas work in practice. I see no reason why this goal of $2500 a month cannot be reached. (And Lafayette is the ideal place to be.)

So instead of getting a job, I have been living on loans of one sort or another, together with group and client fees, and have given top priority to writing the first book. A primary reason for getting my master's and enrolling in the doctoral program was to finance this writing. This all seems to make sense, but sometimes I think it's a crackpot idea, like a novelist who sacrifices to write the Great American Novel but who has little talent, and who winds up a failure. Or a man obsessed with digging up Spanish treasure that doesn't exist. But I think this is different. I have produced one item: Anthetic Values. People have indeed liked it, but there's one problem in all the above: my market is quite narrow. Many people are plugged in to ideologies, Absolute Truth of one kind or another, and don't like Anthetics. Others find it too radical. Or don't want to do the work that's involved. But my requirements (our requirements, now) are modest, especially if we are to live in Lafayette, so I think this plan will work.

Well, any reactions will be gratefully appreciated.

Now, a new topic: spirituality. Since learning to love God (even in the partial way I do), I see how important that is. Eastern religions do not lend themselves to this; they speak of compassion, which, I think, is not strong enough. And not of compassion toward God, either. I think it's important to love God, scary though that is to me, and shameful though I may feel about it—more important than God loving me. So again, I like the Christian tradition from which you come. Please don't vitiate it by believing a lot of ascetic stuff from the East. That love creates the indulgence, extravagance, and voluptuousness that permeate your spirituality.

Now I want to give you my kids' addresses and phone numbers:

Kevin has two girls, Dana and Laura. Carol has Jana and one on the way, as I mentioned.

Just in case, let me give you Elayna's address, too.

I don't want you to feel out of contact with my life.

Kevin works as a computer person in Minneapolis, is making a good income, and plans to move to the Pacific Northwest in a few years, probably Spokane. He and Tami married (eloped, actually) in college. Tami works as a claims adjuster and hates it; wants to be a writer.

Robert is an accountant. Carol is a temporary or part time bookkeeper for an accounting firm. Both families own their own homes. Robert and Carol want to move to the Pacific Northwest, too, perhaps Portland.

Laura is easygoing. Dana loves birds passionately and is just getting interested in horses. (So you will have some lovely built-in grandchildren!)

I just had that marvelous telephone conversation

with you, and I felt so connected to you, and now that I've had a good come, I feel more relaxed and at peace. Blue panties! How erotic! I think blue and pink are my favorite panty colors, with yellow and white a close second. Thank you so much for indulging me. I wonder if I'll ever get so used to our communion that I won't marvel about everything that happens.

Oh, I love you so much!

SATURDAY, MARCH 25, 1989 3:50 PM

My beloved Jim,

I am following my energy – and it drives me to connect with you. Our phone conversation was so tremendously powerful for me. I think our most powerful spiritual connection yet. Transforming for me. You are a powerful man, my love. And a powerful spiritual man. You may not bill yourself that way, but I'm getting to see that you are. Gosh, God gives the best gifts! So your words about The Word cut through some binding spiritual cords and set me free. You are right that spiritual battle was needed there, and it took your strength, discernment, and word to do it. Thank you so much. I am awed that I took a very tentative step with you – concerned that you wouldn't understand about prophecy, about its power to frighten me. But you did and not from already knowing (previous exposure) rather from current, fresh discernment. That is even more powerful to me. Your ability to take all of who you are and what you know and apply it in this new area. Oh, you are a genius. My man is a genius! God, how good it is that you are not a spiritual wimp! So many men (even and maybe especially those brought up in a religious doctrine) are spiritually weak; not at all in touch with their power. But you are. And I submit to you in this. I want a man who is not cowed by my spiritual power, who can stand shoulder to shoulder with me in spiritual expression and battle. And you are he. I cannot put into words how important the spiritual side is to me. I can only trust that you know me and from that knowing know that priority in my life. I am so grateful that you don't have an orthodox or doctrinal background. I need your freshness to foster and strengthen my non-orthodoxy.

Then, I love your parting words to me on "having me." I want you to have me. I am yours. You may have me any time and in all ways. I submit to your having me. And I love that you meet me fantasy to fantasy. I don't shock you. I am so grateful. And you don't shock me. Isn't that something?

I appreciate your comments on Mama's wedding ring. Your caution has me rethinking. Let's do look for a fresh start. And just stay in the question of this till it gets clear.

We are big enough to stay in the question about money too. But let's keep talking about it. There is an interesting shift going on in me. I am not big on rules and guidelines, and you seem to find them important. But with you, I want to explore and name those. It's like I want your maleness and the firmness it brings to me — such foreign firmness — guidelines, intellect, reasoning, budgets. Oh my, and here I am loving these things, welcoming these things. And I don't want them from just any man. In fact, I resist them from other men. But you are like the perfect puzzle piece for me. I long for these things from you. Would you tell me your thought about this dynamic in me? I fear rape — but I want you to take me and ravish me. I hate budgets and guidelines, but it's like a firm foundation with you. I feel like a spirited, wild horse who no one could tame. Then the gentle, powerful wizard came along and it was tamed, accepted the bit and the rider. (I take this image from The Lord of the Rings — my favorite book — the relationship between Gandalf, the wizard, and Shadowfax, the horse.) Perhaps my feminist sisters are turning over in their graves, but this is not a downgrading of myself — this is a fulfillment. Do you understand? Oh, shit on this letter lag. I want to know now. I am so in touch with my power on all levels when I relate to you. Yet I am so ready to submit and surrender to you. It's a paradox.

And you say I really challenge you intellectually — and I am strengthened. And thank you for using such a loving, connected example (jasmine soap) to discuss abstract ideas that helped me stay in the topic with you. You say much pleromatic truth is constructed intuitively. And that feels right to me. Especially in relation to the jasmine soap/heart chakra example. One caution in me is: much pleromatic truth is verified through lived experience: The Word Becomes Flesh. Let's see if I can think of an example. Oh yes, I say, "Oh God I don't want to be promiscuous any more (1979), and I want to get off the pill, and I need your healing touch on my body so I won't be sick every month with my period." And lo and behold, I am healed from the next period forward. After 16 years of terrible periods. I am healed. Of course, the physicalists would say, "okay, one instance, but can it be replicated?" And there you have it — the pleromatic replicates as it will or as the Bible says, "The spirit blows where it will." Resists guidelines! Yet fulfills the law of love. Oh my, thank you, my love, once again for opening the path for me to speak my truth. To give voice to it.

Cali has decided to go to "Journey into Wholeness" with me in May, so that means I won't have to fly. She and I will drive together (it's 12 hours) and so I'll be saved an airline ticket. Which means I'll have more money to visit you or help you visit me. And you'll notice that she copied the enclosed materials and wrote notes to you and highlighted it for you. It's all her work and her messages to you.

I am overcome with love for you, my treasured man.

Your Kathy

MARCH 27, 1989

My beloved husband-to-be —

Ah, what a wonderful thing to write. So you are starting to talk like me? Well, of course, you know our synergy and know that I've noticed just this week that I'm starting to speak like you. And I am delighted! I am sitting at Chad's office for a chiropractic visit. Sitting here glowing in your wonderful love and in the two beautiful, loving letters I received today. You are the most wonderful lover any woman could have. I am bathed in your declaration of manly love acts — defending me, throwing your cloak down, etc. Oh, beautiful. You are my man.

Now re: your preparation for moving, my heart's desire is for you to move here in August. Is there some way I may support you and assist you with the overwhelm you feel about getting things done in order to move early? I'll help in any way I can. I know it must be hard to do it by yourself and to plan and think by yourself. I am here now. I will gladly help you. We are in this together. We can work side by side to have our hearts' desire. (A little part of me is scared that I'm rushing and scaring you, and that to be with me in August is not your heart's desire. Can you speak to me, so I'll know how to support you in this move and its preparations?) I love you so. It's scary to be so in love, so transparent, no defenses — just totally in love with you before you and before others. It certainly feels risky — except when I talk to you or read your letters. And then your mighty love assures and strengthens me. Oh, God, I am overcome with love for you.

Oh, I went to Abdalla's (clothing store) today with Mama and bought some pretty spring clothes. I think you'll like them. I thought about you as I tried them on (it's so strange to think about pleasing you as well as myself, but it's a delight). I bought a red slinky blouse (it's long and covers my thighs and will be perfect for prancing around the house before you with nothing else on — tee hee-- and a taupe slinky blouse, a pretty taupe skirt and a wonderful dress (pink and white striped cotton –fits great — shows all the curves, but is little girl sweet too — like a pink peppermint stick). I want to wear it to meet you at the airport. I want to dress in a way that blesses you and turns you on. Then I went grocery shopping at Albertson's, passed the fruit juices with a heart leap, thinking of when we'll shop together and how sweet, thrilling and glorious it will be to shop together and talk of what we want to eat and have around to snack on. Mama and I talked about you all through lunch — just celebrated how wonderful you are. She loves you already. While we ate at Don's, a fellow USL psychology professor came by the table, all aglow and said, "Guess what I'm doing this afternoon?" I said, "Going fishing?" He said, "No! Getting married." I was excited for him and wanted to tell him of my joy but thought I wouldn't steal his thunder. He said, "I'll see you tomorrow at school." I said, "What, no honeymoon?" He said, "At my age (50 something), the honeymoon only takes about 15 minutes!" Little does he know!

Oh, I'm hurting now. I found out this afternoon that a precious friend was killed in a car accident in California. She was a beautiful lady (Eve) — a spot of incredible love on this earth. Let us honor her by filling up any gap she left with our great love.

Thank you for the Barnyard Shopping Center brochure — what a precious memory. & Yes, I feel just like you — like I've known and loved you forever. & like the intensity and solidity has always been there. I'm so glad we had Pawling together. Yes, let's write love notes after we are married (yum). Yes, things can be this perfect. They are. We are experiencing it. Oh, how you thrill and reassure me every time you write about our wedding ceremony — strawberries, sugar, and cream. Yes, let's keep it sexual. Yes, and a stuffed tiger. I'm glad you're looking already. Oh, you bless me. Yes roses. Yes, I think I'd like to carry them & maybe have them in my hair? And all around the room? I think I know people who grow them. We could pick our own.

You've said your concern about switching your groups to monthly and I've heard a pretty big charge on that concern. So, I think there is where you may be needing support. May I support you, my love? Do you need to talk about your concern, fear etc.? I will happily work with you on empowering you for this. Oh, & thank you for imaging me as a lovely bride. You are incredible, you loving man.

Now about your need for advice re: professional workshops on IC. Yes, I think you can train both professionals and general public. They (the general public) don't know what you are doing with others. I think you can keep them separate and do both.

Oh, and yes, there was something powerful and significant (electric, as you say) at our first meeting and speaking. And the energy on the surface, ready to comingle — uh huh — now that you say it, you are right. We really didn't waste any time moving into getting together. It's like something bigger than us took us up into its life and love and invited us and included us. Oh, it is sweet — like strawberries and cream and sugar.

A little thought, I think I want you to drive the car when

we are married and together.

Oh, and I continue to deepen your work. Sigh.

Oh, your sensitivity to my need for reassurance about wanting to love and marry me after we have had sex. Oh, thank you, you wonderful man. I am totally in love with you, totally devoted to you. I will never leave you. I will not fall in love with another. Not at the May conference, not anywhere, anytime. You are all my desire and more. Yes 100+%. I am incredibly, overwhelmingly in love with you, Jim, my beloved — my all —

your Kathy

MONDAY, MARCH 27, 1989 9:40 PM

My dearest,

I want to tell you how good that orgasm was that I had when I masturbated while talking to you on the telephone, and how close I felt to you, how loving. I continue to be astonished by the things we do—unlike anything I have ever experienced. Again, I felt calmer afterward—not so frenzied with love of you, though still powerfully in love with you as usual. And then I had a thought today: What if our being together, and even our being married, does not diminish this obsession and infatuation we have with each other? Oh, it's got to!

I love the things you write me: "I want to submit to you." "I want the sweetness and the violence of your passion to break upon me." Please keep writing me about sexual things—and about your new blue panties, which have such a profound effect on me. And the pink ones, too, if you have bought them.

Writing that is getting me excited again.

Oh, Kathy, treasure! I miss you so!

About a motel in town: I saw an ad for the Racetrack Inn. It's across from Evangeline Downs. Is it any good? Or can you get information on others for me? (And will you stay the night with me?)

About airline schedules: The Oakland airport is closer to Berkeley, so that's probably the place to arrive and depart from. There's a flight that leaves Lafayette at 8:25 am and arrives 12:48 pm. Departing, it's 1:53 pm and arriving in Lafayette at 9:30 pm. How does that sound?

You say you'd like to visit the English countryside and Scotland. Those are not top-priority items on my list, but I will go with you. Bavarian Alps, yes. Rhine, yes. French countryside, sort of; again, I'll do it. I would enjoy almost anything as long as you are along. My happiness is being by your side.

About moving: I can rent a U-Haul truck for about $1400. Gas would be another $250. Motels extra ($70 a night?). You could arrive on the 12:48 pm flight, and I could pick you up at the airport and zip down to Asilomar, having lunch in Carmel and parking on the beach. I want to look at Curlew again and the rocks on the beach. (Oh, Kathy, what sweet memories we have!)

Then drive south to the beach towns north of San Diego, east to Houston to visit Carol, then home (?).

On the positive side, this would give us a visit to Asilomar (regular cost $650 for air fare), Southern California (another $650), visit to Carol ($400). It would be fun driving with you. It would, as you mentioned, be a rite of passage (if I can get over my feeling of going backward—back East, that is, after having taken that long trip out west from Detroit). Some great memories and experiences, which I'm sure we'd have. (We would get 10 days to complete the trip.) We could stop off for supper at Solvang, which is a sort of Danish village north of Santa Barbara.

Negatively: greater chance of an accident than flying. Traffic through Los Angeles would be fierce. Whole trip would be stressful (for me, anyway), but if we took eight days, it would be okay; just so we don't have to drive like hell all the way. How about six or seven hours a day only? With leisurely stops here and there? I get very stressed from cross-country driving.

This reminds me of a situation in which I might be hard to get along with: when I'm driving with a passenger and I make mistakes (wrong turnoff, etc.). I become very frustrated and jangly and need you to say something soothing to remind me that it's not a life-or-death affair. Will you?

Well, you might see my worst side on such a trip. I hope you will still want to marry me.

Wow, what a powerful statement: that you might (will) marry me! Oh, I love you so much! My precious Kathy, my darling, my dear, sweet girl!

So, if we visit Carol on our trip home(!), we might visit Kevin by air, before our wedding. (Wow: wedding! What a powerful word.)

Well, another negative: We'd have to make that trip home in August, I guess, when it would be quite hot.

I have a little TV, about 13", black and white, and I'm not sure whether it's worth bringing, but I probably will. If I wake up in the middle of the night and can't get back to sleep, I might want to watch it in bed; it has a jack for an earphone. Would that be okay?

About your pet peeve (TV being on constantly), it's mine, too.

About readings at our wedding: Kevin read something at Carol's wedding and so did Tami—something from the bible, I think. I would like to okay whatever is read. If anything is, that is. No I haven't heard "There is Love," but I think I'll like it.

I'm tired after my group (which was a bit frustrating),

and I hope it doesn't show in this letter. I feel scattered.

Wreaths, flowers, baskets, candles for our home (sigh!)—yes, I like them all. Yes, I like the book titles you mention; and I think Kathy Elliott sounds just great. (Though you still might want to keep Vermillion for professional reasons; please feel free to.)

Just think: Mr. and Mrs. James Elliott. Is that too sexist of me? Mrs. Elliott. Wow!

Oh, I'm so sleepy, and I love you so much, and I want to take a long hot bath and crawl into bed beside you right now and curl up against your nude body, hugging you tightly, and not being able to get to sleep for an hour or so because I am so sexually turned on by your voluptuous body. (There I go again arousing myself.) Kathy, I've got to get some sleep, so stop being such a tempting sexual morsel! (No, don't stop! Never stop!) You couldn't stop if you wanted; sexuality just radiates from you naturally. (I'm so fortunate! What if I'd never met you!)

I can't think straight. All I know is I love you desperately and want to spend every minute with you that I can. Preferably naked and in bed. I'm sleepy, so I'll stop now and begin again tomorrow. Good night, my dearest.

(Next day, 9am). I'm feeling a bit down today. I think of California with negative thoughts: there's no place here for—HOORAY! YOU JUST CALLED!—my down feeling is all gone; you are my cure for depression. I'm excited about our May 6 workshop date. I've got to take this out of the typewriter now and write some notes on our group. (OUR group! What a sweet phrase!)

Oh, I love you so very very much
And we'll be together soon —
And the August trip looks viable —
Oh, what rapture!

TUESDAY, MARCH 28, 1989 11:30 AM

My darling Kathy,

Well, this will be a practical letter (if I can stop thinking about your voluptuous body for a few minutes! No; there it goes again; I long so for the feeling of lying naked next to you, soaking up the love your body radiates for me and returning that radiation with love of my own. Stop it, Jim! Focus on practical things! Okay, okay, dammit.)

About the May 6 workshop, here are some items, some thoughts.

And then the thoughts occur to me of couples groups, an ongoing advanced group. How will you have a part to play in that? What would you like? This is all new to me. I don't even know the right way to ask these questions!

How will we divide up the money from the workshop? (This is somewhat scary for me to think about.)

I would like to leave as many decisions up to you as possible; I trust you so. I would just like to see the final copy on the announcement before you have copies made to offer any suggestions or inaccuracies. (Should I be listed as "Jim" or "James"?) (Whose name should appear first?) I never had such sweet problems before!

Shall we pray together about this workshop? Is that what one does when one begins (as I have) to love God?

You are my perfect soulmate,

My ideal woman, My dream come true,

TUESDAY, MARCH 28, 1989 10:00 AM

My beloved Jim,

Now I've started taking notes on things I want to be sure to say to you. (Your influence on me again!) It really helps, I must say. I have so much to say to you that I don't want to forget anything.

A delightful thing happened last night. Cali and I went to eat at Piccadilly (it was so delicious) and as I was walking with my tray to a table, I saw Lanie (my ex-sister-in-law, Andy's sister) and her husband, Jay and children, Tommy (5) and Rebecca (3). Lanie is very pregnant, and I hadn't seen her since she became pregnant, so we visited about that. Well, I went and put my tray on the table and rushed back to her and said, "I have some exciting news for ya'll. I am in love." They were all happy for me. (I love them. They are special people.) They wanted to know how I met you, and I told them. They thought it was great that we're both doctoral students. I said, "Well, it's moving very fast." And Lanie said, "That's how it should be. It should move fast." Then she said, "As it turns out, Noel (Lanie's sister and my beloved friend) is in love too." "His name is Joel," Tommy piped in with his little loving, alive face. And I said, "Oh, well my man's name is Jim." And 5 year old Tommy said, "Tell Jim hello for me." Isn't that precious? So you are already getting greetings from your Lafayette friends! I'm so glad I ran into Lanie, because I want Andy's family to know. They are very special to me. And I know they will be happy for me. They love me.

Then, Chase (My colleague and supervisor) called last night to let me off the hook about some work we were going to do together (required paperwork, etc.) I said, "Gosh, thanks

Chase, for being so kind." He said, "Oh, Kathy, just enjoy this. It doesn't happen often. I'm waiting and ready for a lust/ love relationship myself. I can be empathic with you." So support is all around us.

I spoke with Averill (a vocational counselor who does testing). She says we could use her central area gladly but that her 2 colleagues see individual clients at night. Saturday would be fine. May 6th would be fine. She put it down tentatively (9 to 5). She has several clients who are possible referrals.

…Well, now we've talked (I called you), and we're excited, and the workshop is unfolding. And I'm excited. It's scary to have the marketing to do, but on the other hand, it feels better — less out of control than if Serenity Center were doing the marketing. So please source your thrusting male power to me to market this. I am elated. I want to shout. I have Mama on the prayer rug, and you know how powerful her prayers are!

Well, I must do some brainstorming re: workshop content and get to the bank.

Know that I love and adore you. You are my man. I am ecstatic that your inner decision maker says August for the move. I want to be with you bodily as you move, as a beginning to our together in the flesh in Lafayette life. Shoulder to shoulder — together.

Oh my, I love you so.

your Kathy

WEDNESDAY, MARCH 29, 1989 4:25 PM

My darling twin,

I am aware more and more that what attracts me to you is the fact that you are my counterpart — and that no one else even comes close to being that. At the same time, you are someone other than me: first, you are female, with all the magic and mystery and fascination that that entails for me; second, you have a more highly developed spirituality than I, so I am getting constant surprises from you; third, that you are Southern; and fourth, a whole bunch of other things. So you are my identical twin but not a carbon copy. Sufficiently identical for us to fall into each other; sufficiently different for us to be constantly surprised by each other. It's a nice combination.

Tonight I will make my airline reservations, and I will soon hold you in my arms. How I pine for you! (I never thought I would pine for anyone.) Feels like a tree. Anyway, my one desire is to be married to you and be together forever; to have access to your sexy body, your fine mind, your soaring spirit whenever I wish. Soon, soon. Until then —

All my love, my dearest —

WEDNESDAY, MARCH 29, 1989 7:05 PM

My adored one—

I love you—I hallow you—I bless you—I long for you—I am overjoyed to have found you—to share life with you—My twin—My beloved—My soulmate.

I must go home now, but I wanted you to hear from me Saturday. (I hope the postal service agrees!) To know in writing of my great, undying love for you. You are my all___ Be assured that I will never leave you. You are my delight. I love every part of you—Your beard, your cock, your semen—Your wonderful mouth and hands—I am so glad they are mine—I will honor and treasure them always—I will submit to you as your wife and your beloved. You are worthy of my submission.

Glory—

Your Kathy

P.S. I must share the spirituality notes I gave my class tonight—perhaps for your group? Soon to come—the notes, and me, and you shall come!

WEDNESDAY, MARCH 29, 1989 9:51 PM

My love —

Oh, how good it is to connect with you by letter. I started to make a new cassette tape of music for you but decided I'd rather write. It has been so good to talk to you on the phone. I love to hear your wonderful, warm, loving, sexy voice. I told my Psycho-Social class about you. They loved it. They were all excited and celebrated with me this once-in-a lifetime love. Sat forward in their seats to hear what it's like to be in love when you're 37 instead of 20. (They're mostly in their 30s.) Scott, the only man (a precious young one) said, "I'm listening and taking notes." Like he's learning from us what women want. Our interchange on spirituality was wonderful. Oh, and they want to come to our workshop, just to experience you! And they want to know if they're invited to the wedding! I have a wonderful relationship with them. It's great to have adult students.

As I went through my notes I thought there might be some things I could share with your groups when I'm with you in Berkeley. So here are some brief ideas: 1) Our common desire as humans to be "seen" (truly seen as we are) by others, yet our common terror about being seen. We live in a universe requiring observer participation, the physicists say. We all long to be and need to be/require that we be observed, contemplated, and hallowed. Observed (I see you without judgment; I take you in as you are). Contemplated (I behold you and consider with respect what I behold). Hallowed (I hold as sacred your you-ness). To experience these 3 phases of relating to/knowing each other is life-transforming. I have some stories to illustrate and we could open it to the group from there. (I'm not sure of your group's protocol, but I sense they'd take it from there). 2) Spirituality as search for meaning/transcendence, whether in major life events or in everydayness. (3) Shame — the experience of not being enough, of being flawed to the core. 4) Love — the extravagant possibilities of loving — we're taught to be careful in love, to hold back, to watch our step — but there is another way — the way of spontaneity (the urge to take flowers to my sick neighbor — yes, do it), the way of trusting my inner guidance (I want to smile at that lady pushing her cart in the grocery store aisle rather than waiting to see what she'll do 1st, I initiate); the way of the child (I can sit on this person's lap, figuratively, at times and delight in their presence — fling myself into the experience of delight in the other etc.) So, do any of those mesh with your group? Let me know, my love.

Here is the Ayn Rand quote: "Love is an expression and assertion of self-esteem, a response to one's own values in the person of another." And as you say, my heart, more than values, it is responding to another's isness — a "twinning." Oh, I love that you called and said "Is this the future Kathy Elliott" That was a thrill!

Did I tell you I'd like you to brush my hair? I think I did. Well, I still would like it. Also, I'd like you to bathe me, like I want to bathe you. And I'd like you to rub and caress and stroke my feet. (They feel so neglected — I loved and they loved your kissing them so sweetly.)

You spoke of my being the most pro-libidinal woman you've ever known. And I think that's true. Yet, don't you think it's amazing that I have not acted that out consistently in the last 10 years? Do you have any thoughts from my story as you know it? Did I sublimate? (I think I did.) Was it grace? (I think it was.) Any other thoughts?

Well, I am getting very sleepy, so let me imagine that you are waiting in bed for me, in all your glorious naked flesh. The ceiling fan is whirring the warm air around. I crawl into bed beside you and right into your loving arms, pressing my naked body to yours.

Know of my deep, unending, consuming love for you. I am fulfilled in you, my love.

Your Kathy

THURSDAY, MARCH 30, 1989 1:20 PM

My love —

You are truly my love. I am more in love with you every day.

I have a wonderful naming experience to share with you. This morning I talked with Hale and shared the incredible experience of your spiritual discernment and power re: Greta and her prophecy and my fear. How you cut right through my fear with your speaking of The Word. Our word and its power to overcome and defend us and our love. Well, he got quiet and said, "Kathy, I am in awe. You know what Jim did? He exercised his spiritual headship in your relationship. (Then he spoke of how that term has been clouded and abused by fundamentalists as a way to have power, to put women down, etc. But that the concept is valid.) And I was struck with the truth of that term, spiritual headship. Yes, that's one of the primal urges we've talked about. The desire, need for a woman to experience her man's spiritual power to defend, perceive, protect on the spiritual plane. And it helps me understand why I experienced your words as so awesome, so fundamental. Yes, providing me with a foundation, a feeling of security. My man, this man, has the spiritual power to perceive danger, to speak to it, to do battle with it, to protect me. God, an experience of primal fulfillment. I don't know how you'll take this naming or if you have stuff around it. I'm willing to talk to you about it more. But I want you to hear that for me, it is powerful, so I name you my spiritual head. Will you accept that from me? And perhaps the submission is an extension of that, so it would hold great primal power. Let's talk more about this.

Now, I want to speak to your past letters, especially the letter of Saturday, March 25. Thank you for the affirmation of my financial stuff. And I love how you talk about "making money for us" and "our good life together." Sigh. Yes, your figuring of your part looks right. And as to your own financial shame, I still love you. I accept you and your finances. As to your fear, I am so glad you are big enough to follow your dream, even with the financial risk and sacrifices. I am so happy and admiring of you that you have not sold out your soul to the General Motors model. It would have been more comfortable on some levels. But not on the soul level. And you know I see to the soul level so I respect and love you for being true to your path, even at great cost (literally). You are an extraordinary man, my love.

And so you bring yourself to me (sounds like me) pretty sound of wind and limb. Thank you. Good luck on your root planing and new glasses. And thank you for all you are doing (diet, safety) to keep yourself well. I ate an oat bran roll at lunch in your honor! Piccadilly serves them!

As to your fear re: all the changes, the culture shock, marital shock, etc., I am happy to support you through your fears, to listen to your thoughts and not take them too seriously. I surround your vulnerability with my lubricating balm of my femaleness, my tranquil Kathyness. And thank you for adding that you are 100% committed to me as my husband. What wonderful words. What a blessed fact. I rest in it.

I will be in the market for a flared miniskirt! And white striped panties! It is such fun and so erotic to mutually please each other sexually. I am so glad we are compatible sexually. We are dynamite!

Now, thank you, my sweetheart, for the skill area handouts.

They are clear, easy to read, well developed. I am impressed. I admire you so much…Darn. I got a phone call and a student came by and now I've lost time and have to leave to get supper cooked for prayer group (we take turns) and go to the doctor. I'll continue on the handouts later, when I can duly honor them.

For now, know that I love you and adore you. Oh, our loving is so good. An incredible blessing. Receive an open mouthed kiss from me and the feel of my hand on your cock through your pants!

I love you so,

your Kathy

FRIDAY, MARCH 31, 1989 11:30 AM

My precious twin,

Just in case you are wondering, let me assure you that I will ask you to marry me and that as soon as you decide to say yes, we will indeed be engaged. (I will ask you in Lafayette, I guess; but I need to think about the ring first), and we will most assuredly be married, man and wife, licensed to live together and have sex whenever we want, joined forever and ever, one flesh. There's no question in my mind about this; I am determined to do it.

I am still in awe over your request for spiritual headship and still not entirely sure what it entails; what you said was so overwhelming, I took in only about 30%. Can you tell me again about it?

Now some comments about the dynamic of submission and surrender. (Thank you for posing such juicy intellectual questions for me; they stretch my mind as it has never been stretched before.)

The submission of the woman to the man is, I think, archetypal. In the past, it might have had some value in terms of survival of the human race, either reproductively or otherwise. So I think it's wired in at a deep primal level (and we are certainly touching that level!). It's connected with sexuality, emotionality, intellectuality, and spirituality. It was useful when we were more like animals, and that animal layer is still in there, deep now, but functioning.

With the coming of civilization (reactive civilization, that is), that primal archetype's power got distorted. It must have felt okay to the cave man and cave woman, and it suited them just right. But men (as they became reactively power-hungry) used it not to help women blossom but to oppress them. These men took women's tender and delicate gift of submission and stomped all over it, hoping to crush women's spirit, for their own compensatory needs. At first, women must have thought this was okay because their pleromatic contact made them less strong, and because they knew it was good for them to give this gift. But the result became second class citizenship, and even battering, for women. The feminists rebelled against this, and rightly so. The injustices need to be corrected.

But there is still that archetypal hunger operating in women, and it keeps trying to emerge and become manifest in their lives. I guess if I were a woman, I would keep searching for a man worthy of submitting to (and, of course, not finding one). What a woman needs is a man who has overcome his reactivity. An Anthetic man.

It must be an Anthetic submission, not a reactive one.

So you can now be free to submit, and I can be free to exercise power over you, and it will be a powerfully good thing (it will result in both of us blossoming, each in our own way) only because you, in submitting, will not give up your identity and I in exercising power will not dominate and oppress you but will, as I mentioned create space in which you can flourish and blossom like a garden of beautiful and precious flowers. I will give your life structure so the pleromatic energies you are experiencing can expand to their fullest without fear of splattering and becoming diffuse, or going out of control.

So I name this "Anthetic submission" and "Anthetic

power." Not reactive. And that redeems it.

(Wow! I like those thoughts you have encouraged me to produce!) (You are so incredibly good for me!)

Now about sexuality. I was struck by your report of your colleague's plan for a 15-minute honeymoon. I want to tell you how much I treasure my sexual energies; I've noticed their decline over the past ten years; I want to encourage them to continue as much as possible. Use it or lose it, someone said. I want to use it — and with you. When that sexual energy rises in me I feel a glow; my whole life becomes more pervaded with vitality. On top of that, there is the immense pleasure of coming — heightened a thousandfold by our sexual communion.

So I have a request, which I have formulated before but not with the precision I will now use: Please stimulate me sexually as much as you possibly can. All the time. In letters, on the phone, and above all in person. May I tell you how?

First, just by being who you are. I lubricate at the sound of your voice, even though you might be reading aloud stock market quotations. So a lot of this you can do with no effort at all.

Second, by reassuring me that you accept my semen.

You mention that your pink and white striped dress shows all your curves; I love that statement! I love all your curves! You voluptuous woman, you! I like slinky material, slick and satiny. I like your statement "but is little-girl sweet, too." Can I have all the things I want? I am so hungry for you, my treasure!

All these things will make it easier to overcome my cathexis of California and my office, too. The more tempting you make yourself, the easier it will be to sell my books, throw things away, etc., and overcome my fear of leaving what has been up to now my secure nest here.

As you can see, sexuality is important to me, to say the least, and it has now a spiritual context, with you, which makes it profoundly symbolic of great depths. It gives my life incredible significance. And all that is your doing, my future bride, my future wife, my girl, my precious treasure, my soulmate! My woman!

About your offer of support; it overwhelms me. Apart from the above, I can't yet begin to think about it; I have been so used to doing things on my own and being the one who offered support. Let me think.

Yes, I will drive the car when we are married. For long trips, I might ask you to drive some. I am the man.

I am your man, to do with as you will. A man to protect you, to do battle for you, to guide you, to learn from you, to help you, to comfort you, to support you, to encourage you to blossom the way you were meant to, to surrender to you, to offer structure so you can develop your genius, and to love you so dearly.

P.S. I am impressed by how swiftly and smoothly you respond when I ask for something; e.g., my request for assistance on time zone differences. We surely fill each other's needful spaces!

P.P.S. I suddenly realized why you wanted a man who combines strength with gentleness. If I were a woman, in touch with my pleroma, that's the only kind of man I would want, because I would want to submit to him, and only a man of that type. To submit to a man with only gentleness and no strength would be to submit to passivity, leaving me feeling insecure. To submit to a man with only strength and no gentleness would leave me feeling dominated and stifled. Aha! I am so perfect for you! (As you are for me!)

P.P.P.S. You and I, we are archetypal characters, it occurs to me, in search of something mysterious and miraculous, on a great transformational voyage together.

I pour myself out to you—

I touch the divinity in you and release my divinity to you—

Core to core,

Divine center to divine center,

We melt into each other

At the very center

From whence the whole world was made,

From which it is now sustained

Second by second

Where aliveness gushes forth

Through us,

Ecstatically,

Poured out into the world

To enrich it, to bring joy, to bring

Pure love.

Ultimate P.S.: I have a sense that something powerful is about to happen to me, something is going to open up (as a result of your calling on me for certain things), and I will be flooded with something, some energy of some kind; it seems to be knocking at the door, faintly now, but not yet ready to burst forth. When it does, I will need your sweet help, your receptive presence to speak it into, just as I pour my semen into you. Will you be ready to do this for me?

Final Ultimate P.S.: There is something I must do in this lifetime that I am beginning to have a sense of. I must go all the way to the end of something. So far I have held back because I needed the right companion and haven't had one. Now I have one: you. Now I can go all the way. (Strangely enough your panties and your craving for my semen are important parts of this, although it is a spiritual journey; I don't understand this, but I think I will later.) I need your support and encouragement in this "going all the way to the end." I know I will have it without reservation. I love you so much. (It is scary right now but with a fear that's sweet and anticipatory of great and rapturous events to come.) Oh, I love you.

FRIDAY, MARCH 31, 1989 1:40 PM

My adored one; my spiritual Head —

Ah, what marvelous words — what a marvelous reality. You have touched me to my deepest core in our conversation this morning. Truly, this is deeper than I have every gone relationally. And you (our relationship) are teaching me the meaning of concepts I never understood: e.g., to be in love (really); spiritual headship (purely a concept and a puzzling one before); sexual communion. These were all concepts before; now they are lived reality. Hallelujah! I don't know what else to say to express my incredible experience of transcendence and fulfillment. My god, you are the man for me. You are Gift. You may rest in knowing how loved, adored, honored, submitted to you are. And you inspire my submission, because you exercise your spiritual/sexual headship in complete love. Do you know how rare this is? I've seen Christian men try to live out this concept, and it always falls short. You can't make it happen. You must have to grow into it, as you have done. And I have done. So often I've seen it come out like: the man bullying his wife and children, the wife and children un-lifed, dispirited or on the other hand, defying him. Not so with us. We are living the ideal; the concept. I am steeped in an experience of awe. That this should come to me! And I long to and look forward to our full consummation of this headship in the flesh.

I have an image that this time apart has at least one blessing: we are getting to create a holy/whole container to hold our in-the-flesh relating. And that container is woven of spoken vows; the Word, our word; spiritual principles and concepts; and beautiful sexual love fantasies.

I hold you in my arms, I kiss you sweetly, then deeply. I submit to you.

Your Kathy

P.S. I have a GYN appointment for Thurs, April 27.

MONDAY, APRIL 3, 1989 2:30 PM

My precious darling,

I've just come back from shopping for your wedding and engagement rings in San Francisco. I found one that is equally as good as the one I found previously and will now have to decide between the two—and also keep looking for new possibilities. Will you trust my judgment in choosing one, or do you want to help?

So my mind is on our wedding, and I had a thought. Instead of the clergyperson asking a long question, to be followed by your and my "I do"-- what about that person asking something like, "At this time I ask you, Kathy and James (Jim?), to make a statement about honoring and cherishing and loving." Whereupon, each of us would make our own statement. Then we could be asked to make a statement about submitting and surrendering, and again we would make statements. (I've got mine all prepared.) Then at the end we could be asked something to which we can answer "I do." Perhaps: "In view of the vows and intentions you have made to each other, do you....?" (I guess I want a bigger part in this ceremony; I want to say something from my heart, not simply repeat "I do.") Then the clergy person could turn and face the audience and ask for their support.

Upon re-reading the above, I have a new suggestion for the c.p.'s statement: "At this time, I ask you, Kathy, and you, James, to state your intentions and vows to each other." Or something like that. (Because my memory is so terrible, I might have to refer to a 3x5 card. What about that?)

All the wedding rings I saw are indeed darling, and they all made my heart leap, as did the fact that I asked the salesclerks about them. It must be very satisfying to sell wedding rings.

About letter lag: Our letters now seem to be mostly confirmations of what we have said on the telephone, which is okay. I want to see those things in writing. Can you tell me again, in great detail, two things: 1) What Mama said when you asked her for advice about Cali? And 2) what you told Cali about your allegiance to me? Those things were so powerful that even though you said them several times, I could not take them in completely.

Now about your letter. Yes, me too: this is far deeper than I have ever gone, my twin; as deep as I longed to go but never could. (I think marriage will be good for both of us; it will settle something that needs to be settled and will put a seal on our relationship.) (And we can then go even deeper.)

Yes, I exercise headship in love and caring; I ask for your submission to my love and caring, my deep caring for what's best for both of us. So as head of this family, I say: Let us live in Lafayette. That is best for us. That is my first command to which you must submit. (I require certain sexual things of you also, to which you must submit.)

Yes, headship lends itself, in reactive hands, to oppression. There should have been an "advanced Bible" for special people only, and headship should have been explained in that one, not in the "introductory Bible." How about three phases? How about an Anthetic Bible?

In our letters we are weaving a tapestry with many resplendent threads (and in our conversations on the phone), a tapestry of love and communion and ideas and connections — that will contain our day-by-day life, that will serve as a context and background. We are weaving well. We will be very happy together. I love you so, Kathy!

Oh, it's so painful to be apart. I miss you so. I long for your naked body.

You are my heart's desire,

My dream come true,

The girl of my dreams.

The one I never thought I'd find.

My luscious popsicle of a woman!

HUVAL'S BODY SHOP!
APRIL 4, 1989, TUESDAY 9:05 AM

My love —

I'm waiting for my car to be fine-tuned — some things left undone in the body work. I've loved talking to you — last night late when I was sleepy. You are so dear, loving, giving to me. Thank you. You do and say things that make me feel so secure. (Are you going to say, "I can't make you feel secure?") Well, there is security for me in you. So there. As I waited for my car, Mr. Huval started talking to me about my work, etc. and asked me something about my husband. I said, "I'm not married now, but I will be soon." So we talked about you and it was neat. He told me that he and his wife travel all over the country on their heavy Honda motorcycle. So we had a big visit.

Guess what I've been doing this morning? Calling places in Florida (Fort Walton and Destin) and Biloxi for brochures! One lady was very helpful and when I told her that it was for our honeymoon (yes, our honeymoon), she suggested some special places and will send those brochures. So, today I rest and bask in your love, in our mighty love for each other. It's so good, so enriching, so desire-fulfilling. I love you, Jim. I love you. Next will be my response to your skill handouts (at last).

Skill Area #1 — Feedback — I like that you use 2nd person — very warm and interactive. Varieties of Feedback — It's helpful to see that delineated. How about "I " statements? Do these fall here? "I felt sad as you talked about your day," etc. It says how the person is affecting others and perhaps may help that person identify things in themselves they might have missed.

("Gosh. I didn't realize how sad I was feeling as I talked.")

You say Anthetic training takes place by means of feedback — from trainer or group members — I see a lot of #5 identifying and labeling, which has its place. But I would be cautious about overusing that. One feedback that I don't see in your work and that I would want to use (& do use) is personal story evidencing mutuality — "I feel as you feel, I've been in a similar state" — this heals shame and teaches that it's ok to be where you are. Is there room in Anthetics for this? I hope so. But perhaps we need to talk about it.

Processing Feedback — I love your style. Having experienced it personally from you and provided it to you I know it is powerful.

Difficulty Receiving Feedback — I think this is valuable, and I see an application for it. In chemical dependency work, a lot of feedback is given. But I don't know how much equipping is done of the people receiving it. I think a pamphlet or some in-service trainings or professional workshops on "How to equip a person to receive and use feedback" would be marketable and wonderful.

Yes on giving feedback — good.

Skill #2-- Accessing Feelings — I like that you break down awareness/response into 3 steps. We need specifics, so good.

#4 distinguishes between feeling and body sensation — yes, but I find that body sensations may be the 1st step in helping me identify feelings. When I get a lump in my throat I'm usually sad, moved, anxious, etc. I think it might be helpful to state that body sensations may be a stepping stone to identifying specific feelings. Then we can name them as we talk about them.

I like that you give examples.

Let me gush for a minute. You are doing what Irene deCastillejo said again, performing the torch task again—illuminating the dark places with specifics. They are going to love this work here. And be healed by it. Oh, bless you. And thank you, God, for the gift you've given Jim to bring to us. Oh, my. I am in awe. You have such specific work here. You could do a fantastic book on the Inner Critic and market it to ACOAs etc. Is that "How to Stop Sabotaging Your Life?" Well, may I suggest using Inner Critic in your title? It might bring it into specific contemporary concerns and attract ACAs etc. Wonderful, wonderful, wonderful. I can't wait to learn from you and experience you at our workshop.

Oh, my beloved, it is so good to celebrate your work. I see your strength really at its most thrusting power in the Inner Critic work.

So while I'm on the subject of thrusting power…

My strong man—

Have I told you lately how I desire you? How I want to feel your thrusting power (your spirit and cock combining to inseminate me)? In my vagina—In my mouth—in my hand—Well, let me assure you that I will never leave you. Your hard, shy cock has me captive. Captive to his seductions, to his power. And your loving, expert mouth has me bound. Bound to the feel of it on the back of my neck, on my breasts, on my pussy. And I don't want to go anywhere. I want to be always in your arms. Always lying at your side. Always beneath you as you thrust into me. Always feasting on your luscious semen—fed and nourished by it. I will eat your come every day. And I will relish it. It is a delight to me. You are my man, Jim, my chosen one. I want no other. I will have no others. I desire only you. My mouth, my vagina are sealed to any other. Only you may have me. And you shall have me fully — nothing held back — all the fierceness, all the passion, all the beauty, all the love is yours, my darling. Take me, please. And never let me go.

I love you so —

your Kathy

TUESDAY, APRIL 4, 1989 3:05 PM

My beloved Kathy,

I just talked to you on the phone, dear, and told you about shopping for your wedding and engagement rings. What pleasure it gave me, that shopping! In a day or two, I'll make a final decision—when I get your ring size.

I love planning our honeymoon. Florida! Sounds great! I'm touched that you're calling for brochures. (In my other relationships, I was the one who did everything; the other person just passively followed. Thank God I'm going to be married to a strong woman, with initiative!)

Thank you so much for asking me to wash my hair every day. I will do it. You are going to be my wife, and I want a happy wife. So let me know all the things I can do to make you happy.

I was pleased to hear of your defense of our relationship, Mrs. Tiger. I never realized that so many people would come up with their own stuff about what we're planning! They must think we don't know what we're doing. The nerve of them! An officious bunch of people!

You mentioned on the phone that we jumped immediately into love for each other, right from the beginning. Yes. And I've been thinking about something else—a related theoretical concept.

First, there is the conscious part of each of us. The part that thinks it's the one making the plans and decisions and choices. But deeper, just below the surface, is this other part. I hesitate to call it "the unconscious." It's a big part that runs things. Sort of. If it's reactive it runs things in a driven way, driving us to do things. If it's Anthetic, it's more gentle; it offers suggestions; it acts through strong tendencies, and it serves as a trustworthy guide. There needs to be a name for this part. Not pleroma. Not quite a guide, either, because it's not as focused. It's the part in me that comes up with decisions and solutions to problems, all on its own (if I just ask).

I think that part (Part X?) of me fell in love with that part of you, and wanted to marry you, and spend my life with you, before my conscious part got wind of what was happening. Part X of me saw Part X of you and wouldn't let go, wouldn't deviate from a path that was destined to be taken. And Part X of you saw that and wanted that, too. Your Part X and my Part X created a solid, indissoluble union before our conscious parts knew what was happening. Our conscious parts just went along with what had been previously ordained and decided by these deeper parts. We're just going along for the ride. (Although we do have to give our approval.) (We could nullify the decisions of our Part Xs. But it would be such a hassle, such a traumatic thing. So, we're just letting these deeper parts run with the ball, trusting them, and I think they are trustworthy, because of all the work we have done on ourselves.)

Incidentally, my dear sweetheart, I am committed to working on our relationship. If any conflict arises that we can't resolve, I would be willing to go to a marriage counselor. Let me know your reaction to this, please.

Well, I want my hands on your sweet body, now.

Last night I wanted to touch you through your nightie, just run my hands all over you.

OH, Kathy, what love I have for you!

WEDNESDAY, APRIL 5, 1989 9:50 AM

My dearest soulmate,

Our conversation last night helped me reopen to my spirituality (embarrassment! But I have the right to be spiritual!), and so I thank you. You are very good for me. Now a couple of thoughts; things I have not said precisely enough yet:

What we call God is a manifestation of the transcendent power—a manifestation that we humans are able to handle. Does this seem right?

We can have access to God by calling on him (via prayer) or having a dialogue with him. Right? Any other ways?

When he wants, he comes to us but usually only if we call on him. If we are open to him. Okay?

When he does come, he enfolds us. In his love and caring?

Well, my spiritual teacher, any comments on the above? (And my lower case h.)

I'm about to go for root planing and do some shopping, so this will be a brief note. I was touched by how you felt when I asked about ways of pleasing you. You and I both love to please others and find it ecstatic-and-painful when someone wants to please us. Again, we were made for each other. I'll have more to say about this as our relationship settles into its quotidian patterns. It will be a joyous theme in our marriage. Yes, our forthcoming marriage! We will be husband and wife. What divine ecstasy!

Oh, you sweetheart of mine! How I love you! My

darling Kathy. My love. My woman, my girl. I want you so desperately.

There is some relationship between love (the love I have for you) and spirituality; and between my sexual impulses and spirituality. That love and those impulses are at the core of some powerful reservoir. I want to open my core. To you. To create our own fusion experiment, to generate our own white-hot energy in which others may bask, maybe?

I want to penetrate you

With my penis,

My fiery love,

My divine power.

To insert myself into you to inseminate your own Divinity.

Oh, I love you,

WEDNESDAY, APRIL 5, 1989 2:15 PM

My love —

I am so jangly right now (thanks for giving me that word!). It's been a rough day in some ways. My breakfast with Evan was uncomfortable — my confronting him with his "she's crazy" statement about me. I'll tell you on the phone tonight. I feel pretty alone right now. And I guess that's a necessary step. I'm just getting that — that individuating (including choosing a soul mate/lover/ husband) will call me to stand alone — without agreement from those I might expect or like it from. So it feels lonely, scary, disappointing. But it doesn't deter me. Oh, I see how my voice is developing, Jim. Because I answered all of his thoughts with a counter thought which took him aback with its power and possibility. Yet, I am operating here in our relationship out of some primal, archetypal, non-rational levels. So to try to voice them is difficult. Can you help me? It is okay for me to ask for your help, isn't it? Of course, it is. Well, God is good, because he used the death of a dog (& re-deemed its death I think by using it for me) to teach me. As I had to follow the inner voice that said, "Go back", I stepped into courage, strength, and personal power — also into faith that what I needed would be provided. And it was. I saw the car mat to pick the dog up, and I saw the guy in the parking lot to ask for help. But he wouldn't have done it if I hadn't asked. I provided the heart and commitment; he provided the guts and brawn.

Well, as I process, I am seeing how valuable today was — even with its pain — and it was a pain in the ass! I just stopped writing you to write ideas for our workshop — my part. Because I do feel that I am having to live the experience of doing battle with my Inner Critic (as voiced by actual human voices) and to embrace the positive voices. So I just got that I needed to do a section on the ongoing seduction/compulsion we face with the inner critic, and some ideas on how to work with that. Thank you, God. So here again I get to see confirmation that our God is a redeeming God, turning catastrophe into something valuable.

When I went to Robert today, he said again how fine he thinks you are — how gentleness comes from your eyes and how "he (you) just is, waits, and good comes to him." Are you surprised at his perception of you?

Anyway, I just got another idea on "the microphone effect." I'm experiencing it — how the external world and the voices spoken in it to us can become magnified, depending on whether the inner critic vs. the liberated self is in power. (So, Evan's words are magnified because my inner critic is giving me some shit at some level.)

Well, I also just got that I am being called to grow beyond my inner compliant, people-pleasing part that wants external validation. I say now (in my spiritual power) that I choose Jim. I choose you, Jim. External validation or not, I choose you. You are the love of my life — the man of my dreams. I want you above all else. I am strong again. (I talked with Mama. That woman strengthens me!) Jim, I love you so. I believe you and I have been given a gift — an opportunity to live out a heroic love relationship. (And that does not mean that we have to do heroics but rather just be who we are with each other and let the power of our love and of Pure Love flow through us.) I believe that we shall live and are living an incredible love story — a Rare Relationship. But not rare because other can't have it. Rare because they don't tap it for whatever reason:

cynicism, non-belief, etc. Jesus said, "Be it done unto you according to your belief." "Your faith has made you well." "If you have faith the size of a grain of mustard seed, you can say to this mountain, 'Be moved,' and it will." Look out! I have been fed all afternoon on stories of Jesus coming to my mind: how little agreement he had: "You shouldn't heal on the Sabbath;" "Don't you know that woman kissing your feet is a harlot?" etc. Then these faith statements as I write you strengthen me. Ah, I have shifted, back to center; back to inner knowing.

Oh, Jim, I love you so, my spiritual head, my beloved man, my soul mate, my hungry lover. I wish you were here now to heal any vestiges of bruising with your embrace — your strong, enfolding arms, your loving words, your breath in my ear, your hands in my hair, and your mouth on all parts of my body.

I love you incredibly, I am for you, my love.
The soon-to-be Kathy Elliott

P.S. I wear Ring Size 6!
P.P.S. I bought a new pair of blue panties today!

THURSDAY, APRIL 6, 1989 8:00 AM

My beloved Kathy,

Two letters from you yesterday! And a long conversation last night! On the phone I expressed my fears of your strength, and even that you could encompass and help me with—instead of getting defensive and indignant. In every way we seem well suited to each other.

I want again to assure that depressed little man in your dream that I intend to have an equal partnership with him. He will not be submerged. I will take care that I consult with him. Is he a professional aspect? I want to get to know him more.

Thank you, dear heart, for your wonderful sexual fantasy on the phone. And in your letter. And thank you for thinking about a flared miniskirt and white striped panties. And for buying blue panties again. How important those things are to me!

Now I want to look at us from a purely objective standpoint to assess whether our marriage will be successful.

First, the age difference. Let us look at this boldly, without seeing it through the haze of our love. I am 60 and will be 61 in May. That's more than 23 years' difference. As I mentioned, I bring to our marriage great experience in relationships, partly because of my age, partly because of my expertise which I have accumulated over many years. I specialize in communication, in relationship enhancement, in helping people be close and deal with the glitches and blocks and tangles that come up. So you have my experience to help us, hard won over many years. We are not teenagers or young adults falling in love and hoping that love will conquer all and get us through the hard spots. It won't by itself. We both have solid skills in this area and commitments to the right values. (I guess that's beginning to be an argument for moving quickly, as well as one that addresses the age difference issue.) Anyway, we have gotten very deep with each other.

Other people will judge us by their own shallow and reactive ways of relating, not realizing what we have. Let's keep that in mind when they become officious.

(And now I must go to San Francisco to buy your ticket and shop for your rings.)

(1:40pm) I just came back from S.F. with your airline ticket—and your RINGS! One (1) wedding ring; one (1) engagement ring. Wow! They're cute as a bug's ear; I melt just looking at them. I hope you like them.

About your ticket, I'm going to try to get boarding passes for you, then mail it insured or registered.

Oh, Kathy—this ring (these rings) are so symbolic, so cute. A 1/5 carat diamond with two baguettes, not opposite each other but side by side, pointing to the main stone. You tempting woman, you! How attractive you are—all parts of you.

Just think—when I ask you to marry me (and if you accept, of course), we'll be engaged! I haven't been engaged before, not properly (with a ring). This is the first engagement ring I will ever have given to a girl. (Sigh.)

Now, new topic. I want to pose some possible

314

scenarios for us to discuss. But first, my life goal: Primarily it's to write books and train people in leading Anthetic training groups (and doing Anthetic Therapy). I want to get out of the counseling business and group leading business sometime in the next five years. I want to publish and edit Personal Growth Bulletin. So, given that, here are the scenarios:

You continue your university teaching. Your book is moderately successful. My books and work are fantastically successful, and income (net) is $30,000 per month. You work with me, share Anthetics with me. With $30,000 we can live anywhere (e.g., Southern California) and travel frequently to Lafayette. Or live in Europe. London? Or Hawaii? Or of course Lafayette. Suppose we meet people all over the world that we like. Therapists who lead Anthetic groups, so we must travel often. This would interfere with a full-time job (e.g., teaching) and a practice.

Would you want to stay in Lafayette, continue teaching, while I did the traveling?

Would you want to come with me? Give up your teaching job and practice? (Remember, $30,000 a month income.)

Would your having or not having tenure make a difference?

Your book is enormously successful my books only moderately successful. You write another book, on spirituality. You give lectures and workshops on this topic. You become quite famous. You decide to give up your teaching job and travel. I continue with my own work, but I assist you in yours, traveling with you.

Would you want this scenario?

Any comments or reactions?

You become quite famous for your spiritual teachings. You are offered jobs in several universities, all of them real plums. Would you want to move to any of the following places, provided the job was good?

Southern California? New York City?

Northern California? New England?

Here's a better sketch of your ring—somewhat enlarged.

Your real X-rated letter (with its intoxicating perfume!) came today. Oh, Kathy, I long for you so much!

THURSDAY, APRIL 6, 1989 9:15 PM

My beloved Kathy,

All day I have been feeling exalted, buoyant, refulgent. And I asked myself why. Would you like to hear the answer, you dear woman? Yes, I know you would. Girl of mine. Sweetheart. My darling. (Let's see, where was I? I get carried away with adoration of you. Isn't that nice? Yes.)

Well. Why I was feeling so extraordinarily good; that was the issue. It was, and is, because of something I am wrapped and enfolded in. Several things. Let me list them.

But first let me tell you how desolate I felt before I met you. I wasn't enfolded in anything at all. I felt naked, exposed to the chill winds of the world. I was, of course, searching for my beloved. Not finding her yet, I was chilled to the bone. Hungry for her love. Yearning for someone I thought I would probably never find.

But now — first of all I am wrapped in your love. Surrounded and supported by your total acceptance of me. Your love keeps me warm. It embraces me, holds me close, warms my soul. So even though you are miles away, I am comforted. Your steadfast affection and loyalty hover over me, protect me, give me affirmation.

But there's another sensation: that of your physical presence. Your leg between mine. My open mouth joined to yours, our tongues touching. My hand as it strokes your superb body. The sensations I feel in my skin as I hold you close, naked flesh to naked flesh. Your cheek, your hair, your smooth back. All these sensations are almost as real to me as your body itself. These sensations accompany me and constitute another layer that enfolds me, along with your love.

A third thing is your help—the help you give me. First, your sensitivity to my moods and qualms and fears. (Oh, never before my treasure, has anyone seen me as clearly as you! Your willingness to offer help— immediately, with no thought. Your ability to help. Your wisdom in knowing what I need! How magnificent!) So I am enwrapped and enfolded in your caring and concern. That is always with me—another layer.

A fourth thing is your sexuality. The fantasies and images that we share, the physical experiences, too. All these create still another layer of raw sexual energy that warms me, as I remember first this, then that (your blue panties! Your pink panties! Your sweet spanking fantasy!). This sexual energy enfolds me also.

Finally, the fifth thing is our spirituality. God enfolds us; the transcendent power protects us and holds us in his (its) loving arms. It loves us, Kathy! I feel it. It cares about us; it is not indifferent. It wants the best for us. It guides us in the direction of goodness and contentment.

So all these five things enfold me, give my life meaning, make me feel not alone. I wanted to share these thoughts with you, my precious darling. And there they are.

When you write (or say) "my love," I quiver.

Your rings are in a little ring box, open on my work table, where I can see them whenever I wish. Your engagement ring is darling. (Can I a man, say things like that? Yes.) As you know I want to ask you as soon as possible after my arrival in Lafayette.

You surround me with the lubricating balm of your femaleness, you say in your letter. Still another layer, a sixth! Yes, I feel your femaleness enfolding me, seeping into my maleness, pervading me, soothing me. Yes, I want more. Your femaleness is so good for me. I pronounce it, I name it Exquisite. I cast my strong male look of approval on it; I name it Worthy, Precious, a Treasure.

Thank you for supporting my dream. You are indeed my special woman. It seems so long ago that you spoke of that, that I named you that. We were falling deeply in love then, very fast. Without knowing where our relationship was going. I must tell you that all along I was hoping it would go where it now is headed. I could not tell you that, of course. I didn't want to scare you away. I wanted to insinuate myself in your affections, then I held myself ready for any greater commitment you chose to offer. I hoped and now look at us! About to be married. Oh, dear one! With your rings bought, and all I have to do is ask you!

Again I must comment on your search for a flared miniskirt and striped white panties. And lavender ones, and yellow ones. How about pale green ones? Oh, Kathy, my life is so full of contentment, so happy, now, I could cry.

Does marriage bring fulfillment? Our relationship has already brought me extra- ordinary amounts of fulfillment. Whoever said there is no fulfillment in marriage was coming from an unfulfilled marriage.

Reactive people will judge us by their own puny reactive measuring sticks.

And now, another idea: Whatever we do whatever we think, whatever we feel—whatever ideas we have (whether about spanking fantasies or getting legally married or trying to be totally honest or working on our stuff or helping each other therapeutically or confessing our fears or asking for things from each other or wearing pink panties or defending our marriage to people who would tear it down)—all these things may seem to be our preferences, merely things we happen to like (like people who happen to both like vanilla ice cream, and of which others may say, Well, Jim and Kathy like vanilla, and we like chocolate, and there's no arguing tastes—de gustibus non disputendes est—and we have a right to like chocolate, and so on)—what I'm saying is that it may appear to others (and to us) that what we do is simply an accidental choice, BUT I CONTEND THAT IT IS NOT. I'M COMING TO BELIEVE THAT WHAT WE DO, FEEL, THINK, SAY, ETC.,—THESE THINGS (INCLUDING THE SPEED WITH WHICH WE MOVE INTO THE DEPTHS WITH EACH OTHER, AND THE SPEED WITH WHICH WE DECIDE TO GET MARRIED)—ALL THESE THINGS (NOW GET THIS, MY BELOVED)—ARE NOT SIMPLE PREFERENCES, BUT THESE ARE THE WAY IT'S SUPPOSE TO BE FOR EVERYONE!

How about them apples!

What we are doing, I say, is the way it's supposed to go, if it goes ideally. If all goes well.

What we do is what couples ought to do, and if

others object or find fault or become officious or give unwanted advice or act cynically or try to throw cold water on what we're doing — that's a sign that they don't know what the score is. That their straw doesn't go all the way down to the bottom of their eggnog. That their pilot light is out. That their smoke doesn't go all the way up their chimney. That they're not playing with a full deck. That there's a screw loose somewhere in their machinery. That they're missing some of their marbles.

What I mean to say, Kathy my dear, is that we (perhaps) ought to be questioning them officiously, if we wish. "You mean you got to know each other that slowly?" "You mean you took a whole year to figure out what you wanted? Before you could decide to get married?" "You mean you didn't think enough of your relationship to get married?" "You mean you married someone so young he (or she) hadn't acquired the skills and wisdom and judgment to know how to make a relationship work?"

"You mean you don't share sexual fantasies? Well really." "You mean you don't say I love you often?" "You don't use little love words to each other?" "You mean the woman doesn't know how to submit? The man doesn't know how to exercise headship?" Well, no wonder you're so cynical! The trouble with you is, you have a less-than-optimal relationship. Would you like to come to our couples workshop to find out how to get your shit together?

We — Kathy and Jim Elliott — know from personal experience how to make relationships work. Each of us has been married and divorced before, each of us has had other relationships. We've paid our dues, and we've learned through experience. And now we know how to have an exciting, deep profound, caring, loving, fulfilling, deeply gratifying relationship. We know how to talk about feelings. We know what to do when fear comes up. Or guilt. Or depression. Or shame. You name it. We know more than David Mace or Scott Peck. Yes. We've got solid theory, along with practical skills—which we can teach. Oh, boy!

Well, my precious darling, time for me to go to bed. I love this contact with you. For a few minutes it's as though you were really here in person, and I'm talking to you. It's 10:15pm and I'll sign off for now, my sweetheart. My bride to be. My soon-to-be wife. What sweet words. Good night, love.

And as I sleep, your engagement ring sparkles in the darkness and glows with a life of its own. All snug in its little box. A symbol of our forthcoming marriage, our love for each other.

(Next day, 10am)

I felt great love flowing from you to me this morning during our phone conversation. I'm beginning to see that when you're feeling battered and hurt and insecure, I need to comfort and protect you. When you're needy, my own stuff gets triggered and I wonder if you love me; but it's just that you're feeling bad. So I'm learning you.

Yes, I can make you feel secure. But I think it gets enmeshing if you say I make you feel angry, guilty, depressed, scared, etc. (which of course, you don't). I love to make you feel secure—secure in my love, my caring, my help, my confidence. I intend to go on doing that.

I loved your responses to my skill handouts. Some comments: I-statements do not, I think fall under the category of Anthetic feedback. Of course, everything a person says and does is feedback. I-statements are reserved for later skill categories.

You warn about overusing identifying and labeling as feedback. Yes, with touchy people, it creates problems. That is, with reactive people. But that's what Anthetics is all about: triggering people's machinery so they'll have stuff to work on. Once people have worked on their inner critic, they can handle all kinds of identifying and labeling with the greatest of ease. And there are some people who can never handle it; those people simply can't learn the skills and I want to know it right from the start. Not everyone is trainable in Anthetic skills. I do use this kind of feedback cautiously at first (as with Cali, where I at first mentioned her judgmentalism, then was happy to restate it as she wished: "I experience you as being judgmental." But once her inner critic has been neutralized, she'll be able to handle the more direct feedback). In my Phase III groups, the people are so advanced that they can handle all kinds of direct and powerful identifying and labeling. It's just routine for us.

About personal story evidencing mutuality. That again does not fall under the category of feedback. It's what I call sharing. Right: it's good, it has its uses. But too often it becomes the only mode of communication. X shares, then Y shares, then Z shares—and there's no dialogue. No one asks any questions. But don't get me wrong: sharing is excellent; just a first step, though for us.

Oh, loved one, thank you for your comments on marketing Anthetic ideas. You don't know how that warms the cockles of my heart.

About your feedback on body sensations as an introductory step in identifying feelings. You're absolutely right: I have overlooked that. Thanks for your feedback.

And, oh, Kathy! You write: "I believe in you and your work. And I'm behind you all the way! As I read page by page, I am so excited…" How I hoped for this response. It seems to me that Anthetics is practical, useful, and broad enough to encompass a lot. Broad enough to encompass the kind of spirituality you and I are exploring.

I find myself constantly needing to keep in mind the distinction between my personal idiosyncrasies and the Anthetic principles. (A digression: I guess not all of our preferences can be elevated to the status of general principles for everyone. My choice of pink and blue panties, for example, need not be universalizable! Someone may prefer black or brown, and that's okay.)

In the realm of spirituality, how I dialogue with God may be idiosyncratic. But the fact that I dialogue is an Anthetic principle. In other words, Anthetic spirituality is that which is characterized by indulgence of God (your concept, which I overwhelmingly adopt), lack of guilt and sin, God as a force that works for good in our lives, that enfolds us, not that punishes us. But I must continually keep in mind this distinction, so I don't start teaching an ideology and expect people to believe everything that I believe. Anthetics must remain a broad framework, with room for lots of differing beliefs—especially provisional ones.

But, Kathy your enthusiasm about my work! I have a fantasy—that you will like it so much, you will, as you mentioned, want to intern as an Anthetic trainer; a leader of Phase I, II, and III groups. I would love to teach you this. And I would love to have you shape Anthetics in your own Kathyish way and improve it. And I would love to discuss it with you endlessly!

If you could see the happiness and beginning attempts at love in my Phase III group! And it's a love that is based on practical ways of working with stuff, not blind veneration. It seems easy for many people to say "I love you" and express warmth—but when it comes to caring, especially about the other's freedom, there is a lack of the concept itself. And there is often enmeshment, which is identified as love. And need to control. Oh, Kathy, I love you so! (Is it okay if I sprinkle my letter with my ejaculations? As I will soon sprinkle you with my—what shall I say, semenistic ejaculations? Semenistic? Is there a Semenistic Psychology? OH.

Well, How to Stop Sabotaging Your Life will be the basic book on inner critic work. As you suggest, the subtitle will refer to inner critic work. Spin-offs from the book can be aimed at ACAs (as we call them here). Or anyone.

On, Kathy, what a wonderful life we will have as husband and wife! We can talk any time we want; we don't have to wait for a telephone appointment. We can eat each other as much as often as we want. Just as you say, feast on each other's cream. Oh, my! Your words are so exciting to me. Especially the ones about panties. My fetish.

My God Kathy, what a rich life we already have!

Oh, you darling girl! You sweetheart of mine, you precious creature! You sexpot! You drive me wild with longing for you—not only for your body but for your mind, your ideas, your love, all of you.

I love you so much, Kathy

That sometimes I want to cry.

FRIDAY, APRIL 7, 1989 12:30 PM

My beloved man — my husband to be —

I love you so much. Oh, if I could just show you in the flesh right now. You would see it in my eyes; you would feel it in my hands; you would taste it in my mouth. What a thrill to me to hear you say you were looking at my ring this morning as we talked; that you took things in hand, shopped, chose, and purchased it is so unspeakably loving to me. You are my chosen one. I want you to know how core touching it is to me to have you search for the ring on your own. I love that. It feels like a burden lifted off of me and like you are so committed; this is your choice; your joy to honor and thrill me. Oh, Jim, you make me so happy. We are going to have such a happy, satisfying, incredible marriage and life together. I know it.

So I am headed to my hair appointment, and I will honor your request for straighter hair, while honoring my need to not have limp, hard to work with hair. I want you to love my hair, because I want you in it all the time! I'm also going shopping for nail polish this afternoon. I want to see and have an image of my polished nail hands holding your cock!

In another vein (and it does seem that our relationship can hold a wide range of topics), I want to sit and talk with you about the workshop. I'd like your input about my part. I guess I'll just have to run things by you on the phone. I'm a little nervous about waiting till May 5 to have you suggest some major change, and I'd feel thrown off center. Let's talk about it, ok?

One of my students had a book she was thrilled to show me this week — a new release, and I'd like you to look at it in a local bookstore and tell me what you think: Embracing

Ourselves: The Voice Dialogue Manual, Hal Stone, Ph.D. & Sidra Winkelman, Ph.D. My initial cursory look over her book brought to mind a psychosynthesis approach, but that's out of just minimal knowledge of the book and of psychosynthesis. Anyway, the book was very appealing, might contribute, and suggested to me a validation of a market for your book with a title containing "inner critic" and "silenced voices." Maybe we can work on that together! (Am I intruding on your territory? You can have your boundaries. Let me know when you need space.)

I am enclosing a check for $160 for my ticket. Let me know if you need more for whatever reason.

I love you so much. I adore you. I want you. I want your cock permanently mine — to touch, to stroke, to hold, to lick, to suck, to honor, to love. And your magical semen to drink, to eat, to swallow all down with joy.

Jim, you are my beloved, all my desire. I am deeper than ever in love with you, want to be one with you, to be married to you.

You are my all —

your Kathy

THURSDAY, APRIL 6, 1989 1:55 PM

My one and only love —

Oh my, I have just been so strengthened by my lunch with Jacob. I see from this how important positive input is for strengthening my purpose and for validating the liberated inner voice. Jacob is an assistant professor in Criminal Justice. He moved here from Chicago, was working on his Ph.D. at the time and we became friends as new faculty together. He is getting married May 20th to a local girl, Maria. He is elated at yours and my love. As we talked, I asked him to comment on Evan's words on marriage. He said, "The first thing I'd ask him is, 'Are you happily married — or how is your marriage?' Then from there, I'd put all his comments in context." And I said, "Why do you want to get married, Jacob?" (He and Maria live together.) And he said a profound thing that validates yours and my understanding. He said, "It's mental, a psychologically important thing. Like when you get your Ph.D., you wake up the next day and things have changed. Just by the change in name and agreement. It's powerful." I said, "It's the power of the Word." And he said, "Yes, like the power of labeling." So he said, "Maria and I just living together does not produce the oneness. She and I are not one now. And I want to be." Isn't that neat?

So my love, I guess I needed an external word of support. And Jacob is as rational as they come, so he was a wonderful source for God to speak through. We discussed rings and weddings and honeymoons and you. Well, it was so good for me to celebrate.

Oh, I love you so. I gush love out to you like an oil well gusher. But then, what would I expect from contact with a driller?

So you asked me to write to you what you give me apart from comfort and advice. Ah such a sweet question. (This sounds like you.) Full of opening for me:

You open me. You open me emotionally. I have never loved so effusively. I have never loved shamelessly. I have never loved so extravagantly. I have never laid myself out totally bare in every way. You do that to me. Open me with your gentleness, your seductive invitation, your strength, your maturity. For the first time, I feel so safe that I can be totally open emotionally.

You open me physically. I have never been sexual with so much deliberateness and so little shame. What a glory it is and pure pleasure.

You open me intellectually — make me feel so safe and respected that I can risk thinking, risk speaking ideas, and you affirm me so much that I am reinforced — a Skinnerian delight!

You open me spiritually — yes, I am a goddess with you. You call that forth in me and receive the sacred acts and words I long to express.

You are the container I have found worthy and capable of holding my openness and the contents that spill out of me from all quarters.

You in turn, give me your openness. You lay yourself bare to me — sparing no word, thought, act of love and transparency and honesty. Oh, thank you, I am exalted out of that. I am given equality and even power with you. Oh, my love, you are a special man.

You give me your unsquelched love and affection — giving me all the spoken declarations of love, admiration, commitment

I could desire. I feel so loved and secure. I walk in the glow of that love and security. And you hold nothing back from me in the way of affection. My wish is your command. "Jim, I want my hair stroked." And you do it. I need that so much. You give me mighty unconditional love. I am secure as a little Indian baby in a papoose!

You give me your strength. Your voice, your excellent reasoning capacities, your spiritual discernment and courage.

You give me shared responsibilities. You take up your share (& more) of tasks — getting reservations, tickets, rings, etc. Thank you. I am less in danger of "doing it all."

You believe in me. You believe in me professionally. I can soar with your backing. You rejoice with me as I soar. You think I am a genius!

You give me freedom. Freedom to think, to risk, to speak what to me is the unspeakable. You love my wildest fantasies and join me in them. I am free to dare all thoughts, all feelings, all actions.

You give me attention. I am hungry for attention. And you spare nothing. I felt so attended to in New York and with your letters and when we talk. You are totally with me. I don't feel like you emotionally and intellectually abandon me. You are patient; I don't feel that you have been tapping your foot or drumming your fingers waiting for me to finish.

You give me headship. You are not passive. You take up your authority and speak it and exercise it.

You give me your body fully. Nothing is barred. I am free; have your welcome to know you completely, even the places that you might feel shame about. And you are generous with your energy. You don't say, "Go to sleep, Kathy." You say,

"I am here for you." So I can go with my love and sexual energies with abandon. You give me your sacred fluid to fill me up vaginally and orally. You are so generous!

I have more and will tell you more in the future. It all adds up to you being the most powerfully desirable man in my life. And I want you. I want to marry you; to receive all this on a daily basis; to be one with you. You are the perfect man for me, my love. I long for you to come to me in all ways. I rejoice that you are coming to me. My life is expanded and filled full by your presence, yourself. I will never leave this prize man who has been given to me as a gift. OH, I love you so, Jim.

"Come, north wind, awaken; come, south wind, blow upon my garden and waft its lovely perfume to my beloved. Let him come into his garden and eat its choicest fruits." (Song of Solomon 4:16 – The Living Bible)

"Many waters cannot quench the flame of love, neither can the floods drown it." 8:7

I love you with my whole self, my love. Many waters cannot quench our love.

Your Kathy

SUNDAY, APRIL 9, 1989 6:05 PM

My beloved Jim

If you were here I would shower you with kisses. When you are here, I promise you that I shall do so. Until then, these must suffice —

(Lipstick kisses all over the page)

I love you so. I adore you. You are my man — my beloved head — I am all yours —

Your Kathy

MONDAY, APRIL 10, 1989 10:15 AM

My beloved wife-to-be,

I called Kevin and told him more about us, and about our visit to him in September, and about our forthcoming wedding, and he was very happy for me. I asked him if he thought this thing strange: his father getting married and moving to Louisiana (he was surprised at that), and he said no—that his life with his parents was pretty strange anyway (divorce, etc.) so this was consistent, but if he had grown up "normally," this would be strange. He is looking forward to meeting you.

Your letter came today containing the list of things I give you, and it was so nourishing to me. (One of the things you give me is your responsiveness to my requests, such as this one!) We do open each other—physically, sexually, emotionally, intellectually, spiritually. This is a great gift we give each other that is so rare it probably has never happened before, at least as much. We do affirm each other and accept each other without reservation. What ecstasy this produces!

In my other relationships I asked for the things I ask you, and I got a cold shoulder. Those women were blocked, and so they saw the free flow of my sexual energy as threatening. (And I thought there was something wrong with me; but suspected that I was okay; but couldn't figure out what was going wrong.)

They said things like:

"I feel left out" (because they couldn't empathize)

"I don't want to do that" and "If you loved me, you wouldn't ask me to"

"I don't feel turned on sexually to you, but I'll accommodate you"

"I can't live up to your standards" meaning "I can't be there for you, help you, listen to you, attend to what you're saying."

Very often my conversations consisted of the following:

First, I would say something.

Then there was a silence.

I would ask, "Any response?"

Then the other person would talk.

And so on, for each interchange.

Sometimes the other person would get angry at my question. "I was thinking," she would say. "Just give me some time. Don't ask so quickly."

So the next time, I would wait for a response, without asking. I would wait quite a while—as long as five minutes. And then I would ask, "Any response?" And the other person would say, "Any response to what?" She had forgotten what I said! And was off on some tangent of her own.

Well, I sound judgmental. And I feel judgmental. But I also know that other people are just doing the best they can. Some of them value things that I don't value much: a 100% clean house, no water on the bathroom floor, towels all aligned neatly on the rack, no messy papers lying about, and so on. I like some of those things, but they're not high on my list. What I value more are the things you give: acceptance, openness, expressive love, sexual communion, spiritual encouragement, close attention and great sensitivity, willingness to help with an issue or problem. What I ask of you is only partly for me; it also opens you to new parts of yourself. And you give so generously!

And on top of all this: you are so breathtakingly lovely! My heart leaps when I think of your beauty.

And even more: you are in my field! I can talk to you without explaining a lot of things. We inseminate each other's intellect! You help my work.

It's so rare to find someone so perfect (you), and I must tell you that I still can't quite take it all in. We are still just getting to know each other!

I think I will be celebrating and marveling at our relationship for quite a while until I get familiar with the idea of its magnificence and splendor. As I mentioned, I thought at first you were just being nice to me when you said you loved me. I got over that idea. Then I thought you'd find the struggles too much and would give me up. And I got over that one, too. Now I'm quite sure you really want to marry me. (But can you really accept all parts of me? That's not a big thing, but it's my latest thing. I'll just keep risking and see.)

It feels like the major rocks, whirlpools, and sandbars are past. Now our vessel is just sailing along, free and easy. We are both doing the steering. Yes, we are together. Now, barring some unforeseen problem, it's smooth sailing.

I can almost do a full day's work again. (Masturbation helps somewhat, especially with your dear fantasies. Kathy, what a wonderful woman you are! My sweet girl! My darling treasure!)

And I liked your bible verses. I will indeed eat your

succulent fruits, bite into them as the juice drips down my cheeks. Yes—the flame of our love is strong now (remember my symbol at Curlew?).

Well, a small negative thing. I watched Lolita last night: It's about this older guy, see, who falls in love with a girl young enough to be his daughter, and she leaves him of course for a man her own age, and he's a pitiful character. My inner critic again: "Jim, you cradle-robber; why don't you find someone age-appropriate?" But I think we have to take what we can get; I wish I was younger, for several reasons, but here we are, at the ages we are, and I certainly don't want to miss out on us. And also because of my maturity, I do bring some really good skills and ideas to our communion, which I wouldn't have had were I younger. I might have messed up our relationship completely (I think it would have been a lot rougher for both of us, at least). So, as I have mentioned before, my age is an advantage.

My mare who nips me from time to time! Whose plump round haunches I watch attentively and longingly. Who excites me with her spirited playfulness. Yes, I will teach her to submit to her new rider. She will be happy for it, as her wild energies are tamed and channeled and focused. And I will ride her into some strange and interesting places neither of us has ever explored before. We will be so happy!

I am continually glowing with love for you! I can't believe my good fortune in having found you! (And I don't think anyone appreciates your true value as much as I; or is willing to honor it as much, or worship it as much, or match it as much.)

And so,

I inseminate your very core with my words of love.

I reach right into your deep and mysterious places;

I touch with loving hands the quivering center of your spirit,

Carefully and gently and tenderly and reverently and passionately!

I squirt myself into your being with great spasms of passionate tenderness.

Your sweet petals open to receive my gift.

And I surrender to your exquisite femaleness,

I am the sperm that makes your divineness so fertile.

TUESDAY, APRIL 11, 1989 2:45 PM

My love, my adored one, my Jim

Oh I love you so. I need you here. I can't wait till you come in May and then till I go to you and then till you come back and then till I go to meet you in August and then till we're at home together. Ah, sigh.

I have lots of content to share, so let me get down to business. Do you think we can talk business while you nibble on the nape of my neck? Oh, well… I'm still marketing our workshop; just talked to a former student of mine who is so interested; wants to do it, is just what she's working on. She is so encouraged about our relationship. (She is a young widow who hears lots of negative stuff from her married friends. She longs to remarry but is discouraged by all that.) The world does need our witness, my love.

I love my engagement ring. It looks creative and darling (as per your drawing). Thank you again for heroically shopping, choosing, and buying. You honor me so.

Now, you asked me to write what I told Cali re: my commitment to you. I said, "I have a resentment against you I have never voiced, and I want to do that now. I have seen you speak harshly and judgmentally to your dad, to Mr. Saxon, and to Hale. And I will not have you speak like that to my husband." She said, "Even if he is wrong, you'd still side with him and back him?"

I said, "Even if he was wrong in my eyes, I would discuss it with him. But if he still took the same stand, I would stand with him." And so, I say to you, Jim, my soon-to-be husband, I will have no one speak harshly of you – to you. I stand as your she-tiger to defend my mate. And I stand with you, shoulder to shoulder, come what may.

Then Mama said to me, "He is wise and right to ask this commitment of you. She would tear him apart without your commitment and siding with him. He couldn't stand it. He's saying to you, "I'm moving to be with you, giving up everything here, are you going to be with me; for me? If not, let me know now." And inside I felt a god place say, "Kathy, I have given you this relationship, this love of your life, don't piss it away." I was called to choose, to grow up, to claim my womanhood. And as woman, to choose my man consciously, to choose to stand by you, my man…And now, that has been accomplished without a shadow of a doubt. That was a hard weekend, Jim. I think the hardest, my love. And yet I see how vital it was to have me choose you, claim you as my primary relationship, and pledge my allegiance to you. It was incredibly important and powerful. I love you. I am yours. That commitment has been accomplished. Oh my. It is so good for me. Something inside me needed to be committed. Had never been fully committed before. You are a first – a virginal part you're breaking in!

Thank you for helping me on the phone this a.m. with your clothes and my stuff. I will love to shop with you and to "improve" you, as you say. Thank you for being honored by my interest in you. I am consumed with interest in you.

And thank you, my spiritual head, for your 9:15 a.m. letter with strong words of a blessing – a blessing of a stand and a defense and an exalting of our path. Yes, you strengthen me, you tiger of a man. I love you, my tiger, my stallion. I think you make me swish my tail, toss my mane in pride, and present my haunches for mounting. Anytime my stallion wants it! I am so secure in your love. I receive your tears of love. I bask in your worship, your adoration. I glow in your love. You know, I started glowing when I had an experience of God's love for me. (I'll show you pictures of me, pre-God, and you'll see the lack of light in my face), but the wattage of my glowing has been turned up with your love added. You flesh out God's love in such good, strong, human, male terms, that my flesh is alight. Bring it on, baby. I'll take that enfleshment for the rest of our lives! God, I love you,

your Kathy

P.S. Enclosed is Mama's letter!

APRIL 9, 1989

Dear Jim,

Thank you for your beautiful letter to me. Your words of love and appreciation for Kathy warmed my heart. I have prayed that Kathy would be blessed with a wonderful husband and I truly feel that you are the answer to my prayers.

And so, tonight let me say to you that we are eagerly awaiting your visit and warmly welcome you in our home. I feel that you will love it here. It will be a real pleasure having you with us. My daughter really adores you! I haven't ever seen Kathy as happy as she is today.

So hurry home!

And may God's richest blessings be yours.

Kathy's Mama,

Lorraine

TUESDAY, APRIL 11, 1989 12:50 PM

My darling temptress,

It felt so good this morning on the telephone to respond to your request by pouring out my love to you; I am happy to do this any time you ask, without reservation. I still marvel over your perfection, your charm, your sweet ways, your loving touch, your initiative, your intelligence, your strength, your dear body, your sexy melon-heavy breasts, the tender parts of your psyche that I approach with such care and acceptance. Oh, Kathy, wife-to-be! Sweet companion! Darling counterpart! My twin!

Now, we are in that stage of our relationship where we are adjusting to each other's needs, where we are making requests of each other. It's absolutely vital that we do this, because we want pleasing things in our relationship, and we want to please each other. We are talking now about changes in physical appearance, and this is one of the most problematic of all (second only to who does what chores, perhaps, or how we handle money). I think we're doing well; neither of us has much stuff around clothes (e.g., "Nobody's going to tell me what to wear!"), but we do have wishes.

You have been happy to buy the kind of panties I like, to wear fingernail polish, and to have your hair done the way I like it (as long as it's easy to work with). You have also ordered a garter belt and stockings at my request (You know how to arouse me!) and you have perfumed a letter to me (but only one?).

Now you ask me about my belt, and I will be happy

to change it; and to buy the kind of pants and shoes you like (but the shoes can't be oxfords).

About pants vs. dresses for you, this may be a bit trickier. I know that pants are more comfortable for you. But let me tell you my associations to each.

Dresses and skirts: open, sexually attractive, tempting, easy to get into, arousing, an invitation, flirty, feminine, "I want you to admire my legs."

Pants: Closed, practical, useful, businesslike, no-nonsense, hard to get into, "Let's postpone sexual thoughts for a while."

Well enough about that. I expect I'll get a mixture of pants and skirts, and that's okay.

One thing that strikes me is how free I have made myself even before I met you, almost as though I knew you'd come along. For example: I decided not to sign a lease on my office so I'd be free to move. I postponed buying a car. I decided not to go to Wright Institute (a graduate school), although I'd been accepted, because I would be tied down to daily classes. I focused on group work, not private practice. I wanted to write a book, not get a job. When Danica broke up with me, I decided to stay "broke up" and not try to get back together with her.

About writing a book together: No, you are not intruding on my territory; you never would; I want us to work together in as many ways as possible. But I have a schedule of books laid out for me right now: first, the sabotage book; then one on Anthetics; then one on Anthetic Relationships; a treatment manual; a trainer's manual; a trainee's manual. But I'll be glad to help you with any inner critic book you want to write. Or any book. I think you have a lot to teach, and it shouldn't be lost.

You ask, "Let me know where you need space," and I'm touched by your caring (as I was at Curlew), but you are very, very far from my boundaries; I'll tell you when you get anywhere near; so for now, keep pushing out into your power, into whatever new areas you want; I'll cheer you on, my darling woman.

I love you so much; you are so precious, so tender, so girlish, so perfect for me. My dear one! My treasure! You splendid, juicy, sweet woman, you!

I love you with a great hunger,

WEDNESDAY, APRIL 12, 1989 3:05 PM

My love —

Oh, God, I am out of control in love with you! I long to be with you, to live with you and pour love on you in the flesh.

Well, I'm noticing something: almost all the women I've shared our love with are excited, celebrating of it. The men, however, have been mostly negative! What do you think of that? My preliminary thoughts are: they're scared to death of it and have covered their fear with cynicism. One male colleague today rained negatives on it. But when I said, "Is it so bad to be married?" he said, "Not since my little girl was born. She is a delight." His face lit up and he was telling the truth. So they can tap love, deep powerful, starry eyed love for their children, but not for their wives! What do you think, my wise man? The men who have celebrated with me are those who I know are in good relationships. So there. But how sad that the place we look for love (male-female adult marriage) has become a place of cynicism.

Now, to you spiritual questions/statements of Wed. Apr. 5. 1) God is a manifestation of the transcendent power — one that we humans are able to handle. Yes, this seems right. That our concept of God and his revelation to us must be only an inkling of the full power. My God, people can't even handle the power of our relationship (yours and mine). What would they do with the transcendent fully exposed? So, thank you for voicing this concept. I had intimated it but not put words on it, you animus enfleshed of mine! Moses asked God (in an incredibly powerful love scene between God and Moses in the bible), "Let me see you." And god said, "You couldn't bear it, but if you'll hide yourself in the rock there, I'll cover you with my hand and let you see what you can bear of me." (Or something like that). And Moses was transformed. He came down off the mountain so glowing, he had to cover his face; the people couldn't bear to look at the incredible glow. Oh, when will we grow up spiritually? Sometimes, and now more than ever, I touch the old, wise mature spiritual part of me, and I long to have my brothers and sisters join me. But they aren't there yet. Now, thank God, He has given me YOU, MY SPIRITUAL COMPANION. And I have a sense that I will be needing you in that capacity in the years to come. Oh, how good it is to have you come to me with your spiritual maturity, your ripeness.

2) We can have access to God by calling on him or dialoguing with him. Yes, Other ways: Turning within to that quiet place free of distractions. Letting him break in upon us as he is always ready to do, with his love and support (just like we have to get to a place of letting each other's statements – in letters or verbally – break in upon us). There are others – later.

3) When he wants, he comes to us. If we're open, Yes. I've experienced that he is always there. Always ready. Just like you tell me you are always there for me. Well that's a God Loving or loving like God statement. And he will not force himself on us. Just like you weren't going to force yourself on me. "I want as much of you as I can get." I think that was a God-like statement. He wants as much of us as he can get, but he waits and accepts what we're willing to give. Ah.

4) Yes, he comes with love and enfolding and caring. Absolutely. That is what I have known of him. Great, transcendent love.

My Jim, let us continue to relate core-to-core. It is life-

giving to our relationship. I want you so.

Now, I talked to Caroline re: birth control. And she says she waits until she's ready for intercourse to put in her diaphragm, and that Jerry likes to do it for her. And that the spermicidal jelly is safe for oral sex. But that she just waits. We had the most fun discussion of sex over lunch. Including her telling me of her recent ventures into multi-orgasms (100 or so!). And that it just happened and she never thought it possible. She just made space for it as a possibility and let go of it. So, in case you just got activated, I declare you free from having to make me multi-orgasmic, and I declare myself free from having to have multi-orgasms. And if they show up, great! I love sex with you — our lovemaking; truly love sharing, our openness, our fantasies, our joy in pleasing each other. Oh, I told Caroline about wanting to have your baby, and she said with a laugh, "Oh yes, Kathy, and the desire will get worse. You'll want it even more." "Just be with it." Isn't that neat that she could identify? I thought she'd be scandalized.

I'll sign off now. You sexy man, you. I adore you. You have me wanting you like I've never wanted anyone before. So maybe we can sleep together, and you can show me the things I've heard other girls talk about. But you won't come in me, will you? And you'll just let us look and not touch, right?

Until we speak again,

I adore you, Jim.

Your Kathy

THURSDAY, APRIL 13, 1989 10:30 AM

My beloved sweet woman,

Everyday I think of you and sense my love for you, and it feels stronger and deeper than I have ever loved before, and I think: This is as deep as I can ever love; there is no room for any more of it; I've reached the absolute limit. And then you say or do something (like, "I want you to sexually inseminate me so I'll have your baby"), and I get a rush of even more love for you, and I think, "What could I have been thinking of yesterday to think I was loving as deeply as I could?" Today, I say, I am really loving to the maximum, and then I think, "Well, what about tomorrow? I may love you even more then." So I realize that I can't put any limits on how much I love you; there will always be room for more, impossible as that may seem at any one time.

Today your contentless letter came with its kisses, which I experienced as a surge of love from you (though I do like content). The kisses were quite erotic and arousing, and there was the faint smell of perfume from your lipstick, and I want more kisses on my letters from you. (And some perfume?) Oh, I love you so!

I'm enclosing a reprint you might find interesting.

Now about my inner critic work. When I began leading groups in 1964, I used very few techniques. I kept quiet for the most part and asked people what they were feeling from time to time. Then I heard about Stew Shapiro in Sherman Oaks, Calif., who was doing subself work, 1966, I think. I interviewed him for an article and learned very quickly how to do empty chair work, just by his telling me what he did. I had also previously attended a psychodrama workshop (how to do it). Stew spoke about the inner critic, and its importance, but I didn't grasp it yet (nor did he, really). That is, I didn't grasp how central it was.

So I began doing empty chair work in my groups, and the first inner figure that was elicited was usually a critical one. Stew's technique consisted simply of eliciting the critic (if it came) and commenting on how powerful it was. And that's all I did at first. For many years.

Somewhere along the way, as I ran groups, I hit on the notion of getting released from the power of the inner critic, and I experimented with releasing statements, beginning with Fritz Perls "I'm not here to live up to your expectations." These were statements to real people, not inner critic. Sometime in the late 1970s I helped people who were being attacked, by suggesting releasing statements. I remember one instance, where a man named Reiner was attacking Archie for being a wimp, a jellyfish. I told Archie to say to Reiner: "You think this is bad, you ain't seen nothing yet." Before, Archie was feeling depressed at Reiner's comments; now, he brightened up and got released.

Somewhere around 1984 or 1985 I began an intense interest in cognitive therapy. From it I took the idea of challenging. Cognitive therapists asked patients to challenge beliefs (irrational in the case of Ellis, dysfunctional as termed by Beck), and I saw that it was the inner critic that needed to be challenged. So I gradually focused on inner Critic work more and more, creating an elaborate set of principles and challenges. My group members (and individual clients) took to these ideas quickly and began using them often. So that's how it happened.

About my differences with Ellis. Al was a psychoanalyst for a while and discovered it wasn't working, so he began challenging his clients' irrational beliefs very actively and found that this did work. Here are the differences:

1. Because of Ellis's argument with psychoanalysis he now maintains that going back in the past is worthless; the beliefs, he says, are in the present, so all you need to do is dispute them. And you should forget about how they originated. I, on the other hand, find that exploration of the past is important, but only to unearth the dysfunctional beliefs. Because I use the empty chair, which Ellis does not, I find that the people who implanted the beliefs (mom and Dad, usually) need to be challenged, too. And that means stuff from the past. (Strangely enough, Ellis says not to worry about the past; then he uses the concept.)

2. Ellis thinks beliefs have content that can be challenged by bringing up evidence against them. His approach is logical. To me, many inner critic statements are immune from logic. When the inner critic says, "You are a jerk," Ellis would say, "Where is it written that I am a jerk?" This is vague. Suppose a client would say, "Right here in this letter I got; that's where it's written." I say the inner critic statement must be challenged not through evidence pro or con but by realizing that every judgmental statement made by the inner critic is

not a factual statement at all, but simply an emotional expression of the inner critic. It needs to be challenged not by adducing proof but by saying, essentially, "That's just my inner critic, being judgmental again; I refuse to believe it." No need for asking, "Where is it written?" And useless to add up evidence pro and con re: jerkiness.

3. Even more important is my concept that in challenging the inner critic, you must take back your rights; e.g., "I have the right to be what you call a jerk." Ellis hasn't addressed this at all, but if he did, he would probably say, "That's not disputing an irrational belief at all; in fact, it's agreeing with it."

So these are the three main ways that my work differs from Ellis's. (I like answering your questions about my work.)

I seem to be running out of ways to say I love you, except just: "I love you. Very much. My love grows every day; I cherish you; I want to warm myself by lying the length of your soft female body." And I want to wake in the night to feel you beside me. And wake in the morning to have you there, where I can have you whenever I want.

And sometimes I think: This is so incredible, it can't be happening. That woman in Louisiana must be some stranger I've seen in a dream; her love for me is merely my own wish-fulfillment. It's all a figment of my imagination. When I get off the plane, there will be no one to meet me; the pink and white striped dress is a fantasy of mine, never to be fulfilled (never to be lifted). But I know you are real, you are a real girl, my girl, my own. The bride I will marry. My precious darling. You are not a dream, you are a real woman. But it's still like Christmas morning.

I love you so,

FRIDAY, APRIL 14, 1989 4:25 PM

My dearest soulmate,

My client has come and gone, and I guess you and Cali are out to dinner, because you didn't call at 4:05, and I am going to call you later this evening, because we have some loose ends lift, and I want to tell you how proud I am of us and how overjoyed I am at the way we handle glitches. I have always been able to process them, but the other person I had been relating to was unable to, and so the kind of work you do on these problems is so important to me (your willingness, your understanding of how to do it, your skills, my skills), and your special abilities are so important to me that if that were all you had, I would ask you to marry me. I think that ability you have is of paramount importance in a relationship, and as I said, the closer one gets (the more merged) the more skills people need, because stuff will get triggered if we get close. And we are trying for a lot of closeness, because of the remarkable people we are. And we are equal to the task: we know how to deal with the tangles. That is more precious to me than gold and rubies (I don't know where I'm getting the allusion).

Anyway, I'm quite pleased with us.

You thought you had to anticipate perfectly what would trigger my stuff, to predict in advance, and not do it—because then I would go away. This was not a simple withdrawal, this (to Little Kathy) was death, if Daddy went away. Maybe because he was the primary care-giver for a while? So to survive, you had to do the impossible: know in advance what would make him go away. So now you lay a should on yourself: to know in advance what will trigger Jim's stuff, because he too might go away. But, of course, I am not Daddy. I will never go away. Never. You are too precious to me for me ever to go away, to abandon you. How could I abandon my right arm? You are part of me. But you see me through that old Daddy filter. So we soothed Little Kathy, and I think we did a fine job (and if we ever have a B---, we will be very good at soothing, I can tell). You did excellent work in disengaging from Little Kathy and knowing what she needed. She thinks she needs validation from other people, but you are the only one who can really take care of her; I can help, but what I do will be secondary.

So, good for us. I feel confident we can weather any glitch or crisis that might come along. It will just take a little time, but each of us is willing to take that time.

We are playing for big stakes. And we hold top cards.

Mama's letter warmed my heart. "So hurry home," she wrote. That woman knows what's best for me.

Your letters warmed my heart, too. For example, when you wrote:

—"God…has given me you, my SPIRITUAL COMPANION." Oh, I melt.

—"Let us continue to relate core to core. It is life giving to our relationship." Oh, yes, Kathy, my precious one. Please call me to that if I falter.

—"You can show me the things I've heard other girls talk about. But you won't come in me, will you? And you'll just let us look and not touch, right?" Oh, Kathy, how powerful these words are: like a drama, building suspense—am I going to get what I want? Maybe not—and then my dreams will come true! My girl will give in to me, out of her own need! How precious you are! How can I tell you what these dramatic sexual episodes mean to me!

And then you wrote about Caroline, about discussing sex techniques with her. It's so erotic to think of you talking about sex with a woman—that her man likes to put in her diaphragm for her. OH, my! Oh, you sexual creature, you!

About multiple orgasms: yes, let's try, without having to perform.

And your words to Cali! How secure I now feel! And you say: "I stand with you, shoulder to shoulder, come what may." Powerful words. What I need, exactly right.

And Mama's wisdom: "He is right to ask this commitment of you. He is asking, "Are you going to be with me, for me?" And you're being called to stand by your man. That is so precious to me; it is something I will never forget in that it has created a bond between us that means (and this is meant again to reassure you) that I will be loyal to you, too; I will never ever abandon you. No one has given this before, and it is what I always wanted. Yearned for. You recognize my worth, and you are willing to back up that recognition with action. Your loyalty to me means more than any wedding ceremony.

Kathy, I love you.

I am yours forever.

About your responses to my scenarios: my heart is again warmed; I want you with me all the time; I never want to leave you. I am more and more committed to living in Lafayette; my second choice would be southern California, but there are earthquakes there (except in La Jolla). I'm so glad we agree on geographical location. Anyway, I would like to visit S. Calif. Often. (What about going there on our honeymoon, dear one? Just a thought.)

And in your letter, you call me your stallion (sigh).

Oh, Kathy, this week is almost over, and before I know it, I'll be well into the next one, and then there's only a full week before the week when I'll fly to you, my darling. Oh, pink-and-what striped dress! Oh, pink panties! That night will you bathe the dust of travel off my weary body? Can I touch you all over? Under your beautiful new dress? May I reassure you of my love?

What love I feel for you!

Jim (entwined hearts)

SATURDAY, APRIL 15, 1989 1:50 PM

My beloved Jim,

Oh my, I just got your wonderful card. Oh, Jim, you are so thoughtful. And what comes from you to me is so life-giving to me. You are an incredible man. I'm so glad you're mine. (Is it okay for me to say, "You're mine"?) You haven't proposed marriage yet, so perhaps I'm presuming. No, that's absurd. You are mine. Yes, and I claim you and honor you.

I am learning the applied power of our love. I mean that you and I are practicing loving each other in such a miraculous way. I'm thinking of our work on glitches. That was so good. Nothing has to be kept undercover or stuffed. We can work with each issue. Oh, how did such a marvelous man come to me? I must have been ready for you. And for us! Yes, I was ready.

I went searching for invitations to our engagement party. It was very exciting. I think mainly to be declaring our love to others in writing. And this will be our really 1st time to include others in our relationship. I ran into some friends at the store, and they were very excited and celebrated with me about our love. When I told them, "I'm in love," all heads in the store turned to me! People love to hear about love and to see it. I guess they're just scared to live it!

I'm waiting for your phone call at 2:30. Oh, I love these phone conversations with you. They are so good. Your voice is so warm. And you are so immediate in your responses to me.

As to your April 11th letter…I love your marveling at me and who I am. And your willingness to pour love out to me. And your willingness to get new clothes (no oxfords, agreed). Now about pants and dresses. Yes there will be times where my psyche will want or need to wear pants, and I'm glad you're okay with that. And for the most part, I like to wear dresses.

I love that you freed yourself for me even before you knew me. It seems like divine order.

And I love that you call me "so precious, so tender… your dear one, your treasure, and your splendid, juicy, sweet woman." Oh, don't stop, Jim. And keep loving me with a great hunger.

Do you know what is so sweet to me, my love? On page 3 of your April 6 letter you said, "Well, my precious darling, time for me to go to bed…" I felt like I was with you as I read it. Oh, you are a lover; the most loving man I've ever known. Your love and expressiveness to me are so free flowing. It is a delight. If you want to know how to keep me close to you; loving you, here it is: Just keep speaking these words of love, these love names, these affirmations of your love for me.

There are writings I have done in the past that I want to share with you — personal journal writings. But these are very special to me — not a diary, more an expression of the soul. I don't know how to describe them. But I do know they are very precious to me; I don't share them with people. (I haven't even shared them with Cali.) But I want to share them with you. Your love is so enfolding, and you reach into my soul core with such gentleness that I know I am safe. And I want to expose even more of myself and my journey to you. Oh, Jim I want to sit together for hundreds of hours — talking — where we've come from; what was significant along the way — and where we are now. Then, where we want to go. And you'll read my journal, and we'll commune.

But let me not miss the preciousness of this stage of our

journey — writing these heart exposing/soul touching letters. And speaking these core touching phone conversations. And I am so touched that on p. 4 (Apr 6 still) you say Anthetic spirituality is characterized by the indulgence of God. A Kathy concept you've incorporated. And I do believe we are living out Anthetic love — caring about each other's freedom, working on our stuff. And yes, please sprinkle your letters with your ejaculations and sprinkle me with your magical fluid too.

Oh, Jim, I adore you. I have absolute faith in you. You are just the man for me. And my longings are surfacing! What a sweet, painful joy. To think that you will fulfill those longings for me. That you attend to them, care about my slightest qualm of longing. Oh, I treasure you, Jim. I will never let you go — never leave you.

Your Kathy

SATURDAY, APRIL 15, 1989 11:30 AM

My sweet girl,

And you are sweet. How nice to have someone who is not contentious, judgmental, jangly! And who is sexy. And beautiful. And accepting. And who is committed to resolving conflicts not by escalating them and acting out but by working on stuff, as I am. You are so perfect for me, it takes my breath away when I think of all the ways you are.

(Sunday, 12 noon). I want to tell you in writing about the bonds I feel we are forming, the bonds anyway that I sense. Strongest of all was your pledge of loyalty to me. Something powerful shifted in both of us when that happened. But another one was the come I had when we talked on the phone yesterday. It doesn't seem that this would create a bond, yet it did. I felt very cared for and accepted and very much in synch with you; very much with you. And you said you did too. I guess I need to feel safe with the other person in order to let myself go sexually. Safe and loved and enfolded.

Another bond happened when you hugged me in my room at Asilomar. And when we hugged at the airport, and you pressed your full body against me. And of course when you said you wanted to spend the night with me. And when we actually did. Each time there was another bond. The nights at Pawling were strong bonds. But the strongest there, almost as strong as your loyalty, was when you came to my room, sensing that I was feeling bad. Oh, how important that was!

And there are many little ones, each important. When

you brushed against my arm at Pawling. And each time we work on a glitch. And when you said you would wear only dresses during my visit.

I'm looking forward to future bondings, because I think there'll be more.

I want to say again how much I treasure your sensitivity to me: your sensing when I get overloaded with the powerful things you say; when I've got some stuff to work on, too.

I like it when you tell me of the things that are good and necessary for our relationship—like our daily calls. Sometimes I think they're a luxury, not necessary that often. But you are right: we need them to build our communion.

I also like it when I give you some feedback (e.g., "I like such-and-such that you said") and you say, "That's important for me to hear." Please do as much of this as you possibly can. (I like our rich and complex feedback to each other. It warms some place inside me that has been cold and deprived for many many years.)

I like the fact that you are courageous about saying things, that you never hold back or withdraw. "Like" isn't strong enough, I cherish it; I dote on it; I find it essential. (How can there be so many perfect things about you?)

Well, I've got to get my group room ready for my evaluation group.

(Next day, 10pm). Let me tell you again about the things I love you for, that I don't find in any other woman.

First, your willingness to work on your stuff. You

are so good at this; it makes me feel very secure that we can move quite deep in our relationship. You will not withdraw, which is what I have had to endure from others. I can't tell you how important this is to me. You are committed to working, to processing. And we are both so good at it.

Second, you are willing to help me with my stuff. And you are sensitive to me; often asking if you can help. It's so lovely to have this!

Third, I love it when you take the initiative with things. When you use your fine imagination and come up with, for example, the image of a mare.

I crave you, Kathy Jo. I yearn for your voluptuous body under my hands. I replay again and again our meeting in the Lafayette airport: my hugging you and kissing you; again in the car only now with fondling; my proposal and your acceptance, our brief (?) stay at the prayer group; our quick dash to the motel; your bathing me, perhaps, and my hands all over you. Oh, sweet girl!

I love you more each day,

My beloved Jim.

Here is a heart gift — the tape of songs that have a message for you in each.

I'm also including the invitation to our engagement party. It was very sweet to do these this afternoon. And made our engagement seem more real. Wow! To write it and declare it to others is so bold, strengthening, and yet scary!

Well, my love, may this package touch you and bless you. I love you so,

your Kathy

You're Invited
To a Celebration of Our Engagement!
Kathy Vermillion & Jim Elliott
Date: Monday, May 8, 1989
Time: 7-9 p.m. Drop-In
Place: Lorraine Shoemake's

SUNDAY, APRIL 16, 1989 7:25 PM

My love —

It's Sunday evening — the first really spring like day we've had. It's been a delight. I went to Acadiana Mall and bought a new slip (white ½ slip) and the invitations to our engagement party. I went into Victoria's Secret and checked out all the pretty lingerie. They also had sexy men's nylon and silk underwear. Oh, I want you to have some! I'm learning what I like too, under your loving tutelage.

Oh, Jim, I loved your observation about our bonding. It's true. We keep having these incredible bonding experiences. And I'm so grateful for them and for the fact that you see them and recognize them for what they are. You are an incredible man, and I'm not about to let you go, mister.

I'm still so touched that you sent me the love card. Oh, Jim, you are the most thoughtful, most romantic, most loving man I've ever known. And you want me! At last, I have found my mate! My man. God, thank you so much for giving me my heart's desire, when I had given up on it. You were just getting him ready all that time, weren't you? And getting me ready, and keeping me free to marry him. Oh, thank you, God, for your provision and your protection.

You know, Jim, I love your desperate love for me. It really touches me. I have that kind of love for you too. So let me tell you how far above any man I know you are. You are heads, no, miles above any man I know. Specifically…Take Hale… He can be a brute, totally into himself, unthinking. He wants to be a man, mature but instead of sitting when he needs to sit and acting when he needs to act, he often does the opposite. You, on the other hand, my love, have the maturity to discern correctly when to speak and when to stand. Now take Evan. Evan is a gifted therapist. Allows lots of space for his clients' magnificence to come forth. But on the personal level, he often seems withdrawn. You do not withdraw. You hang in there. And you are present to me always. And you come back quickly when I say, "Did you go away?" And you are warm, outpouring. And you are a gifted therapist. I am receiving much therapeutic benefit from you in our interactions. Thank you, my beloved. You bring forth my magnificence. Mama says Evan is probably threatened on some level that he is losing a wonderful client to her therapist husband. Sweetheart of mine, no one even comes close to you in my admiration, my affections. You have catapulted into 1st and primary place with no close second. So be secure, my beloved, you are IT! I have never experienced myself as being so solidly committed. But then I believe God was saving me for you. And you for me. Truly, neither of us has ever loved like this.

I'm enclosing a couple copies of the flyer. Hope you're pleased. Then, I'm sending a copy of the invitation with the tape and a short letter in a separate envelope. God, I love you and I long for you. I had a really hard longing pain for you a while ago. I almost called you, but I thought I'd better not because of the money.

Jim, you are everything to me. Kind of scary for me to write. But I think I just want to somehow find words for the great deep, life-changing love I have for you. Why you even changed my panty color! Now that's something. (I have a drawer full of beige panties — their days are numbered!) Oh, we have such beautiful and precious things we share. I just had a de ja vu of walking arm in arm with you at Asilomar on that cold moonlit night, with the moon on the water. Giddy on our wonderful campfire with our colloquiumites and on our budding love for each other. And that bud has begun to bloom and has turned into many buds and is blooming profusely. Oh— (longing pain).

Be enfolded in my incredibly deep and abiding love for you, Jim.

Your wife-to-be,

TUESDAY, APRIL 18, 1989 6:35 PM

My dear sweet juicy plum of a woman,

Yes, yes, yes! — I am yours! Never doubt it. It is okay to say, "You are mine, Jim." We are each other's. Till the end of time. And beyond, to whatever is there. As far as I'm concerned, we are already married, and what comes next is just the formalities. Are just the formalities.

Your perfumed letter sends me into ecstasies when I sniff it. Oh, Kathy! Your perfume is so perfect; it evokes so many memories.

I have just heated up a can of mushroom soup and made a turkey sandwich and finished eating them — delicious! And had some See's candy for dessert. Polar bear paws. Would you like some polar bear paws? Would Cali? You bought some candy for her in Carmel Valley, didn't you?

I'm going to write some checks in a few minutes, but I can't do it until I write this letter to you. This love letter for you. This is a love letter for you. Your love letter. (How I like to say those things!) I hope you like your love letters!

I love you, Kathy Jo!

I think of our shopping for things: Do we need spices? Sugar? Flour? A timer? Etc. Going up one aisle and down another, outfitting our new house. Our home. (Let's keep our eye open for bassinettes on sale, huh? Hmmm? What's that you say? A baby? Well, just one! I thought we could use the bassinet as a bed for the dog. Well, I guess a baby could sleep in it, too. Once the dog was evicted.)

You sweet woman, you will shower our baby with love, won't you? (You won't ignore me, will you?) Baby. Yes, our baby. The baby you will bear for me. The one I will implant in you. And our baby will be conceived. Yes, "baby." Ours. A little creature. It will have 99.99999% verbal ability, won't it? Will it start talking right away? "What is this?" it will say. "What am I getting myself into here? Where's my mama and my daddy?"

Ah, sweet girl, you say I can keep you close to me by speaking little words of love. How easy that will be! (I love you, my treasure!). And you can keep me close to you by continuing to speak at great lengths and in great detail of panties and semen—those magic terms.

And putting perfume on your letters to me. And holding me close.

It's so important to me to know that you like sex, not only by stating that fact but by demonstrating it, as you do. You reassure me so much. Girls do like sex! They like it a lot.

Yes, dear, it is a sweet painful joy—our love for each other. And yes, I will fulfill all your longings. Attend to each one. Satisfy your every desire.

I want you with me always, dear one. There was a time back in the '60s when people were saying no one person can be all things to another, but I think we can come pretty close. I do not need anyone else but you; I have no thoughts of open marriage as I did with both Gail and Elayna. And Anna, too. You are enough for me; you fulfill all my desires. You are my woman, forever.

Oh, I long for you! Well, I think I'll go to the store for some milk. I'll finish this letter later, maybe tomorrow.

(1:45pm Wednesday). I've just talked to you; you have some very heavy things to get through, and I know you'll be able to do it. I wish I were there to help you (mostly by holding you). But I can hold you a long time in about two weeks.

Oh, you temptress! You ballsy woman, too!

About Cali: I think that this separation is necessary for each of you; and I want to say it was an inherently unfulfilling relationship for each of you. Partly fulfilling, of course, but not enough for you and because of that, not enough for her. If she processes this thing the right way, she will come out ahead.

Well, I'm going out to find some lunch now and maybe take a third look at the post office.

Know that I love you,

I adore you,

(Not just the sexual parts)

All of you — your mind,

Your ideas,

Your naked body (whoops!)

Well your fine breasts

(I guess I can't stop praising those parts I love so much.)

So I'll just have to attend to them for a while.

TUESDAY, APRIL 18, 1989 3:20 PM

My sweet girl,

I just got back to my office from having my tooth root-canalled (ouch! But your love was enfolding me, and I felt protected), and I found your sweet message on my answering machine, about going to bed early (great melting sigh!) and getting plenty of sleep so I'd be up when you called tomorrow at 7:30. I love it when you speak so caringly (maternally) to me! Please continue.

Oh, Kathy!

We are well into the week before the full week that comes before the partial week when I'll fly to you, so things aren't so yearningly miserable as they were before. Now I've got to get to work on the handouts for our workshop. Remember when it was just an idea? We move fast don't we dear one?

Oh, sweet Kathy! How I love you, my darling!

Well, how about some theory for my beloved? About your thoughts on replacing feminism with your own philosophy. I find the concepts in Anthetics very useful in thinking about such new things. Anthetic sexuality, for example. Anthetic politics. And what about Anthetic feminism? That which takes into account the primal differences between the genders? First it must be established that there are some. And that they are not demeaning for women. Then, I suggest an analysis of women's rage, Anthetically: it's revenge, and it's bound up with trading. Then finally a revisioning of such concepts as headship, surrender, submission, bearing children, and so on. With a strong attack on conventional female roles, the ones that lead to oppression. If you write such a book, you can count on two things: 1) a lot of publicity and 2) a lot of angry women. Such a book would make a small fortune for you, and I will help you all along the way. Let me know what you think of these ideas.

Oh, here's another surge of love coming up! Stand by! Oooooof! There it is! My sweetheart! Did you feel that?

I finally found your surprise today, at a UC library. You'll already know what it is: a poem. You will have already heard it. Anyway, I've been looking all over for it.

Some thoughts on what I like: Two kinds of special soaps for men –Aramis (any product in their line) and Tabac. The scents are marvelous. (I filled up my flight bag with some Tabac soap I bought in Paris once.)

Let's go to Florida on our honeymoon and postpone the Los Angeles trip till later.

Well, sweet Kathy, I have to work now and get ready for going to a lecture tonight, which I wish you could come with me to attend. As I walk around Berkeley I say to myself "Kathy would like that" and "No, that wouldn't interest Kathy" and "If Kathy were here, we'd stop by this little brook and talk." Oh, damnit, I love you so miserably!

Maybe the same stars shine on you and me,

But it's not the same as having the same light from the bed lamp.

TUESDAY, APRIL 18, 1989 9:20 AM

My darling Jim,

There is such tenderness in me toward you this morning. (It is so fun to explore this loving country with you. At times, it's a place of passion, other times it is a place of well-being; today a place of tenderness.) As I was driving to work, I recalled your pain at Pawling over your group work and over our struggles together. And I felt compassion pour out of me to you. Oh, you are such a tender man. I am so grateful that you are.

I love your love greetings — always creatively calling me new, loving names (beloved sweet woman). You keep naming me, and I am enlivened! I love your first paragraph — on going deeper in love. "I realize that I can't put any limits on how much I love you; there will always be room for more." Oh yes, that is a Word you are declaring, and I join you in it. Love's nature is to grow-to multiply-to bless-to be fruitful. So why should we be surprised (or as the world thinks that it cannot grow)? Thank you for being willing to open yourself to more and more expansion with me; more and more love.

And thank you, darling, for your inner critic work history. I loved it. I admire you so much. You really are an original, creative professional — taking the seminal work of others, expanding it, and creating something new and fertile. (Oh my, I can't help but use sexual images with you. I think my baby-making part is very near the surface!) And I am in awe of you professionally, that you have stuck with this work, persisted in the evolutionary development of it over many years. I love the challenging work you do — such a nice application of cognitive therapy. I was surprised that this part of your work was so recent (you said 84-85). Oh, and I love your differences with Ellis. I agree that exploration of the past is important. It will surface sideways if we don't recognize it consciously. (Like little Kathy's stuff last Friday.) And what power for release and healing there is in this work. I absolutely believe in work on our past stuff. And from experiencing your helping me, I like the way you do it a lot. I also like what I've learned and how I work. (I must say that Ellis's work really helped me right after my divorce in 1976. But I think it was all I could handle at that time. Later it became necessary to work with the past. That was in 1980 when the critical inner voices became so loud and so abusive. I am very grateful for the healing work on my inner child that I've done since then.) And thank you, marvelous man for Pt. #2. Logic falls short for me. So I love that you don't deify logic — but work at emotional levels. Hooray! And I love your Bill of Rights! Now, the only thing in all this explanation I'm missing is your personal story. Why is Inner Critic so important to you? Would you tell me your personal work with your own Inner Critic? I'd love to hear it, my love.

Oh, Jim, it's now 1:05, and I still love you! I adore you. Words are inadequate to describe my great, deep bonding to you. And I want to stay bonded forever. I want to celebrate that bonding in our wedding ceremony. I want to join my life to you in marriage as soon as possible. My mind and heart are in accord. We want to be yours.

April 14th letter — Thank you, my love, for speaking specifically to our glitch. Even though I'm complete, reading your perspective is so helpful and affirming to me. Thank you for not "dropping" our finished business. Some of it deserves "afterglow." And the little Kathy work was one of those. You say, "I will never go away. Never. You are too precious for me ever to go away, to abandon you. You are part of me." God, Jim, your words are so powerful. You are the most wonderful man in the world. How could I ever leave you? You and I are bonded. We already are one, I think.

And yes, we are both so creative and open. We will continue to create and live out wonderful dramatic sexual episodes. Catch me if you can, you Tiger, you. And yes, I graduated valedictorian of Temptress School! A very proper boarding school.

Thank you for telling me what you always yearned for, and that I give it to you. "Your loyalty to me means more than any wedding ceremony." Wow! I didn't know how very important that was to you. But, you know, my love, it is for me too. It is vital (& this is a primal sense I have) that I be loyal to you. It's good and important for me too.

So, my beloved, let me assure you that I am real. And that I am really for you. Our extravagant Lover God has graced us with each other, perfect as we are for each other. And I will prove to you that I am real from the moment you arrive May 4th. I will fling myself upon you and hold you and kiss you and join with you, as we meet. I will be in my pink and white striped dress and in my most provocative Temptress mode! I will press myself full-length against you – so the curves you see will be the curves you feel melded to your solid body. And in the car, I will offer my legs to you, to lay your hands upon, to run your hands up under my dress. And I will deep kiss you, as I've longed to do. Oh, my. And in the motel, I will bathe the dust off your travel weary body. And I will offer myself to you – "Jim, will you touch me all over with your wonderful hands?" Well, there's more, but this needs to get mailed.

You are the man for me. My Whole Desire. I love you,

Your Kathy

WEDNESDAY, APRIL 19, 1989 2:00 PM

My love —

Well, I am growing furiously — the dream last night, which you so beautifully helped me with, and now the shift in me (which I'll tell you about on the phone this afternoon) that says, "I must move out of the living situation with Cali." I see now that for her, the mate part is primary. She's relating out of that, and I've been in denial about that. So, given that she is there, can't help but be there, it is absurd for me to remain in the house. So, now my life changes again — a move. My mind is full of....We've just hung up, my love. And I feel more calm. Yes, I will move — probably June. I'll look for a house and will be trusting God to provide and lead.

...I've just hung up with Mama, and I've been talking to her re: a minister. I have one in mind, whom I know and like a lot. But he's been transferred to a church in north Louisiana. So I want to talk to you some about this. Oh, "why a minister?" you say. (Do I know you, my darling?) And I laugh and say, "For our wedding, my love." You keep me honest, you know. And you keep me voicing. Thank you for that. I need to keep giving voice to this and all those other things I've been silenced about: my Temptress voice, my Ballsy voice, etc. See, you are my spiritual head, evoking my personal power to come forth. (Quite different from headship in fundamental churches where women are silenced. That always enraged me!)

It's getting very close to class time, and I want to be able to mail this to you after class. So, my love, let me just remind you how much I love and adore you. How right and good you are for me. How much I admire you and love our collegiality and comraderie. I love that you are my lover. You are the most romantic, verbal, ballsy(!) lover I've ever had. I am so grateful that you love me, that you'll let me go down on you. That you'll let me eat your semen. Because I want to. It feels good to me. And if you resist, I'll have to make you lie down and receive my mouth on your cock. And I'll make you touch me through my pink panties. You must! I'll take your hand and put it on my pussy. Now don't run away, Jim. You must stay and touch me and let me suck your cock. You'll see. You'll like it. I'll make you like it. You might even come in my mouth. You might even make me come with your mouth on my pussy. I'll teach you how to make me feel good. You, Tiger, you.

Well, my beloved, more to come (double entendre).

I Adore you, love you, am your woman, will be your wife. You will be my beloved husband. We are meant for each other.

God bless you and enfold you, my love —

Your Kathy

APRIL 20, 1989 4:25 PM

My beloved man, Jim —

I am filled full of love for you. So let me pour it on you. Thank you, my darling, for walking side by side with me through my stuff. You are being true to your word, and I am learning that you are a man of your word. "I will stand shoulder to shoulder with you," you said, "With my skills and your gleaming sword." And we are doing that. Oh, what glory to share this love with you.

You are my gift from God. Thank you, Lord, for this incredible gift; this man, Jim, this desire of my heart. You are extravagant to give me all my heart's desire, when I didn't dare to ask.

Oh, Jim, I adore you. Be enfolded in my love, my blessing, my feminine embrace. You have all of me forever.

Forever I kiss you
Forever I hold you
Forever I go down on you
Forever I drink in your semen
You are mine —
I am all yours —

Your Kathy

FRIDAY, APRIL 21, 1989 9:20 AM

My beloved man,

You exquisite romantic lover. I've been reading your love card (on marriage) and your wonderful letter on bonding while I went through the car wash! (Car washes were never so wonderful!) And oh Jim, your words are so powerful for me. The things I have done, some very deliberately ("I think Jim would like this"--like pink panties); some out of just being myself (sitting close to you at Pawling); and more than some at great risk ("Jim seems to be hurting. Dare I go to his room and see about him? Yes, I must.") To know how these have been a powerful bonding for you; a restoring of things lost long ago; and a necessity for our communion is a huge blessing to me. You are God's best gift to me, Jim. The most wonderful man and partner God could have given me. And I intend to enjoy you today, every day, forever. Your delineation of my virtues is such a core touching experience. You name me, Jim. Why, you even name me "perfect." Oh my.

I got a call from a lady at the school board who heard about our workshop (our workshop! Thrill!) through someone at the hospital(!) and wants to participate. So, I sent her a flyer. It's exciting to me to see how the grapevine is working, because I didn't send flyers to the hospital, and I didn't know the lady she said told her about it. Perhaps you're accustomed to that, but for me it's exciting.

I just spoke with you my darling man. In your agitated state. I'm so glad I called. I want to always be there for you when you need me. Always, Jim. I love you so much. I will never leave you. Your struggles are my concerns too. I will always listen to you, soothe you, hear you out. You have a loving ear here in me. And when you are ready, I will hold you and cover you with my feminine Kathy balm.

Oh, the love in me for you grows deeper every day. And has stronger roots each day. You are rooted in me, my love, inside me.

I adore you.

Your Kathy

FRIDAY, APRIL 21, 1989 2:15 PM

My darling sweetheart,

Three letters from you today! Two of them nicely perfumed! (Your perfume is powerful, dear one. It evokes for me your precious body and all the touching and feelings we shared. I love you so much, Kathy.)

And what an impact I received when I read your sexy words. (I guess I am into sexy words as you are into love words; and we each like both.) You wrote: "If you resist, I'll have to make you lie down and receive my mouth on your cock." (Oh, how glorious!) "And I'll make you touch me through my pink panties." (Oh, best of all—panties! Oh, do keep writing me about them. (Can we pair them with your music?) "I'll take your hand and put it between my legs." (Oh, ecstasy!) "You'll see; you'll like it. I'll make you like it." (Oh! Oh!) "I'll teach you how to make me feel good." Yes, Kathy, please teach me that; please write about it (and Panties) and make me do what will make you feel good. I want to, and I want you to make me. Oh, you adorable girl, you. You juicy wench!

And you describe the meeting we'll have in the airport. "I'll be wearing my pink and white striped dress" —even that line is sexy for me. "And in the car, I will offer my legs to you, to lay your hands upon, to run your hands up, under my dress." (Oh, more ecstasy!) Thank you, my darling girl, for writing that which pleases me and warms me.

Oh, you temptress!

And you will dance for me! Please do. You morsel,

you; let your powerful sexual vibrations enfold me as you dance. I'm getting wild. You are indeed pulling me out of Berkeley, as though you were a strong magnet drawing an iron filing. I will cling to you, sweetheart. Lure me away from this terrible place (which is now terrible, but was not too bad B.K.)

You sweetheart!

Thank you for writing that your drawerful of beige panties — that is, that their days are numbered. Yes, away with celibate colors! On (and off!) with lustful clothing!

You terribly attractive woman, you! (How could Andy ever have needed to even think, when given a choice between you and that other woman?) You were right to believe he would have chosen you. Any man in his right mind would instantly choose you — and would not even put himself in a position where a choice needed to be made! (Thank God Andy didn't know, as we said in the Navy, his ass from a hole in the ground. Poor dumb Andy!)

Again, dearest darling, teach me to give you pleasure. Sexual pleasure. Make me do it. Tell me I must serve your lust. Be wild. Oh, Kathy. I love you so much.

If this letter sounds incoherent, it's because I am. Thank you for calling me this morning before your orals. I don't know what's happening to me lately. You certainly soothed me, however.

I love you, Kathy Jo —

SATURDAY, APRIL 22, 1989 2:00 PM

My darling Kathy Jo,

Thank you, dear one, for signing your letters with the name I love so much—your sweet full name, the one that makes a corner of my heart melt when I read it. Kathy Jo. Sweet, girlish, sexy, childlike, trusting, innocent, warm. I bask in your name. (Thank you, God, for not giving me a girl named Olga or Gertrude.)

Oh, Kathy, I love you! (And as I will tell you on the phone tonight, I am having some fear of change. When I think of it all at once, it's unsettling. One slice at a time, though, and I can handle it. This is the most radical change I've ever made in my life. Please help me.)

Now your letter. Yes, please pour your love on me. Tell God again and again (so I can overhear) what you think of me. Tell me again and again that you will go down on me. Tell me I may put my hand between your legs while you do it, and touch you through your slick panties. Pink ones. Please tempt me! I need you so.

Your words sustain me, give me hope; your declarations of love are vital to me now. In the next three months, dear, I will need you a lot. I am your lovesick swain. More than ever I need your care, your tender concern, your loving words. To get me through this time of transition. To get me to you.

In one of my groups recently, we talked about the power of love words. Statements like, "I love you more than life itself." One man said, "I wouldn't want a relationship where someone said that. That's too much: more than life?" "People in love," I said, "Have a special dispensation to express hyperbolic statements." And they all suddenly realized that people in love speak on a poetic level, not a physicalist-literal one. (Yet it surely seems like it's more than life itself.)

Well, now to theory. I've been mulling over your comments on the meaning of hemorrhoids. Louise Hay (right name?) said it means such-and-such. Something felt wrong about that. Suddenly I realized what it was. It's a dream book interpretation. A cigar means a penis. A key means one, too. And so on. That's too logical for me. I want to be more open. What I would do is put the hemorrhoids in the empty chair and ask them, "What are you about? What do you mean?" I want to give the thing a space for it to tell me what it means. That goes not only for dream symbols (including temptresses on bicycles), physical ailments, and jasmine soap. "What's your function in my life, jasmine soap?" And the soap will answer with its own power. No need to look it up in a dreambook. Tell me what you think of this line of thought.

Even more on this subject: In the world of the pleroma, things are charged with meaning, and they will tell you if you dialogue with them. I think the chief method of pleromatic work is the dialogue. (Don't look up in the bible what God means; just ask him!)

You temptress, you! How I love you, Kathy Jo! I couldn't believe at first that you were perfect for me. There must, I thought be some flaw here somewhere; it can't be this good. She'll get to feeling crowded or suffocated; she'll get bored with my affirmations and expressions of love. (She'll be like Danica, who said, in effect, "If you can't leave me alone, I'll find someone who will.")

I think in the next 500 years, if this whole personal growth movement continues, there will be many more people like you and me. For now, we are the avant garde, the pioneers, the harbingers, the forerunners of what full humanness ought to be. For now we two models live in a world of reactive people who will express their cynicism, judgmentalism, anger, pessimism, warnings, etc., to us. We must continually remind ourselves that these negativities, while they might apply to some, do not apply to us. We are special, Kathy Jo. We are (yes, let me say it) the elite. We are not ordinary people. Warnings may apply to average people, but not to us. We are like creative geniuses, growing up in a dull-witted family, thinking there's something wrong with us if we don't conform to the norm we see around us. Not realizing we are here to set some new norms. For them to aspire to. Let us not forget this.

We must give each other strength. We must cling together as one, in the face of a world that might not understand us very well. (The women in that world seem to understand us better than the men, don't they?)

Kathy Jo, you are so wonderful. So marvelous! Such a splendid creature! You ripe fruit, you. You juicy woman. So intelligent—a genuine genius. Creative. Highly verbal. Attentive to my needs. Able to receive my help. You toothsome wench! So kind and sensitive. So lovely! Breathtakingly beautiful! Exquisite! A dazzling beauty! And your slow, calm sensual movements! The sweet motions of your body! You dear woman, you! Capable of such deep emotions, such spiritual depths. And so sensible. Not stuck in some ideology. Thank God for you, Kathy. Kathy Jo. Soon to be my beautiful wife.

I love you, my darling woman,

MONDAY, APRIL 24, 1989 3:00 PM

Oh, Kathy, my sweet sexy temptress —

This morning you said the most beautiful things to me on the telephone — full-blast sexuality, no holds barred, about panties and eating men's semen — Oh my! Something shifted in me very much. And it was somehow integrated with spirituality, as though all those things are not bad at all but really part of God's unfolding power, working through our bodies. All good things. All to be completely unfolded and expressed in the context of God's spiritual energies. How sublime it was! How lost in it I was! Your dear voice, the sweet things you said — all this was so powerfully affirming of my sexuality! It was something I have never had before! How nice to have a darling woman who can handle such high voltages! Oh, I love you more and more, every hour more.

I'm working on the handouts for our workshop.

I'm thinking about you standing next to me in your wedding dress, sweet, lovely, my bride! Kathy — my bride! I bet you will look both demure and sexy. And romantic and ecstatic and glowing.

My mind is still a confusion of thoughts and feelings: anxiety, hope, lust, love, awe, guilt (re Cali), sadness (at leaving Berkeley), anticipation, excitement, adoration (of you), bliss. More feelings than I've ever had before at one time. Please go on helping me make this transition.

Kathy, don't rent a house until you check with me first. Okay, dear? Why? Well, can you guess? You clever girl, you. (I mean don't rent a house-apartment-for-you-to-live-in-until-I-get-there.)

I've just been shopping and now I'm going to throw away some boxes of envelopes I've been hanging on to. In preparation for relocating to Louisiana. To marry you.

And live with you the rest of my life. As your husband.

Kathy, I love you!
It won't be long now till we're together
IN bed,
Flesh to flesh
Our legs entwined.
My arms holding you tightly,
My mouth saying, "Kathy?"
And you saying, "Yes, my love?"
"Kathy? Can I go down on you?"
And my head is already on its way
To the sweet place
Between your legs.

MONDAY, APRIL 24, 1989 8:45 AM

My love —

Hooray! The last week before you come! Oh, Jim, I can't wait to see you, to be with you, to hold you, to sleep with you, to make love with you. I can just imagine all the wonderful things we'll share. Yet, it will be just a continuation, deepening, fleshing out of what we already share daily in our letters and on the phone. Thank you my beloved, for joining me in this extravagant love-making we are doing as we talk every day, write every day. It's vital to me; to us. And you are not stopped by money considerations, holding yourself back, conventionalities, whatever. You are truly the man for me. We are both flowing freely. It's a gusher, isn't it?

Now, I'm still in awe of the voicing we did about your spirituality — how it is tacit. Not taught, learned, indoctrinated, just a given. That is such a blessing for me to experience. Your spirituality is so open, so fresh, so pure, so unadulterated. That is exactly what I needed for spiritual headship. I couldn't have submitted to a man with indoctrinated spirituality. I would rebel. From where I stand, your spirituality seems to have so little stuff attached to it. It's just fresh — a real mixture of childlikeness and maturity. I love that you cannot label yourself spiritually (Hindu, Christian, etc.), but rather that you call yourself "a man who loves God." Oh, God, you are so good to give me this man. I see him as a reflection of you, God. Open, unboxy, creative, full of free-flowing love. And so extravagant. Yet wise and discerning. You knew I wouldn't, couldn't submit to a man who was any less. And so you gave me Jim. Thank you, thank you, thank you, Daddy! Oh, Jim, I do want to ask you about your lower case letters on him

(Him), he (He) etc. for God. So tell me about that please.

The desire of my heart would be for us to be freed up enough to gush with each other sexually. I believe that is for us. That we already are free with each other — freer than either of us has ever been before. I guess this is just my longing to pour my love on you in great waves of sexual expression and to feel you pour your love on me in the same way. We shall have it, I know. I suppose people who can make a powerful sexual connection on the phone, long distance no less, can certainly do so in person.

1:30 — My love, I have lost all previous train of thought. We have spoken, that incredible experience of your speaking the Word to me — the experience of power, discernment, God's love, pouring through you to me. Do you know you become deepened, strengthened when you are in that space? Yes, you know. Oh, Jim, that experience was so incredible to me. I was stunned, trans-ported, all through my lunch with Mama! I'm still in awe — held up by your Word. Yes you are to flesh out God to me. And I am ready to receive you and Him. I want this in all its depths. Bring it on, honey, my spiritual head. And I will continue to evoke it in you, just by being myself.

Your opening, submissive flower,

your Kathy

TUESDAY, APRIL 25, 1989 1:50 PM

My dearest sweet girl,

Yes, it gets worse and worse. God has not only guided me to Asilomar to find you, he has implanted in you a terrible attractiveness—spiritual, physical (snuggling), sexual, intellectual, emotional, loving—and he has implanted in me an openness to being attracted to such a supremely desirable person as you. The result: it gets worse and worse, every day. Every time we talk, with every letter I get from you.

Kathy, I'm a gone goose. I'm a pigeon. I'm a fool for love. I'm lost in my love for you. It's my calling, calling me to my cosmic relationship, my divine-inspired relationship with you. God calls me to this. If I don't answer this call, I will blow the biggest chance of my life. There's no question as to what I will do. I am in the grip of forces bigger than I've ever felt in my life. I willingly surrender to them, to God's call to be your mate. He brooks no opposition. He will have what he wants. I can do no other.

What all this adds up to is my fierce and potent love for you.

And it's getting worse and worse.

Oh, Kathy! My sweet bride. My girl with that divine and mysterious secret place that I love to eat. To me the center of my universe. (Right now I'm obsessed with sexuality.)

Now, to your letter. Thank you for liking my words about bonding with you. Yes, you have named my redemptive quest with you: "A restoring of things lost long ago" and a "necessity for our communion." (We certainly bond with each other through our complex and complete feedback, don't we, my darling?)

"Your struggles are my concerns, too," you wrote. That will be hard for me to accept. I'm so used to being self-sufficient. But I'll try.

(Kathy! You're going to wear that wedding dress and stand next to me — right there before all those people — and we're going to pledge ourselves to each other, in public. We can't take it back! We're going to be married! I love you so passionately!)

The pleroma, it seems to me, is unlike the physical world in that the former is malleable to our thoughts and feelings. I want to push this idea again: I cannot make a computer do things simply by thinking and feeling (although in the future this might be possible). But for now, the computer — existing as a physical object — is implacable, obdurate, unforgiving. It does what it does no matter how nice I am to it. If I don't push the right sequence of buttons, it won't work. I can get mad at it, and it cares not a whit. It will not change unless I rewire its circuits.

But the pleroma is plastic. My word (backed with the power of my assertiveness and my emotions and intention) has some effect on the pleroma. I name jasmine soap with the words Love and Protective Armor, and it now has those qualities. I name our love Good, and it is. I pour my love out to you, and it transforms you. (Though it has no effect on a computer.) And it transforms me. The realm of the pleroma is mutable.

And therein lies some dangers. Another person's

Word can affect me, simply by my hearing it. A prediction can have power over me, if I let it. (Whereas a computer just does its job.) A negative word said to me can possibly transform me for the worse.

Special defenses and weapons (all noetic and/or pleromatic) are needed to swim around in this world. One is critical thinking. The Nazis didn't have it, and they succumbed to Hitler's Word. Likewise, the Jim Jonesers.

Someone can say "You were born under this sign, and you are destined to be such-and-such." And we can give away our power by not challenging this.

I think what I'm saying is that swimming in the pleroma safely requires firm boundaries, along with the realization that you yourself can create with pleromatic material. That is, you are a co-creator with the pleroma. By your word, you can make reality, change it, transform it—pleromatically. (But not a computer.)

So you need the right values. At least two: inner freedom and caring. Love. With those values, you can take pleromatic material and shape it properly. With self-centeredness and vengeance, you will shape it for evil ends.

Well, dear sweetheart, let me know what you think of these ideas.

Let's hold each other close and feel the divine glow that God gives us for making love so spiritually and lustfully. We are fulfilling his plan. He is pleased.

Oh, I love you Kathy!

TUESDAY, APRIL 25, 1989 2:45 PM

My beloved Jim —

I'm sitting under a tree in the bank parking lot. I just deposited $290.00 of workshop registrations in my account, and I want to get a quick letter off to you.

Are you open to a quickie? Would you be open to my unzipping your pants quickly and tearing your slacks off? And ripping my dress off and my bra and slip and pantyhose off? (Oh, you did it already!) And then with just my cream panties on, I fling myself on your body and we kiss deep, tongue to tongue and feel our bodies press against each other. Feel my breasts against your chest? Do you feel my slinky panties on your stomach, your cock? Feel my legs intertwined with yours — Feel our arms holding each other. But now I untwine one arm to place my fingers in your mouth and to feel our tongues probing each other — telling our insistence. Hear our hot, hushed words — "Jim, I've got to have you." "Have what, Kathy darling?" "I've got to have your cock in me." And you say, "You shall have it, my darling." And you roll me over until I am beneath you, and you look down on me and see the burning desire on my face — my dilated pupils, my enflamed nostrils, my parted lips, my flushed face — And desire engulfs you — engorges your cock for me. You rip off my slinky panties and say, "Open to me, Kathy." "Wider, Kathy." "Open all the way to me, Kathy." And I unhesitatingly open myself to you completely; to your insistent, hard cock. And you plunge into me, not hesitating. And you feel me rise to take you all in. And we move passionately, trying to join your loins to my pelvis as deeply as we can. And we are wild for each other, with each other. The intensity of our love driving us to express it in as fierce and passionate a way as our bodies can speak. And we breathe in moans and gasps. And our love is an engulfing flame. And God is in the flame, adding His love and power to ours. "Oh, Jim," I cry. And your tears splash on to my chest as you cry your love and communion with me. And you drive hard and deep, because you want it, and I want you to. I must have your power in me. And you come with a great cry. And you fall upon my breast, and I hold you —

Then knowing that I need more, you recover and move your body down over me, look me in the face and say, "Kathy, I'm going to go down on you, because I know you need it." And I arch up to you in gratitude to your wisdom, your caring, your virility. And you do go down on me. And I am so aroused that your tongue just touches my pussy, and I enter an incredible rolling orgasm, and you don't let up until I cry and squirm for mercy —

Then you move up to be with me again, and as we enter each other's arms, we laugh together with delight. And we hold each other in great love and affection and satisfaction. And fall asleep in each other's arms.

Oh, I love you, Jim. You are my spiritual head. I give myself to you; submit to you totally, as you require. And you are my incredible, exquisite lover.

Come to me soon, my love — (lipstick kiss)

Your Kathy

WEDNESDAY, APRIL 26, 1989 12:15 PM

Dear sweet Kathy Jo,

My love for you continues to get worse and worse every day. How I long for you! How desirable you have made yourself for me! And most of that, you don't even have to try; all you are is your sweet self, and I come buzzin' around like a honeybee, to see if I can get inside your petals. You wildly attractive girl!

I sensed your insecurity during our telephone conversation this morning (about group sex and open marriages), and I want to tell you again in no uncertain terms, without any equivocation whatever:

I want only you. No other woman. Ever. You are woman enough for me. There's no need for anything else.

But anyway, I'm committed to monogamy and fidelity. It's the only thing that seems to work. "Open marriages" look attractive but are actually destructive. We need the focus of our fusion generator. "Openness" dissipates our sexual energies. Not only that, it endangers our relationship. I want to safeguard it against any threat. (Any sexual variety we need can be taken care of in our fantasies.) I was committed to monogamy and fidelity before I met you. Ever since I saw Fiddler on the Roof.

You are my woman. My one and only woman. What we have is so precious to me. (Well, there's another good thing about loving a mature man: he has gone through all his wild oats cycle, and is ready to settle down.)

Kathy? I love you. I'm going to be your husband! You're going to be my sweet wife! We're going to be married. You're going to marry me in your new wedding dress. We're going to be happy. We're going to live happily ever after. ("But first I've got to plant these beans I got for the cow.")

By the time you get this letter, my beloved, it'll be only a few days before we'll be together. (God will not let that plane crash, will he?) (No, he told me he won't.)

I've been thinking about your question about my inner critic work and my life. I think as a child I had a lot of freedom. No guidance whatever, which I disliked. But the freedom I did like. And although I made a few mistakes, I was glad to have had it. So I grew up valuing it. I never wanted to follow custom and tradition; I always wanted to go my own way. I disliked orthodoxy wherever I found it. Se when I began leading groups, I saw that other people weren't as free as I was, and I wanted to help them become free. I saw that what blocked them was inner critic stuff. And then I saw that it was blocking me, too. So I was determined to get free from my internal oppression, also. It was always easy for me, doing inner critic challenging — as easy as it was for you, once I suggested it to you.

And then I realized how much I liked to be around people who had also worked on their inner critic. And how much I hated to be around the others — those judgmental, reactive, neurotic, driven ones. So I created Anthetics — to form a community of free people.

I want to create my own therapy, my own religion, my own work, my own version of a close relationship (with you, yes). My own versions of things, not hand-me-down versions imposed by other people. And I needed inner critic work on myself in order to do that. I have always exulted in being original and creative, so as to get something that suits me just right.

I want my own kind of sexual expressiveness, my own political stance. All these versions have come together under the rubric of Anthetics, now. It seems to me to be a great unifying idea.

As I rejected orthodoxy, I didn't want to rebel, either, and simply choose the opposite of what existed. I wanted to retain the good from the past within the new forms I was creating.

Thus, your Anthetic feminism.

I guess I was led to group work by God. And to find my own way in it, not get a PhD and follow someone else's way. And find all systems wanting, so I had to create my own.

There have been many mistakes along the way, but I wouldn't trade what I did for the safety of orthodoxy. My life has been exciting. And it has been a preparation for our relationship, Kathy, my sweet. Everything has gone along just right, just the way it was supposed to.

Karl Jaspers, the existentialist philosopher, talks about boundary situations—things you can't ever get past, because they form the paradoxical boundaries of your life. Like death. Like wanting you to be fully experienced sexually, yet doing everything with me for the first time. Or wanting you to be 37 and still 10. Isn't life funny? Aren't we experiencing it to the full? Another paradoxical boundary: being totally free, yet in the grip of god. Grip? Maybe not grip; arms? Well, somehow surrendered to God.

Or being human, yet enfleshed God. Or divinized

flesh? I think when you get down to such basic levels, paradoxes grow like truffles. It's like getting into sub-electronic levels, where the ordinary rules no longer hold.

We are God, aren't we, Kathy? In some sense? Surely, God flows through us. We express God to each other. We embody him? He is intertwined with us? He energizes our sexual experiences and praises our boldness? He unfolds in us; yes. We have let him into our lives. He shares in our joys, both sexual and other. He is quite intimate with us. He pervades our being. Or do we pervade his? Or both? He bestows his blessings on us and what we do.

But don't we have something to say about what kind of God we have chosen? He is not the punitive god of the Old Testament. I read where in the time of Moses, God hardened the heart of Pharaoh against the Jews. Our God would never do a thing like that. I don't think that means that god has evolved, as much as that we form a partnership with him, and that is what has evolved. There is an interaction that has improved; we humans have taken pleromatic material, with its potential for goodness, and called forth the goodness of God that was inherent in it, rejecting whatever propensities for evil were there. Any reactions?

Sweetheart, my client will appear at any moment.

Oh, I love our interchanges on all their many levels!

You are my darling girl, my only one, my single choice, my fidelitous wife. My beautiful, wise, genius of a woman!

FRIDAY, APRIL 28, 1989 2:35 PM

My beloved Kathy Jo,

Two letters from you today—both sexy! Oh, my! I love your image of tearing off clothes, especially panties. Just ripping them off your body, tearing them to smithereens, being so wild. Ravishing you. That's what I'd love to do: ravish your sweet body. (Thank you for flinging yourself on me still wearing your panties.) Yes, I want you to rise, to raise your hips, to take me all in, as deep as I can go. I want to go deep into you when I enter your sweet body.

And I love your saying "because you want it." Yes, Kathy Jo, I do want it. And you do want me to do it.

And then you say you need more. I want you to say that: "I need more, Jim." You write: "Kathy, I'm going to go down on you, because I know you need it." What a sweet theme, upon which I can happily elaborate. I want to have intercourse with you, Kathy Jo, because I know you need it. You need it pretty badly. You need to have me eat your pussy, too. And you need to eat my semen. It's very good for you, isn't it?

In fact, when you eat my semen, you absorb my masculine qualities: strength, hardness, aggressiveness, potency. Each spurt you swallow gives you these empowering magical elements, just as bathing with jasmine soap armors you with my love and protection. I want you to know that I give these things freely. I pour them on you by coming in your mouth and your vagina. You partake of maleness through me. I pour out on you, and into you, my sacramental sex fluid.

And now about lower case pronouns for God. Upper case, it seems to me, is too distancing. I want to be intimate with God. He is a Presence (hmmm, that cap seems right), and I want him to intertwine with and inform me, as your sweet presence does. It's more difficult to have communion with an upper-case-pronoun God.

Now, about money. Let's both ask questions of married couples re this issue. I guess we decided on individual checking accounts plus one common one (for rent, etc.?). Many of my expenses are tax write-offs; e.g., the trip to the APA. Well, let's talk about this.

Now, things I would like you to say to me:

"Would you like to have intercourse with me, Jim?"

"Do you want me to take off my panties?" (Or touch them)

"Jim can I eat some more of your semen?"

"Would you like to look up my skirt while I take off my panty hose?"

"Would you like to see my panties?"

"Would you like me to show you my panties?"

"Would you like to see what panties I'm wearing today?" (Or "I have on today?")

"Would you teach me how to have sex" or "how to have intercourse?" (Et al.)

"Do you think I'm too young for you to have intercourse with me?" (The "too young" theme is very nice.)

Oh, Kathy Jo—just writing these things turns me on!

Well, I went to San Francisco today and finally got my glasses. My first client today said they make me look like a college professor. So far so good. I like them. I think. I'll see what you say. From now on, you have a say in how I look.

Kathy Jo, the closer I get to Thursday, the wilder I get for you.

Oh, I love you!

You sweet temptress!

APRIL 26, 1989 1:30 PM

My beloved man,

Yes, you are beloved to me Jim. My whole desire. I'm sitting under a tree at Abdalla's which I'll be entering to look for your birthday present. Such a new and thrilling feeling — to be buying birthday presents for my man. I feel so close to you, so intimate, so belonging.

Thank you again, my love for calling me last night; for loving me enough to step out of rationality into extravagance. And thank you for wanting to move things up from August. I am thrilled and ready. (Well, almost! Ready, that is.) I'll have to think about wedding plans and we'll have to talk. Preparations must be made, you know. Like for food and reserving Paulette's home and obtaining a minister. All those little, special things that we need for the occasion of exchanging our vows — speaking our vows to each other, my love. And thank you for your magnificent headship. I'm thinking of how you handled my terror this morning — terror of the wild sexuality in me and in you. Thank you for discerning that I needed your protection and your strong stand for monogamy. You said exactly the right thing. And then my wisdom came in knowing that we needed to pray. And then your powerful prayer for God to contain our white hot love in himself. (Oh dear, lower case "h"). Oh, more bonding, more power, more deep love. I continue in awe at us and in gratitude for you. You are the only man for me. I want you alone. Yeah, alone in our room, on the bed, naked, white hot, enfolded in each other's arms.

You will be here next week, THANK GOD! Come on to me, my man. Everything you need is here. Nothing will be lacking. OH, well, there won't be any panhandlers and much less crime. But I guess you can do without those.

Oh, I can't wait to be living day to day with the man who makes me laugh, till my stomach hurts. Really, by the time you got through with me on the phone last night ("Bye-bye" BaBa) I could feel my stomach muscles aching. It was a delight, my love. Life with you is so wonderful. Quotidian life with you will be glorious, I can tell.

God, I love you, honey.

You fill me up.

BaBa—

your Kathy

FRIDAY, APRIL 28, 1989 2:20 PM

My beloved Man —

God, I am in love with you. It really is intensifying all the time. I am bonded with you, Jim. I am yours. And I remind you that I submit to you totally. It is so good to have your headship. What glory!

Yes, you and I each have a couple of approaches to our sexual communion which are core issues. Yours is that little boy who needs assurance that he is okay as a sexual being; that sex is good; that girls like it; that girls will let him touch them. And now you've found the girl just made for that boy. I think she'll let him do all those things. And I've got the core issue of needing to be dominated, to have my wildness, my raw sexuality harnessed. I need to experience a man who will dominate me sexually, so I have to come. And I've found just the man for all these things. We were meant for each other. (Did I tell you that I love the way you say the word, "fuck"? And that I think you say "shit" adorably? Well, I do love those words on your mouth!) God, Jim, I am so glad I don't have to shut down any part of me for your sake. You'll take all of me — naughty, raunchy, wild, everything. Thank you so much. I want you to take me. To move with you. I want you to soften with approval for my obedience to your domination. To cast your strong male look of approval over me — to name me — whatever creatively you come up with as you make love to me. To claim me. Oh, God. This is primal stuff for me, Jim. My heart is pounding just thinking about it. I guess I must need and want this bad.

Jim, next Friday, we'll be together. Oh, I can't wait.

Oh, God, you have surely opened me, made me ready for

Jim — ready for deeper living, deeper power, delving into my feminine to depths I've never been before and living with the masculine. Jim's and mine. This is such an amazing thing you have given us — this raw, wild, sweet love. Please protect it and us, Lord. Help us to relax into, to surrender to it. This man, God, this Jim is surely your pick — straight from your heart to me. And I see you in him so much. I learn of you from living with and loving him. Thank you for anointing him for this task — loving me.

I adore you,

your Kathy

SATURDAY, APRIL 29, 1989 8:30 AM

My love,

This is probably the last letter you'll get before you come to me. Yes, come to me. Oh, Jim, you'll be here so soon. Thank God! We are swimming in very deep waters, you and I. And God is en-folding us, following along behind us watchfully — seeing that we stay out of danger — there to protect us if we should meet danger. Oh, Jim, I love you. I love all these facets of you I'm learning — the little boy, the spiritual head, the colleague, the romantic lover, and more. I will be so glad to experience them in the flesh.

Come to me, my love. Let us continue with this great work, In Which:

Things lost are being restored.

Arms emptied are being filled.

Jewels devalued are being delighted over.

And a new life is being created.

God, I love you, Jim.

Come to me, honey.

I am wide open to you,

your Kathy

Of the pink panties

MONDAY, MAY 1, 1989 1:00 PM

My beloved Kathy Jo,

Today (if today is Thursday) I will be with you! In the flesh! Tonight we will be in each other's arms, in bed! I'm not as wild now as I was this morning but I am wild. Frenzied. I've got to have your sweet body!

Now I want to talk about a theoretical topic. Forgiveness. People talk about forgiving each other, about getting forgiveness from God, and about forgiving themselves.

I've always felt uncomfortable with this topic, especially the last one. To forgive someone means to me that the other person has done something bad or wrong. To forgive means to pardon, to give up on punishing the other. Now, that might be okay if one has committed a crime (against a person) or a sin (against God—but I hope we don't believe in sins). You forgive by saying, "I will not punish you." But it's still a crime or sin.

But forgiving oneself can occur only if one decides not to punish oneself (through a practical, physical punishment). Not to atone, that is. (I think I'm not saying clearly what I want to say.) A clear statement would be: I'd rather disarm my inner critic; then there's no "crime" or "sin"—nothing to forgive. So I'm not so keen on self-forgiveness, since it implies that there is badness—to forgive. Maybe we'll have time to talk about this. (Maybe we'll be too busy with other things, too. What do you think?)

Anyway, by the time Thursday is over, you will be an engaged girl. With a sparkling ring on your third finger, left hand. You will be taken. Owned by me. Cut out of the herd. My girl. My fiancée.

Tonight, sweetheart, will you say, "Jim, would you like to look up my skirt while I take off my pantyhose?" Will you let me? Then can I hold you and touch you? Lying on the bed? Then will you bathe me? Wearing your new negligee and pink panties? (Can I kiss you and touch you while you do it?) Then back on the bed, can we use our special birth control method? Can we have intercourse, too, without your putting a sponge in your vagina? Just to take a chance? Oh, Kathy, I guess I'm still pretty wild about you. All these sexual thoughts and fantasies. I long for you so. I desire you so fiercely. And I love you so much! Be assured, dear one, that I fully intend to marry you; to make you Kathy Elliott. There are no doubts whatever about my doing this, even though there are fears.

I'm so excited about being with you,

And I love you so much

And I want to come up behind you and give you a hug and turn you around and give you a very deep kiss.

Part 4

Engagement!

On May 4, Jim flew to meet me in my home town. His plane arrived at 8:30 that evening. As we got in the car, Jim directed me, "Drive to Girard Hall." So, I drove to the building on campus where I taught and had my office. When we arrived, we got out of the car, and he took me by the hand. At the building, we walked halfway up the outside steps. He took out his handkerchief (it had rained, and the steps were wet) and knelt on the step beneath where I stood. He said to me, "I don't have much, but my prospects are good. Will you marry me?" I without hesitation said, "Yes!!" He then took out the sparkling engagement ring he had told me about and placed it on my hand. We were engaged!

We spent the next 5 days together. It marked a new era in our relationship. Not only were we engaged (and had celebrated it with an engagement party hosted by Mama), but we also had begun our work life together, presenting our first workshop to the public. Our letters take up after Jim had left to return to Berkeley.

WEDNESDAY, MAY 10, 1989 9:15 AM

My love —

The bonding grows deeper! Glory! I am more in love with you than ever. My mind is full of you. I can close my eyes, and you are right there! I adore you. I submit to you totally. I love you with every inch of me! You are a delight to be with, Jim. I loved every minute with you. You are so congenial (well, it's deeper than congenial, but I can't think of the word). Anyway, I loved waking up with you right next to me, and then immediately feeling you reach out to enfold me in your arms. I loved going to sleep in your arms. Waking up at 2 a.m. and making love was glorious. I loved sitting right next to you as we shared meals and dishes and sodas! I loved working through more stuff with you. God, my heart and my body are pulling right now, a kinesthetic experience of how much I love you. And oh, God, I love working together as colleagues. That was a high above and beyond the romantic, sexual, and heart relationship we have. Jim, we work together great! I want more! It deepens what we have. God, communion on all levels — spiritual, sexual, emotional, affectional, and vocational! God! Thank you.

Oh, honey, I started my period right after you left on Tuesday. So no conception on this trip!

I got some wonderful feedback on the workshop. That was wonderful. I'll share it on the phone today or tomorrow.

Jim, dear, I love you. You are everything to me! I want to show you with my eyes and with my body.

I mailed the thank you cards for our gifts. And as I signed both of our names, it felt new and wonderful. I'll be glad when I can put "Elliott" on the return address!

Well, my love, I need to get ready to leave for Florida.

Have a very good week — soaked in my love for you — a love that will cosset you, arouse you, and satiate you for the rest of your life.

A very deep kiss,

Your Kathy

(FROM KATHY)

Extravagance Lesson:

Actually, love, these are my thoughts this morning on parable stories that speak of God's extravagance. This was new interpretation of familiar stories, so it was good for me. First, I thought of the Prodigal Son. In this parable, the son asks his father for all his portion of the inheritance, right now, before dad dies. And if we see Dad as God, we see how God doesn't say, "No, you'll just go squander it on loose living," or "Are you sure this is what you should do?" No, he just gives him the inheritance — a verification to me of our work Sunday on God's laying it all out before us and leaving it in our hands to take charge of. And a validation of God's extravagant love. Extravagance has open hands; doesn't fret or point the finger at motive of the receiver. Then the son returns home penniless, filthy, a wreck, and the father runs to meet him with the best ring and robe, and then he throws a big party, kills the fatted calf. Extravagance again — no chiding; no tight-lipped, parsimonious welcome. Oh no, an extravagant welcome.

… Jim, honey, so much time has passed since I started this that I've lost my train of thought. I'll just put this in the mail and seal it with love.

I adore you, you marvelous man —

Your Kathy

WEDNESDAY, MAY 10, 1989 6:00 PM

My beloved sweetheart,

Well, the bonding is getting stronger and stronger. I'm not feeling very frantic now. More secure, maybe. I guess you really do like me. And really do want to marry me. You wouldn't have introduced me to all your friends at the engagement party as your fiancé if you didn't. So I guess you do, huh? So you probably will go through with it. Right?

Anyway, I love you desperately, solidly, incoherently, inexpressibly, immoderately, and cherishingly. I have so many beautiful memories of my trip:

Your cosseting me. Oh, deep pleasure, beyond words! I sank into some pleromatic womb as you ministered unto me. It was so precious, darling.

Our fantasies. Fantastic! Our quick acceptance of each other. Our sexual frenzy as we lived through them. We merged with each other, didn't we?

Strawberry ice cream sodas. Creamed corn with bacon drippings. Chicken fried steak. Spinach salad. Apple cobbler.

Putting on a good performance at the party. Not all performance, of course—jus' bein' mahself—it was so easy to be warm toward all those warm people. (But I did put on a good performance, didn't I?)

Our work on your jealousy-of-Mama glitch. You were such a good girl! And now I want this thing from you—

Thrusting into your voluptuous body with my hard cock. Oh, Kathy! It was so good. (I feel shy now.)

Lying entwined, our legs braided together, our arms clasping each other, our thoughts and feelings merging, as though we were one person talking to itself. We were so intimate. I still have the kinesthetic memory; my body longs for it again. We will have so much time to spend doing this once we are married! To go to bed at night this way. To wake up in the middle of the night and do it. To wake up in the morning and braid ourselves together, to intermingle our bodies. Oh, I love you so terribly much!

Buying you a pair of peach panties and you not only enduring it but actually liking it!

Your office, the desk of which I hope will now be somewhat transformed with new meaning.

The steps of Girard Hall, likewise.

Hale. A nice guy.

Our workshop. The topic of a whole letter itself. (Kathy! We did it!)

Debriefing our workshop over Juliuses. How sweet.

Your intention to participate, to join me in my work. (Even more bonding. I think you will indeed like it and find enough space in it to do anything you want.

Your wish to mingle money. Boy, are we ever mingling!

The fact that your dear Mama provided such an abundance of food, then didn't know what to do with it afterward.

Acadiana Mall

Aramis soap and cologne

Blue Jockey shorts. Nylon. Sleek and shiny.

Our bathing each other. My learning of the special

little soaps and products for each part of your sweet body.

Making wedding plans in Sadie's. (It's really going to happen!) My crying, and your not caring what other people were thinking. Your reminding me that it's our wedding, and we can do it any way we want. (You care about my inner freedom, an Anthetic value. No one ever has before!)

Your quick discernment of what turned me on, and your doing it and saying it.

Your perceptiveness in knowing when I did not receive the full impact of what you were saying. And in perceiving when I went away then calling me back.

(9:50pm, same day). My group is over; they talked about my forthcoming move to Lafayette and decided they'd better learn some leadership techniques fast so they can continue to meet. They are very dear people, and they are looking forward to meeting you.

(11am, Wednesday, May 17). We are both going through some tricky rapids now. You with Cali, I with moving and school and my student loan. And we are giving each other support. (But I'm sorry I turned off my telephone this morning, sweetheart. I was sure you wouldn't need me, and I wanted to avoid being awakened by salespeople who have been calling lately.) Well, I'm glad you are feeling better.

I am in a task-oriented, practical, problem-solving mode and will be until you get here this Tuesday. (Oh happy day!) I'm getting things done, but slowly, and I panic from time to time, wondering if I can get it all done. In seven weeks. It seems like a long time, but I have so much to do. Well, if it takes longer, I'll just spend more time here. But I do want to go to you at the end of June. And start living together. (I think everything will turn out okay.)

Now I want to say some things about friends. At our engagement party, there was Lou inviting us to go sailing and Hale, who wants some contact with us. Then there's Cali — a question mark.

Here are my priorities:

I want to spend as much time as possible with you. In bed with you (sometime even sleeping). Eating meals with you. Hanging around you. Touching you. Hugging you. And so on. Travelling with you too.

Then there's my book. I'll work on that at home, so I can be with you, too.

Then my group work in Lafayette (and Berkeley). I want you with me as much as possible, here, too.

Then my UGS work. Seminars together. Peer days.

Then all the administrative things I have to do: correspondence, processing any orders, making books, etc. I'll do this at home too.

This leaves only a small amount of time for friends. The older I get, the more selective I become. For example, I don't want to spend time with people who are well-defended, armored, and walled up. At one time I was interested in working on getting through to people but no more. Life is too short.

I also do not want to spend time with people who are not motivated to work on their stuff. I want depth in my friendships as well as my love relationship with you. To get that depth, to handle it, you need to be able to work.

To not only be motivated but to have the skills.

In addition, I do not want to spend time with people who are so wrapped up in themselves that they are uninterested in me, who are unwilling to express that interest by simply asking me questions about myself.

At the engagement party, Hale was the only one who seemed to even come close to these criteria. He was interested in me and my work. Evan was interested in himself. Jacob was more fun to talk with but was also self-concerned. As you can see, I have high standards. (I'm enclosing some Anthetic criteria that I recommend to my group participants.)

In addition, I want to relate to people who are intellectuals—who are interested in discussing ideas—who are open and nondogmatic about it, too. And especially ideas in the fields of psychology and psychotherapy. And spiritual growth. Perhaps philosophy, too.

Some people have liked me and have wanted to be my friend, and I have acceded but then found they didn't meet these criteria. They wanted a listener, but they didn't want to do any listening. Or they wanted to put me down and didn't see this as their problem. So I had to give up these relationships, and the people felt hurt and angry. I don't want to do that again. I want to make sure my relationships are what I want. (That's why I choose you.)

So in Lafayette I will be pretty choosey about whom I relate with. Maybe they won't understand this. I'll say I'm very busy with my book and my work and my schoolwork, and that of course will be true. I guess I'm just warning you about what to expect. You and I may have somewhat different friends, although I hope you are with me on this issue. Let's discuss it.

Kathy, our telephone conversations while you are at the conference represent a new stage of our relationship. We are becoming more bonded. (Kathy, we're going to be married!) Something constructive is happening between you and Cali, too. Please do not buy into any responsibility stuff with her.

I want to say again the parallel: It's as though you were a latent homosexual man, married, who tried to conform to heterosexuality but realized he had to fulfill himself and come out of the closet. And relate to someone of his kind. With Cali, you were trying to be what you were not. You have not been bisexual for ten years, Kathy. You are a basically heterosexual woman (who needs a man), who resigned to a close relationship with a woman, and who finally found the man she needed. Cali said she knew you would do this sooner or later. Yet she continued in the dependency. I'm not saying she has only herself to blame; I am saying that her feelings are family-of-origin-based. Her great dependency on you was unwarranted. If you were both committed lesbians, the whole thing would have been different. Especially if you were having a fulfilling sexual relationship. But Cali knew you needed fulfillment with a man, and she was in denial. This denial formed the basis for her dependency. What she needs to do is work through the pain and grief and anger and use it as a clue to work on her emptiness. She needs more self-sufficiency, for her own happiness. That's what this lesson is about for her.

How to be the source of her own strength. It's a painful lesson but a necessary one.

Now I want to tell you how much I love you. All my words are too little; my feelings are so inordinate, inarticulate, inexpressible. Monumental. Powerful. Oh, Kathy, you are so precious to me! I need you so much!

I'm in a disrupted state of mind, not only by your absence but by the projects I have to accomplish. I need you here by my side and soon, dammit. Tuesday. You'll get this letter on Saturday. Only a couple days between it and Tuesday. Fly swiftly to me, my darling girl, my own, and keep pulling up on the armrests to keep the plane up in the air. I'm glad I've taken that flight, so I know what your experience will be.

Kathy Jo, I love you with all my heart;
Even though I can't be rhapsodic now,
Know that I adore you and long for the day
When we will be man and wife.

MAY 14, 1989, ST. SIMON'S ISLAND, GEORGIA

My beloved Jim —

I have a moment before the next session. I tried to call you and missed you; I'm so glad you have an answering machine. I'm sitting in a very idyllic spot overlooking a pretty courtyard with a fountain. I'm anxious to discuss this morning's talk by Robert Johnson and "The 3 loves." I'll tell you tonight when I call. It was interesting to hear delineated the avenues of love we're living and integrating. It's so good to be able to talk these things out with you and to especially live these things, this love out with you.

I find that I want us to connect on all levels each time we talk! If one is left out I miss it. So our not connecting on the sexual level leaves a gap in me too. I will be glad to talk to you tonight and share our sexual communion. I will be even more happy to be with you next Tuesday and share that communion in the flesh! Truly we do commune on each other — feasting on each other's cream, pouring our life to each other. And at the same time experiencing the ecstasy that comes with that outpouring. How important it is for the one experiencing the sexual arousal to have an other to receive that outpouring in reverent lust. We want that so badly as humans that we'll pay prostitutes to simulate reverent lust for us. Do you know what I mean? What do you think of that? It just occurred to me as I wrote it. I want to hear your thoughts on this, my love. I wish I could have told Robert Johnson of our love and the synthesis we are doing of all the levels, but I'm not willing to expose such a precious, fragile thing yet. Yet you say our love is strong. And I agree. The fragility perhaps is in the representing of our experience in words. Well more later, my darling man,

I adore you.   *your Kathy*

THURSDAY, MAY 18, 1989 1:00 PM

My darling Kathy,

I feel a great sense of relief at knowing you are speeding westward to Lafayette, closer and closer to me, where you will soon climb aboard that cute little airplane with the propellers and fly to me in Oakland. I didn't know I felt so unhappy at your geographical distance in Georgia from me. Hurry, sweet Kathy. I love you, my sweetheart. My soon-to-be wife.

Sometimes our relationship seems like a dream I'm having, a wonderful dream, and I'll wake up from it and find I'm back in my relationship with Danica (whatever that was) and my now-dreary life in Berkeley. But then I remember that you are a real girl; I have actually touched all parts of your dear body; it is not a dream at all. (Except that you are my dream girl, and my dream has come true.)

I still feel a little fear that you will listen to some lecturer or guru or read some book and say, "Oh, now I see that my relationship with Jim is impossible." Dammit, Kathy, stop giving away our power (yes, our power) to some outside influence! As your spiritual head, I command you! (But then you are really doing quite well developmentally, considering what used to shake your ideas.) (And you are right: You are not Danica; my fears are coming from that relationship, not from ours. You are indeed totally committed to me. And yet I hope you understand my fears. I guess even the ideal relationship has its glitches. And we are very good at working on them. I suppose I just need you with me;

this long-distance love is okay but only temporarily. I need day-to-day contact with you. I do see things more in perspective today, too. I was just having middle-of-the-night inner critic thoughts last night, not to be trusted at all.)

Anyway, I visualize you in Cali's car speeding west. Very nice. You will get this letter Monday, and it will be the last one before you come to me. Oh, Kathy, I love you so! I need you in the flesh so badly! I think our touching and holding each other means more to me than any words of commitment.

You keep surprising me; e.g., your not only acceptance of my anger but your asking me twice to repeat it, along with your statement that it gives you strength. We are exploring new ground I have never even considered before. Our relationship is truly destined, truly necessary for my work. We will look back on our glitches as little ripples on the surface of our deep love and connectedness. (Please go on reassuring me of your determination not to be disempowered by Jungian garbage.)

Kathy, no more seminars and conferences alone, dammit.

You sweet girl, I am so wildly turned on by thoughts of your body. Our legs intertwined; our bodies pressed together in bed as though we were one organism. The whispers into each others' ears. The breathtaking speed with which we endow everything we do and see with immense meaning. The relationship legends we are creating for ourselves. We are like an old married couple, except that we have the eagerness of youth and newness. (And I expect that will continue forever.)

Anyway, our bonding is continually increasing.

I love you inexpressibly,

FRIDAY, MAY 19, 1989 10:00 AM

My dearest darling Kathy,

Your note came today. More like a letter than a note; so gratifying. Often I focus on only one aspect of you — e.g., your sexuality, your physical affection — and forget about the others. Now I am reminded of your fine mind, and it's still (my exploration of you, that is) like suddenly being transported to a large mansion and looking through the marvelous rooms, being surprised by each one, forgetting one, then coming back to it and again being surprised. What a rich person you are!

Well, what I am now taken by is your intellect. Your creative mind. I want to encourage your use of it as much as possible. Let's take the concept of three loves. Let me free-associate. There's sexual love. Nurturing love, of a parent for a child. Freeing love, of a therapist for a client. Partnership love? Love of God, which seems different, too. God's love for me, which is also different. (Partnership love is a companionate thing, the love of people for each other who are engaged in a project; e.g., comradeship of soldiers in battle.) What about sacrificial love? Submissive love? The love of Anthetic headship? There seem to be many more than three. Any comments? (Merging love?)

Yes, the challenge is to stay conscious. But about bridging any differences that occur (one person being in one love the other in another), can you say more about what you mean?

Yes, we experience and live those things; we can also theorize about them and analyze them.

Now about callings. There seem to be two modes of living (at least): one, where we simply plod through life, doing the next routine thing that happens; another, where we are called by something to bring forth our power. My work can be a calling, in which case it is something that grips me; or it can be a mundane job. In sex, I can be called. (By my fantasies? By the requests of the other? By the relationship itself?) Or I can go through the motions. In a relationship, I can be called by the solid presence of the other. With God I can be called. A lecture (or a Jungian conference) can be the occasion for "milk-pitcher learning," in which the speaker pours out information into the glasses of the audience — or it can be an occasion where I am called to think, to question, to formulate my own ideas, to challenge the speaker to delve deeper.

What are the characteristics of a calling? It expands me, not just adds to me. It evokes, not just provides supplies. Instead of "giving" me strength, it evokes my own strength. It helps me exercise unused muscles. It fulfills me. It requires that I take the initiative, that I be accountable. Responsible. It stirs my depths, not rearranges my surface. It gives intensity. It makes me alive. It enlivens me. It makes my life an adventure.

But it has more risks than (what's the opposite of calling? Of being called? Is it being rescued? Being passive?)… I must deal with my inner critic, who tells me to play it safe. But calling connects me with my primary energy.

The opposite of calling is gray everydayness, dull routine, etc.

Being called is maieutic, in the Socratic sense; the caller is a midwife, not a charismatic guru who requires dependence.

Well, Kathy Jo, thank you for being intellectually receptive. Thank you for being my counterpart-genius. My intellectual companion. The one who calls me to my greatness. The one whom I in turn call to her greatness. We synergistic twins!

Now, I can't quite believe that you need to connect (via telephone) on a sexual level. (Do girls really like sex? Do you?) I guess so. I think I will someday be convinced. Keep up the demonstrations, girl.

You write: "How important it is for the one experiencing the sexual arousal to have an other to receive that aroused outpouring of reverent lust." Oh, yes. It gives us affirmation. It calls forth more sexuality in us.

Yes, we crave reverent lust, and so much so that we are willing to accept its simulacrum. You wrote: "It just occurred to me as I wrote it." The fact that you were writing to me; that you knew I would read your words, meant that I (even without knowing it, without actually doing anything) was calling forth your ideas. Your great ideas (much, much better--more profound, more practical at the same time, more carefully reasoned, more solid—than the ones you heard at the Jungian conference) sometimes occur in our interaction, as I call you to greatness, to your genius. I love that, Kathy. Some day we will put on a seminar that the Jungians can attend in order to straighten out their thinking.

Yes, what we know now about relationships is in

the process of being formulated and our knowledge is not as clearly articulated as it will be later. I don't think it's fragile as much as provisional and partly tacit. Once we formulate it, it will be strong and ready for public presentation. (Much of it would be totally misunderstood at this point.)

Oh Kathy darling, we've got to get married!

The world needs us, dear. Please don't underestimate this. I have spent the last three or four years positioning myself—finding where my position is in the hierarchy of modern thought. And it's pretty high, my position. It just needs some further development and elaboration and articulation. The fact that not only can you join me, but that you and I are on the same level and can co-create something quite new—this fact is so wonderful I can hardly believe.

God, thank you again for giving me the gift of this dear woman, and thank you for making me the gift that is given to her. We revel in what you have done for us, and we want you to infuse our lives with your love and care and enjoyment of us.

Oh, Kathy, I love you so much!

NOTE: On Tuesday, May 23, I flew to Oakland to spend 10 days with Jim. When we walked into the motel room where we would stay, I was charmed to find that he had been there earlier that day. On the desk were fresh flowers and See's candy. It was an important ten days—the longest we had spent together in the flesh. We began "twigging," our name for buying "twigs" for our nest; i.e., home items like dishes and comforters. Our sexuality deepened. Jim introduced me to his group people. And he showed me Berkeley and San Francisco, where he had lived for 25 years.

FRIDAY, JUNE 2, 1989 11:35 AM

My darling Kathy,

Two more months, sweetheart, and we will be married! We sure are working hard on our differences and glitches. I think we will continue to find elegant win/win solutions, and we'll learn enough to (if you want) do couples groups and write a book on relationships (also if you want). With each glitch or difference, I sometimes think "Oh, this can't work," and then you or I say some magic words, and the thing gets resolved. I think we have worked on all the deepest ones. From now on, we'll just have to deal with chocolate/vanilla issues. I'm glad we did all this before we got married.

Let's see what our remaining differences are:

Jangly places with bakeries and restaurants (Telegraph Ave., Soho in London, Left Bank in Paris). I'll hold your hand tightly as you walk with me, and I'll quit when you've had enough. (Maybe you can be somewhat desensitized and disengaged.)

The Ashram. We'll decide whether to go together, or you separately. Maybe we'll create an Ashram of our own, a better one.

Extravagance in restaurants and clothes. I will take extravagance lessons from you and try to improve.

Stating qualms and dislikes. If I see that you're deep in something (whether play, grief, anger, or whatever), I'll bracket my feeling—unless it's a powerful one—and talk about it later. If it doesn't seem to me that you're in such a feeling, I'll bring up my item. If your child feels hurt and disempowered, you and I will help her. (I may make mistakes and not be aware of the depth of your feeling.)

I have many happy memories of your visit. Going to sleep while spooning you. Braiding ourselves together. The horse story with its long plateau. Going down on you in our new position, and being able to do it all night. Your buying red bikini panties. (Oh, my!) Bathing each other. Buying powder for you at Crabtree & Evelyn's. Cheese Danish at Just Desserts in Embarcadero Center. Chinese food by the ounce. Shopping for a wedding band. Meeting with my group people at 9 o'clock. The sweet notes you left for me to find. Leading your group. Processing our glitches. Stopping for pastry and coffee. Your brushing my hair (exquisite heavenly experience!). Talking about Heidegger. Looking at flowers; smelling the roses. Exotic food at Bubi's. See's candy. Your feeling distant. The deepening of our love for each other (deeper than an infatuation) as we do the hard work necessary for our complex relationship. Our delicious kissing, our mouths and tongues so soft and yielding. The roughness scenario.

Now I want to restate something I said before: I honor and respect your work on callings. I will give you loads of help, not only with content but also with writing. You will finish the book in a year.

(2:10pm) Kathy! I just hung up after our conversation—we're getting married July 28th at 7pm!

I love you Kathy Jo,

Not for just an hour, either,

SATURDAY, JUNE 3, 1989 3:20 PM

My darling Kathy,

I want to tell you: how much I love you…how happy I am at the thought of living day by day with you…how pleased I am at the way we bring up issues and glitches and process them immediately (I know there's nothing seething inside, and that makes me feel calm and secure)…how gratifying it is to be with a woman who is hungry for connectedness…how well we function together…and now how well we discuss professional matters. Oh, Kathy it gets better and better, worse and worse!

We move very fast, darling, and we dig very deep. I love you. Kathy, Kathy, Kathy, Kathy!

Am I ever going to go back to Danica? Never! Even if you were to leave me, I wouldn't. I have now tasted heaven; who would want to return to a concentration camp?

Kathy Jo! Guess what ? By 7:30 pm July 28, 1989, we ought to be married to each other. Joined together by our public declaration, never to be sundered from each other. A unit now. All mingled up.

All I can do is rhapsodize.

I have been looking forward to each of our visits with each other; watching day by day as the days go by impatiently. Now I am waiting for that bigger event: not only my move to Lafayette to live with you but our marriage, our wedding. Our union. The sexual, emotional, and now legal union. Intellectual, too. Affectional, also.

And Kathy! (Yes, my love?) We laugh at the same things! Did you notice? We have a similar sense of humor.

Oh, Love! Oh, love! I am full to overflowing today with love of you.

You are my heart's desire, my dream come true, my dream girl—in the flesh! Soft, warm, comforting, yielding flesh. The flesh I love to hold tightly as we sleep spoonwise. So secure. So expressive of my love for you.

Just rhapsodies here, no content. I guess I am in love. Do you wonder if I want to marry you? I do! As we work through issue after issue, I feel more and more certain. More and more bonded. What will it be like in five years? Solid bonding. Day-by-day ecstasy! Deep satisfaction and contentment. Oh, Kathy! (Yes, my love?) It's just that I love you so much. You sweet girl. Pink-pantied. Voluptuous and sexy.

Oh, I love you!

SUNDAY, JUNE 4, 1989 9:05 PM

Jim honey,

I am still glowing and afterglowing over our conversation today and that wonderful liberating work on my wants and God. Oh, Jim, that was so fantastic. Thank you so extremely much for your love, mentoring, and companionship through that process. It was incredible for me. I love you, Oh God, I love you. We are fantastic together. And Jim. I want you. And I intend to have you as my husband! Oh, Jim, every time we work together I get a lived glimpse of your genius. And each experience is a solidifying of my desire to join you in this work. And to create a work together. To Kathyize it, as you say. & to further Jimize it! & to Kathy & Jimize it!! I feel like I have my swimsuit on and am entering this enticing pool. But I'm cautious. Yet with each step deeper, I am more and more taken with the joy of the water, and its rightness for me. Perhaps soon I'll plunge in!

I'm enclosing the copies of the reminder I sent out. Also the comforter. (I still like our Macy's one better. What do you think?) And here's also a copy of a set of dishes I like, although there's one I like even better that I'll show you when you come. Oh, Jim. I adore you. I can't wait to be husband and wife. God, I long for you. God, I long for Jim. I want him. I want to be his wife. I claim him as my love, my husband. Thank you for giving my life to me, for bringing him into my life.

You are my all, my beloved.

your Kathy

MONDAY, JUNE 5, 1989 3:45 PM

My beloved Kathy,

As it gets closer to our wedding day, my love for you gets worse and worse. Oh, Kathy! Anyway, I can work now. (But I didn't get any book-packing done today.) You darling woman! How I love you! And miss you! (I still seem to think I won't be seeing you until July 28, but I'll be in your arms a week from Thursday, won't I?) (I'm having quite a jumble of feelings: a complex mixture of feelings about you—mostly longing and love—feeling supported by Mama; pain and uncertainty when I think of Cali; pain and sadness when I think of Danica; fear when I think of leaving Berkeley, mixed with excitement and repulsion; fear when I wonder whether I can meet the packing and moving deadline of June 30; worry about getting enough people in my group in Lafayette. I've never had such a mixture of feelings, positive and negative, in my life. I accept and include them all. This I think will be the most growthful year of my life, exceeding even the year I began leading groups.)

Again I am listing all the reasons to get married to you. First, because I love you so much. Then because you and I are having what I always wanted: a perfect Anthetic relationship—and you are a colleague—and you love me, too. Third, because you like to talk about ideas, we share the same interests, and our sex life is so ecstatic. Finally, because I really would like to live in Lafayette. These reasons are hierarchical, the important ones first; the first two are really important. Oh, Kathy, darling! I mush for you. You adorable girl, you! (And you want to please me so much; that means so much to me!) (My gay client asked about our relationship, and I told him how well we related, and he was envious, and what he heard gave him hope and inspiration for his present relationship. He's coming to realize that if you punish someone by withholding yourself from that person, you can't be warm and close, and so it doesn't feel very good.)

Kathy, we will create a masterpiece! (Mama said so.)

You sweet girl! I can't stop telling you how much I love you! (This is another in a series of rhapsodic letters.)

Yes, I will be bringing my clothes to you. My masculine clothes to hang in your feminine closet. (Oh, sweet, sweet Kathy! You dear girl!)

We are bound together by so many things now. Not just glitchwork. But also professional exchanges, interest in words, favorite positions for snuggling in bed, places we like to be touched and touch, restaurants. Oh, Kathy!

I have no content for you; just an outpouring of love.

I love you so much! Please marry me. I'm tired of burning.

I love you,

TUESDAY, JUNE 6, 1989 10:10 AM
(WRITTEN ON BLANK GREETING CARD WITH MARE AND COLT GRAZING ON FRONT)

My dearest love —

How precious you are to me. I have never loved like this, with my whole self — all open; nothing held back. And that is what I bring to you — my whole being — for you to love, honor, cherish, worship lustfully, lay, dominate, go down on, feed, bathe, hold, braid, deep kiss, ride, etc.

Why is this mare looking so content? Because she has been on a high plateau for quite some time with her beloved, wild driving stallion!

Jim, I want to tell you how many things I cherish from my trip to be with you: lunch in the walled garden; spaghetti and pizza; kissing before we brushed our teeth in the morning; bathing each other; walking hand in hand; your coming in my mouth; my finger in your rectum; feeling you holding me in a tight spoon as I wake up; riding BART; pastries & coffee; special juices; our new position for going down on me; brushing your hair; washing your hair; your honoring my candy by resisting your compulsion to eat it all right away; meeting your dear group people; meeting Grace, your barber; working through glitches, both of us hanging in there tenaciously until we're through it to the release and joy on the other side; your singing in the shower; your holding me as we watched TV in bed; middle of the night fucking, you on top; 1st thing in the morning fucking, me on top; pulling your balls up between your legs; sitting in your back office and reading your notes in professional books and reading your novel and knowing you so intimately; our roughness scenario; negotiating dishes;

sitting on a campus bench until we could talk through the emotional stuff; holding each other and drawing comfort from each other after glitch work; walking and walking hand in hand with you; feeling your life energy and feeling myself strengthening physically. There are many others. I'll continue later. I just typed my letter requesting my divorce decree copy and will mail it today. I think July 12 or so is great timing for you to move. I love you so. I'll be waiting for you with our little house by the side of the road all in order! And a paper on the toilet saying, "KATHYIZED"! I adore you, my love —

your Kathy

WEDNESDAY, JUNE 7, 1989 5:01 PM

My dearest Kathy,

I am feeling some stress now; I missed your call, and I needed to talk with you. Thank you for your declaration of love on my answering machine, which I can now play over and over. I'm not sure what's happening to me. I feel some anxiety. Some disorientation. (I feel confident I'll get everything done before July, now.)

But I'm eager to marry you, to have the thing done: the move, the wedding, our house, everything all settled. As I will tell you when I call you, I will need about a week or more to decompress when I arrive in July. Can I have that?

Also as I will tell you, the one image that impels me to work hard at moving is you in your pink and white striped dress, with your pink panties and your promise that I can ravage you wildly as soon as I get there. Ravage? Maybe ravish is a better word. Well maybe just "have my way with your body." I hunger for you so, and you are so delectable and delicious. I am disoriented. Will we be able to rationally plan our wedding?

Oh, Kathy, I love you so! I am so wild and dysfunctional right now. (Will we be a dysfunctional family when we're married?)

Kathy, we must be married soon! I am burning. Being with you a few days at a time is not enough. I am eager for my life to start. Up till now, it was just the preliminaries. I am mad for you, crazy in love with you. I desire you. I must have you. I love you so much. I miss you so much.

Oh, Kathy, please help me;
I'm so distraught.
Love, oh all my love —

WEDNESDAY, JUNE 7, 1989 9:45 PM

My love,

We just spoke an hour ago, and my heart still goes out to you. You are so in need of cosseting. So, sit back, my darling, and let me kythe my love, comfort, and care for you through this letter. Here I am, dear one, coming to you in my pink and white striped dress. Would you like to know what I'm wearing underneath? Well, there's my new pink bra—and my pink bikini panties—and my white garter belt—and my white stockings. Now that you know the smorgasbord that's before you, would you like to see some of it? Oh, you would! Well, would you like to see my pink panties? There—Do you like them? Oh, you want to touch? Well, I'll let you. Oh, so you want to eat my pussy through my panties? Yes, I'll let you. Oh my, I like that! Would you like to rip my clothes off? I'll let you do that too. There goes my dress, my slip, my white stockings—no, let's leave those on, shall we? My bra, my panties. So here I am in my white garter belt and stockings, my cunt hair calling to you. Would you like to lick my cunt? I'll let you, Jim. You do that so well. You expert lover, you. Our new position? Oh yes! I see you looking up at me from your position at my feet. And you lick away at my cunt—and I cream extravagantly! Feast on me, my love. All night. And you see my deep pleasure as you take me to a high plateau. And you feel my nails scratch you and dig painfully into your shoulders as a sign of my rolling exquisite come.

Then may I go down on you? And put my finger in your rectum? To the hilt? And may I hear your gasp of pleasure? And see your face contorted with ecstasy? And will you let me suck you off? And may I beg you to let it all come out? And will you come spurting warmly and generously in my mouth? And will I hear you scream your orgasm to the world? And shall I delight in you and your wild sexuality? Oh, yes! And then will I leave my mouth on your cock to suck off the final spurts when you are ready? Then slowly pull my finger out from its warm, tight place? And then I hold you and hear you lose yourself in a litany of whispered "Kathys."

Oh, Jim, I love you, honey. I adore you. I want to be married to you — to be settled. To give you ecstasy whenever you want it. To receive your lovemaking whenever I want it. To bathe you. To apply very warm wet cloths to your forehead until all your anxiety is dissolved. To soak you in the tub until you are totally relaxed. To dry you off and lead you to our bed where my naked flesh ministers serenity to your naked flesh. I am your oasis. Rest in me.

your Kathy

THURSDAY, JUNE 8, 1989 12 NOON

My sweet fiancée,

Two cards came today! Kathy, I need your written notes and letters so much! I need both: phone calls and letters. I love all the things you say. I love your dear horse cards, and now the horse has new meaning for me. I still can't believe you are so perfect for me.

And your letters! Mine seem so banal; yours are so thrilling. (Say, we don't have a stuffed tiger yet. See how disjointed my thinking is?)

Kathy, keep telling me about pink panties (yours). Those things inspire the part of me that needs to pack.

Yes, kissing before we brushed our teeth in the morning: how exquisitely extravagant and accepting! About glitch work: we both did hang in there, didn't we? We're pretty good aren't we? There's always release and joy on the other side, isn't there?

I forgot about watching PBS in bed, in each other's arms. How nice! And more, you leaving your panties lying on the floor; the little brook on campus.

Kathy, the card is wonderful! Those verses (on all the cards you sent) seem written just for us. Thank you for not wanting to let the sun set on our anger or unresolved hurt. I never had that before; many times I have lain stiffly beside a woman who did not want (or was not able to) resolve glitches. That's a concentration camp.

Yes, let us plight our troth, my betrothed one. Let us betroth each other. Troth is associated with truth and means fidelity. Plight means to take care of, to pledge.

You are my betrothed. We celebrated our betrothal at our engagement party. And after our wedding, you will be my uxorial woman, and I will be uxorious, too (excessively fond of a wife).

You write that you will climax on our wedding day. Will that be part of the ceremony? Should we announce it in advance so people will know what is happening? Would even Mama be freaked out by it?

Kathy, I love your statement that you will reach into my core. I want that in our vows. A vow is a promise, but I want our vows to be avowals: open declarations. To avow: to declare openly, bluntly and without shame. I don't want to promise to love you, because it sounds too much like a should, and my love for you must be free-flowing; it would be like promising you that I will continue breathing, or continuing to speak English to you. Yes, let us have avowals, not vows. What do you think? (Or have vows and by the term mean avowals.) (Is that a word you can say so often that you no longer know what it means?) (Does it sound like the opposite of consonants?)

Oh, Kathy dear, I love to hear your words of endearment for me! They sustain me, those sweet buffers! Bring them on, amass them, deploy them, pour them out right into my yearning heart.

I long for you so much,

MONDAY, JUNE 12, 1989 12:45 PM

My own sweetheart,

One by one I am snapping the cables that keep me tied to Berkeley. The first, some time ago, was my relationship with Danica. It was the easiest. The second was when I announced my intentions to my groups and clients. That was more difficult; I felt guilty. But it was done. The third was my phone call to my landlord yesterday. Then this morning I delivered to him the letter I am legally required to submit: giving him 30 days' notice. We talked in a very friendly way; he offered to store some of my gear if I needed it. (He's a nice guy; a former math teacher.) That last one was difficult. Now that it's done, I feel freer. (Now I've got to move!) (But can I do it? Maybe he'll give me extra time if I need it.) I'm thinking more and more of taking Eastern Airlines to New Orleans. Well, we'll see.

The next cable will be snapped when I call the bookstores and then when I call a moving company. One by one, the ties to Berkeley are being cut. Each one is difficult; each one is freeing. Free, my darling, to come to you. To live with you. Then to marry you. It's getting set in concrete now, our marriage. We've got to go through with it.

Yes, I am leaving Berkeley. Going to a heavenly new place in Louisiana. Who would have thought it! Me moving! Out of the state! Down South no less! To Louisiana, of all places! And to Lafayette, not New Orleans! (Thank God for the good restaurants there, especially the Piccadilly.) And Thank God for you, my sweetheart and soon-to-be wife. Yes, I will be bewifed. Is that right? Will you be behusbanded? I will make good on the troth I plighted. Plaught? You have my troth. But I have a trothache for you. Is there a dentist in the house?

Is it all right that I am so sexually wild and desperate about your sweet body? Will I try to fuck the tray table, even when it is in an upright position, on the airplane? Will the flight attendant come? Will I come? Will I stop talking about coming? Will the sweet vision of you in your pretty pink bikini panties stimulate me so much that I'll leave everything here and start running toward Louisiana? Yes, to the last one. Maybe. Well, you know how much I adore you. Or if not, I'll tell you when I see you. Kathy, I'm wild about you! I love you so much; it's so deep and powerful! I pour it out onto your soul, to comfort it, to warm you to the bone, to infuse your mind and body with the warm liquor of my love and adoration. Oh, Kathy!

And today, dear one! Today I'll be with you. This afternoon! This very afternoon! To hold you in my arms. To grab you in a wild frenzy! Oh Kathy! Sweetheart of mine! You belong to me. You are mine, Kathy. I own you. You are not your own any more. Rest in comfort and assurance that you are owned by a gentle tender loving man who cares for you in his strong male way, who protects you from danger, who attends to your slightest qualm, who surveys you with his masculine glance and casts his strong male look of approval over you, all parts of your body (including your dear pimples and sweet thighs), and over all the intercourses and

couplings and sexual experiences you have ever had —
who blesses them all, who loves them all, who loves each
and every one of the sexual partners you have ever had
for whatever pleasure and/or love they have brought to
your dear self and body.

Oh, soon, Kathy!

Love,

TUESDAY, JUNE 13, 1989 11:50 AM

My dearest love

Day after tomorrow we'll be together. Oh, glory! I need you so. I need to be with you. And you need me. We are for each other. By the time you get this, you'll be back home (Berkeley, that is), and I know you'll be needing a connection with me — a letter. So I want to have this waiting for you — as a sign of how much I think about you; how I look to your needs; and how I know what's best for you. It's very good for you, Jim, to have frequent contact with me.

Oh, this archetypal matrix we're living in is incredible. I feel that we're doing very well in it. We're conscious of it, and we're respecting our limits. Yet, the limits are expanding all the time. And we're more and more able to swim around in it. God, you are the man for me. You are so huge! And I need that. You know that I am living in surprise, as new levels of my own psyche are revealed (e.g., the men in my life and the part they've played).

Now it's Wednesday, and we've just hung up. I love talking with you. We are so close, my Jim. We are one; you and I. We will ritualize that oneness at our wedding, but we are already one.

And you are doing so well in your extravagance lessons. You are doing what every teacher hopes her students will do: putting the lessons into practice. Yes, you are allowing your life to be transformed by me, by my touch on you. And I too am being transformed by you. Amazing that despite the fact that I'm staying in Lafayette, my relationship life has been re-ordered. You are now at the top, the focus, the primary one. All others have been displaced to make room for and to support your primary place for me.

It was a joy to read your Anthetic Values Manual and to see our relationship described. Jim, honey, you are living in your most intimate relationship a fulfillment of the vision you have for ideal relationships. Truly you have come to a time of ripeness. The fruit is full and luscious on the vine, and I get to share its harvesting. So I bite into the fruit (succulent like a peach) of your maturity and ripeness and let the juice run down my chin. Every time we work on a glitch; every time we have wild, open and free sexual communion; every time we care and empathize with each other; every time you verbally pour out your love for me; every time you take a risk to change, actually transform your patterns (e.g. extravagance, moving to Lafayette, letting me influence your thinking) — every time I rapturously experience your ripeness. I love walking through this orchard of yourself and of our relationship hand in hand with you.

My engagement ring is shining, sparkling with life and love on my hand. It must be picking up the power of our love that's coursing through me.

Now I am ready for our quotidian life (thanks for the new word). I want to lie in your arms in bed (under our beautiful comforter) or sit leisurely at our dining table and discuss transpersonal psychology and Eugene Gendlin and any other ideas that come to us. What a rich intellectual interchange we share. And our intellectual communion will lead us to a desire for sexual expression. And reverent lust will reign as I push you back on the bed. And we will bring each other to a high plateau. And you will see my face transformed by intense pleasure and you will hear my voice released in a rolling come.

Oh, Jim, I want to be married to you, to share life with you. I love how your influence is freeing my love voice (the voice which expresses the love within me in all ways).

God, you are my perfect lover. The man I have awaited.

Your Kathy

MONDAY, JUNE 19, 1989 10:15 PM

Jim, my beloved one —

Oh, you've only been gone 5 hours, and I am already longing for you. However, my longing is moderated, because I'm still pulsing and glowing from your visit. Oh, darling, this was our best visit yet! Some major reasons for my saying this are: 1) the recognition I had of how solid our relationship is. For me it is as solid as a rock. I felt this from the moment you arrived. Our lovemaking that arrival day reflected that for me. The communion was all fleshed out, no gaps, no boniness! It was total communion, like I've never experienced before. This communion was possible because: 2) I was more surrendered to you and to our love than I have ever been. More surrendered; more given to it; more laid wide open. 3) Our skills are sharpened now so that we are negotiating more smoothly. And I am able to rest in the fact that our love can contain glitches and negotiating with great strength. 4) I am seeing that you are totally committed to the deepest relationship possible with me; that you want as much closeness as I do. 5) Our creativity is blossoming; for example, our last night tub bath, soaking in the pleroma, I can't tell you what bliss that was for me. Actually our entire time together was pure bliss. Another bliss: I just washed your clothes! Oh, Jim, I have a man's clothes to wash! And I hung your shirts and slacks next to my pink and white striped dress in my closet. That is such a satisfying feeling to me. And I folded your underwear and socks. Mmm. I'm so happy that you left your clothes, etc. with me. It helps. I'm also following your flight tonight, praying for you, thinking of you and checking with American to find out how your flights are going. I'm so sorry for you that your

Dallas plane was late. I know you'll be so tired when you get home. Bless your heart.

Oh, Jim honey, the joy of waking up in the night and plastering myself to your back, throwing my arm over you. Then waking up in the morning to your loving greeting: "Good morning, sweetheart."

Jim, I tell you again: I am totally sexually satisfied with you. You are my man — a superb lover — the Best. I love being held in your arms so much. I just want to live there! And even in your arms while you read! Oh, you just don't tune me out ever. What a delight! I even love how you talk me to sleep! Actually it's sort of sweet to me how I fall asleep in your arms while you're talking. I know it's annoying to you, but it's very sweet for me. Your arms are my haven (and my heaven). Jim, I want to, am ready to, and am committed to going even deeper, if that is possible. Let's call each other to the deep places. Your call upon me was magical! Do you remember? What a rich visit. And Jim, honey, thank you for calling me to pretty panties and other lingerie. It's a joy to celebrate and explore my femininity. And I love my new love names: "Kitty Kat" and "Pet." They are so full of love for me. I feel it. You don't know how much I bask in them.

Thanks too, love, for all the twigging. It's all piled up in my room now. And I'm so excited to make our home together. Even our twigging was delightful. Thank you, sweetheart.

Jim, dear, you were more open and surrendered to me and to us this visit too. It seemed so to me. Did you feel it? I love our intimacy. Your proprietorship over me and my things — like my checkbook, my writing tablet, etc. Oh, I am full of bliss. And I celebrate you, us, God's gift. Glory — you singer of songs, reciter of poems, and lover of mine.

I am all yours from my polished fingernails to my Jim-kissed toes.

I adore you,

Your Kathy

TUESDAY, JUNE 20, 1989 12:05 PM

My darling wife-to-be,

I want to mention all the blissful experiences we had on my last visit to my new home: red beans and rice at the Cajun Café; apple pie and roast turkey at Osborne's; Crab salad, banana pudding, fruit, and vanilla pudding at Piccadilly; hot fudge sundae at TCBY; our bath ritual (yes, Minx, food first, then physical contact); our smoothly functioning oral sex; waking up in the morning and finding you there—someone to reach for—grabbing your dear buns in my frenzy; my crying as we talked to the minister; getting things clear with the attorney; your fear that the only place I'll want to eat will be cafeterias; deciding on dishes; buying two lamps; buying towels and shower curtains (especially the yellow one from that nice Southern gentleman); meeting people as we go about our errands; the sudden rainstorm (I'm glad there's so little rain in Southern Louisiana—and not many hot days, either)—(Yes, that was Jim's little humor); the two groups, Phase I and II; the cool Wesley place, and outside the warm summer sunshine; (Aren't you glad I proposed to you on the steps of Girard Hall—so you don't have to go so far to see the place and remember what happened?); our McDonald breakfast; getting everywhere on time; sodas at Borden's; my loud cries as I came; singing Christian songs on the way to Rayne; your dismay about my not liking any tables; showing me your new pink panties and white ones, too; how incredibly desirable you are, you little minx!; your strong feelings when I didn't like the table; our new way of indicating dislike; Oh Kathy dearest! I love you so!

And now I feel despair at looking over what I have to do here. Despair and strong motivation. You mention in your letter that you look to my needs. Yes, Pet, I want you to. Please do. It means so much to me. Please be invasively intimate with me, even at the risk of making mistakes. I'll try not to complain too sharply if that happens. You do know what's best for me. It is indeed very good not only to have, as you've written, frequent contact with you, but continuous contact with you.

Yes, our archetypal matrix. We are living it. Freely and as fully as we dare. Our limits are indeed expanding all the time. We've come a long way since Asilomar, since Pawling. We were so tentative then, so timid, checking each other out: Can he accept this? Can she bear to hear (and do) that? And he did, and she could. You are living in surprise, huh, Kittycat? Good. I am too. I didn't know you were, so much. You seem to take everything so easily. Thank you for your fruit image. The ripe fruit being bitten into. Ripe and mature. As you say, the orchard of our relationship. The fruits ripe for our plucking. And feeding to each other.

Oh, I will pack fast and furiously today.

All my love, Kittycat,

TUESDAY, JUNE 20, 1989 5:55 PM

My darling Kittycat,

Here are some things that thrill me so much that I feel a ripple, a pulsation going through my body, centered somewhere between my stomach and my heart, a kind of little earthquake of love, a weak feeling that is also poignant and sharp as a love-bite:

When you tell me you like oral sex; that you love to give me pleasure, that you feel merged with me as I roar out my ecstasy while coming. You like this too!

Holding your warm, large, soft, tender, grabbable body in bed: in the middle of the night, or while we go to sleep, or when I awake in the morning and open my eyes to see you there beside me, easily accessible, wanting to be touched, wanting to be grabbed and held

Watching you in your pink bikini panties, white garter belt, white stockings, pink bra. A vision of loveliness, of intense desirability; as I mentioned, far far better than any Playboy picture

Any adjustment of my clothing you make, or arranging my hair, or stealing a bite of food from my plate—any intrusive act you perform on me

The awe and deep feeling in your eyes when I speak to you of spiritual things from my headship; your responsiveness to the power that pours from me

Your tears when I confirm your femininity with my strong masculine approval and validation

Your boldness in washing me in the shower

Your intense pleasure when we agree on, then purchase, a new twig

The slightest whiff of your perfume

The tangy sultry sweet slightly-musky smell of your skin

6:10 am, Wednesday, June 21. Now I must write about two things you told me last night: That I have great power over you and need not be so brusque to exercise it (that's the first one) and that you take great pleasure in doing things for me. These are two blind spots I have. I think I have little power over you; that you will leave me at any moment (my scared child thinks this). I can't imagine that you take pleasure in doing very many things for me; my programming tells me you will quickly get tired of doing something (programming from my past relationships) for me. But you said I was nowhere near your limit for granting requests: 40% you said. I need to let all this sink in. I feel chagrined that I didn't know it before.

Oh, sweet Kittycat, I didn't know! How dumb I am. I didn't really know how much you loved me. My Inner Critic told me no one could love me that much, so I thought you were just using lovers' words, like "I'd do anything for you," where you mean, "a lot" but not "anything at all." Yes, I've got to let this sink in.

(3:30pm Wednesday). Well, we have gotten through a big glitch, sweetheart. You are seeing that perhaps there were destructive (disempowering) aspects of your relationship with Cali. Infantilizing. (No, I'm still not sure of the exact idea here, but that something is not quite right, I am sure.) Your enmeshment with her—especially her drive to give you advice—these things are danger signals to me, though I can't quite tell what the issue is. Her statement that you might get pregnant (as though you don't know what you're doing), and that she would have to raise the baby (as bizarre a thought as I've heard in a long time)—Yes, I want you to see that these are not ordinary concerns of a caring person. Her judgmental statements to me: "Jim you've got her where you want her." And: "You say she doesn't have to have sex with you, but there you are, standing next to her with your pants unzipped." This is not caring, not loving. That she should think this is perfectly normal; that she should say it—well, there's something funny about it.

That you should defend her to me also doesn't seem right. I'm thinking: Can Kathy see her clearly? Can she really see the judgmentalism? Is she immune from it?

And then when you yourself are just a little bit judgmental toward me; rarely, of course. But not easily detected.

Anyway, sweet Kathy, I want us to be a unit, one flesh. With no interference from anyone. Mama has been a dear about this: no advice, no officiousness at all. She respects us. Has learned (as I have with my kids) to keep hands off. (It isn't easy for a parent.)

Well, we'll see. I am with you as always. My hand in yours, holding it tightly. My love surrounding you.

Now, look: I love you with an infinite love; you are the one for me, with no doubts or hesitation at all. This bond grows stronger with each glitch we work on. I love the way you process. You are so open. I would not have picked a girl who could not process. You are superb! It is so necessary for the intensity and depth we want. Without our ability to process, we would be lost, sweetheart.

I am for you. I am moving to Lafayette to marry you and live with you for the rest of our lives. In Heaven. With occasional trips to a restaurant but mostly in bed with you, your dear sweet naked flesh entwined in mine. Our mouths touching so we can easily kiss as we whisper love words to each other. How rapturous!

I choose you above (way above, as a matter of fact) all other women.

Sweetheart, I love you so much! I want us to create an indissoluble unity.

Kathy, I feel very solid with you!

Love,

WEDNESDAY JUNE 21, 1989 4:45 PM

My darling,

Yes, tell me what you would like from me, like calling you darling. I want to thrill you, heal you, fill you, delight you. I want your life with me to be fruition — fruit bearing of all the dreams you've held of relationship. So I gladly call you darling. I gladly wear pink panties and rehabilitate my panty wardrobe. For you, I'll do anything, Jim. You are the love of my life. My man. I forsake all others and cling to you. And I know you receive me with open arms. Darling, I love that your arms are always open to me, morning, night, midday. When I ask and when I don't ask. I want to live in your arms. And we come pretty close to my living there.

Jim, I just got through skimming Pathfinders, by Gail Sheehy. I wanted to read her chapters on satisfying relationships. Well, they had some good points: the desire to spend lots of quality time together; fun making; risk taking; being devoted to each other and to the relationship above all else. And all of these things are good. We're doing them. But our relationship surpasses even the ones she surveyed that were exceptionally good. They mentioned nothing of the primal nor of the archetypal nor of the spiritual. So our primal layers and headship dimensions are superlative. They catapult us to a place beyond where even the best relationships live. I see all this. And I celebrate it. Oh, Jim, the communion we share is so beautiful, so deep. I am in a place of awe now.

10:50 Thursday, June 22… Dearest one, we've just spoken. And you asked that I write the words I said to you. So here they are, my love. I have the strong conviction that I want to enjoy every moment, every second of our time together. The glitch work, the rapture, the talks, the affection, the phone calls, the longing — all of it. It means we're alive, we're fiercely in love, and we have a now, a past and a future.

I see that we fulfill the multilayered ages of our lives. By this I mean, we meet and hold each other as babies, parenting, soothing, loving, and celebrating our life spark. I love holding you as my baby. But we don't just minister to our inner babies, we also love the 4-year old in each other, and now we are going to play together, share toys, set up our own playhouse. We also love the awkward pre-teen in each other, the one who's attracted to the other, yet is painfully shy and self-doubting. And we are the teen lovers, who pass notes and walk home arm in arm and love to neck! And we are the newlyweds infatuated with each other, wanting to spend all our time in bed, to dehydrate ourselves with sex! And we are the young professional colleagues, developing our work together, joining in a project we both believe in and can find full expression through. And we are the old married couple, sure of each other's love, comfortable with each other, replete with a rich past; our own mythology and symbols.

This is awesome.

I am so proud of you. I see the worth of your work and am glad that therapist and Chevron see it too. You are a powerful theoretician and practitioner. I'm proud to stand shoulder to shoulder with you.

I told Mama that you said about her, "What a dear woman. How I love her." And again she was blessed and touched and healed. She said, "I guess you'll have the house all ready for him when he comes." And I said, "No, I'll wait till he gets here. Jim wants it to feel like his house too. We want to do it together." And she was so affirming and said, "How great that he cares. Most men don't care."

Talking with you, love, gives me such opportunities for clarifying my stand. I'm thinking specifically of this morning as I spoke to you of the closed doors in rehab practice. I hadn't articulated that yet. So again you perform the animus function for me. Thank you for listening and being so interested in me. Thank you too for the generous gift of opening your work to me, now even more, sharing our processing of possibilities. And the gift of wanting me to work side by side with you. I want to work with you, Jim. I want your umbrella for the development of my spirituality work. Again you deepen the work you began at Asilomar when you said that my primary gift was in spirituality. And I thrilled and blossomed to the recognition and affirmation of myself. You see me! You really see me! And revere me! Oh, glory.

Oh my beloved, I am speechless with love, deeper than love for you. Soak yourself in it as you pack, work, and prepare to come home to me.

I adore you, my darling.

Your Kathy

TUESDAY, JUNE 22, 1989 12:15 PM

Dear Sweetheart of mine,

I've just come from shopping, and I have some bad feelings that I'll tell you about when you call me this evening after prayer group. I love you, but I'm feeling wounded; hurt, dismayed, a bit angry, forlorn. I know that by the time you read these words, we will have processed it all and everything will be okay. Damn this letter lag! But writing you about it helps. I don't want to mention content at this time. I do love you, Kittycat.

But I'm so troubled by this thing; it's like a dark cloud. I'll be glad when we're together, and there will be no delay in talking things out. I have faith, sweetheart, that we can work on this and come up with a good resolution. Oh, I feel so bad!

I do love you; I am committed to you; I can't wait till we get married.

Forlornly (temporarily),

And lovingly (permanently),

FRIDAY, JUNE 23, 1989 5 PM

Dear Little Bunny,

Well, we have done some good work, haven't we? I feel even more solid about our relationship, even stronger in my love for you—which must mean that maybe today I don't feel as solid or as strong, since by tomorrow, I will feel solider and stronger. Well, I guess that's true. Right now, it's more than I've ever had before, more than I know other people usually have. So this is pretty damn good. But I can see a gap here and there. Will she go on processing at the superior level she has been doing it on? Will she turn on me and start accusing me of this and that? Will she try to punish me by withdrawing? Will she zing me? Can I trust that our glitchwork will continue to be resolved? Will she still love me afterward, or will she say, Oh, Jim, this is too hard. I'll give up; it seems hopeless. Too much of a hassle to relate to you. I don't think any of these things will happen, but the fact that they are questions means I have the capacity tomorrow to love you even more than today as my fears are allayed.

Your wonderful card came today. With the shower. Yes, Kitty Kat, I want to be showered with heavy affection and mighty love. We each need that, after our glitchwork. I do want to grow into trusting that you love me a lot. (And I want you to grow into trusting that I will not return to Danica, that I will always be there for you, that I will never go away.)

We are calling each other to great things, Pet. We each call each other to greater depth, greater merging, greater union. Our marital union. And we each call the other to maintaining identity, not losing oneself in the other. I call you to your femininity, in terms of lingerie. You call me to my masculine headship. We each call the other to surrender to the love that wants to flow through us and give it its strongest voice possible, its most expressive and spontaneous voice. We call each other to inclusive growth—I to include my shamed child, you to include your little girl who feels such pain at not having gotten what she wanted and now feeling she never will. We call each other to spiritual gifts. You call me to accept and trust your love.

And we are each growing into what we are called to be and do. It will be difficult for a while, but soon we will have the results of these callings as a foundation upon which to deploy and express and exercise our personal power, making a big splash in the world.

We are eagles, my darling, and let us not forget that.

So our glitchwork gives us, ultimately, more power. Power to confront a negative feeling in the other. Power to trust. Power to soothe our little child parts, as they feel scared by the high voltage of this relationship.

Your letter came today, too, all scented with your marvelous perfume. It evokes you very strongly for me. Yes, we surrendered to each other and to the love that flowed. I'm glad you wrote: "I am seeing that you are totally committed to the deepest relationship possible with me, that you want as much closeness as I do." Yes.

Dear Kathy, I love you so much. I feel like a teenager in high school with my girl, each of us fully committed to the other, ignoring others who would come on to us.

It's very sweet.

You write, "Jim, I want to, am ready to, and am committed to going even deeper." Me too, Little Bunny. Yes, me too. As deep as we can go, with all engines full ahead, nothing held back, everything right out there for the other to see.

Thank you for liking your new pet names, my sweetheart. I feel some shame in telling you them. (I'm supposed to be tough and strong and not use love names.) As you write, they are indeed full of love, vehicles for my deep love for you.

8am Saturday—Today I will call you at noon! My love is indeed stronger today than it was yesterday; I trust more today that you love me than I did yesterday. Oh, I love you, Little Bunny! You are the woman for me out of all others. I choose you. (And our work together needs you.)

Oh, Kathy, how much I love you!

Little Bunny of mine!

My heart longs for you.

My wet tongue misses yours; it yearns for its partner.

My body feels lost without yours.

TUESDAY, JUNE 27, 1989 8:35 AM

My darling Little Bunny,

I have now sold all the good books, the ones I have delivered to bookstores, and all that remains bookwise is to call a bookstore and ask them to pick up the rest. Time now seems to be going by very fast; I hope I can accomplish everything I have to. Well, it looks okay; these fears are just stuff. I think.

Now, dearest wife-to-be of mine. I want to remind you of some things. (I uncovered some notes from Pawling). Remember eating that muffin in that little grocerystore-restaurant? And my quart of chocolate milk? (90 cents I think it was or more.) And the woman in the LaGuardia airport I told we were getting married to? And your telling me, "I can abandon myself only to a man." And your asking me (for the first time, I think), in the Pawling restaurant, "Are you going away?"

And now I want to tell you how much you mean to me. First of all, that you wanted to be with me in San Francisco at my Chevron workshop. No one has ever wanted that before. I felt very loved. It must be what you felt when I said I wanted to be with you at the Pawling seminar and got airline reservations so we could fly together. It sure is a nice feeling, a solid feeling, to know the other person likes you that much.

And now I want to list all the things I love about you, that (most of which) I've never gotten before.

First, that you do in fact want to be with me. Actively. You are attracted to me.

Second, that we can talk about ideas in our

field. Psychotherapy, personal growth, Anthetics, spirituality.

Third, that you are intelligent.

Fourth, that we are colleagues. This is not the same as #2, since many colleagues do not want to talk about ideas. We are both working on books; we can work together leading groups; there's no need to explain things to each other at great length.

Your liking for physical closeness. Snuggling, cuddling, flesh-to-flesh touching. You body soothes me. I've had physical closeness before but never this voluptuous, languorous, relaxing.

Expressiveness of love. You like to express love to me, and I to you. This is quite rare. It's rare for me to find someone who can receive my expressiveness; not just rare—it has never happened. And who can match it.

Willingness to work on stuff. Hardly anyone is; hardly anyone can do it as well as you (no one, in fact, that I know, except me). This permits great depth and honesty and closeness in our relationship.

Great depth and honesty and closeness. Emotionally, that is. I can say all the shameful things to you I want. I can express and exercise my power as much as I want.

Your strong need to resolve conflict. I love this. I never had it. I match it with my own. It's very rare. You do not withdraw.

Your nonjudgmentalism. You accept me. I've never had anything remotely close to this before.

Your valuing of critical thinking. Many women who are capable of emotional closeness aren't interested in thinking critically. Very rare combination.

Our paradoxical relating. Your submission to me; my Anthetic headship of you. How strange! How wonderful! How liberating! I never dreamed this was possible, though part of me yearned for it, without clearly knowing what it was. We create and invent our relationship as it goes; we discard any cliché tendencies. (We craft the kind of sexual relationship we want; the kind that gives us the most communion, intimacy, and pleasure—and to hell with what the sex manuals call normal.)

Your commitment to marriage. Our devotion to this state. Not abandoning each other when the going gets rough or the strong feelings arise. I've never had this, either.

Your nondogmatic experiential spirituality. Not orthodox or doctrinaire. Your acceptance of my spirituality.

Your commitment to pleasing me. Oh, Kitty Kat, how intensely pleasureful this is; how much I value it, appreciate it. (And I'm committed to pleasing you.) We have little or no stuff around this; our wishes to please are free-flowing. Panties, Dishes, Massages. Hairpulling. Cossetting. Dining out. Saying things. (Not saying things.) Pants. Shoes. Hat. And so on. I've never had anywhere near this much, though I've always been willing to give.

Our verbality. Wordplay. Concern with correct usage. I've had this before, but not with someone so smart.

Your being responsible. Dependable. Sharply focused.

Usually with people who can speak emotionalese, there's a don't-give-a-damn attitude, which you have none of. Very rare combination: emotional expressiveness and responsibility.

Of the above, I've had some of the following with Elayna: #5, #6, #11, #16, #17. But none of the others.

Oh, here's #18: Your sweet temperedness, your optimism. I've been with too many gloomy and disgrungled people (I wanted to write "disgruntled," but I think "disgrungled" is better.)

Anna had some of #1, #5, #6, #9, #10, #15, and #17; also #18.

My ex-wife had #17; tiny bits of others.

It's rare to find #2 combined with the others. It's very rare to find #7, #8, #10, #11, #12, #13, #14, #15, #16, and #18. (And I've got them all in one girl! Plus all the others!)

Well, this is by way of telling you how ideal you are; how you are in fact my ideal woman. There is no flaw in you: I would not want you more intelligent than I (you might become pedantic); or younger (you'd be too callow); or older (I like young girls, like you).

Oh here's #19: You are creative; you offer original input instead of just following my lead. No one has ever done that. Very rare.

And here's #20: You read about relationships and share ideas with me instead of just slogging blindly along. I love this! I am excited whenever I think of this. Also rare.

And then there's #21: You challenge my ideas. No one has ever done this thoughtfully and intelligently.

You give me pause. You make me think. I love that. This is very rare, too.

What about #22: You have a sexy body; you are lovely; you are a vision of feminine beauty; your body is better than any Playboy bunny I have ever seen pictures of. You excite me: just looking at you, just hearing your sultry voice, my cock begins lubricating when you talk. The truth is I have never been with (or seen) anyone who is nearly as sexually desirable as you.

You also are with me sexually (Number 23). Very, very rare. We merge, even if it's just me masturbating.

Also there's #24: You ask me questions about myself; you are interested in me; you are concerned about me; you think about me, telling me you think I'd be tired (I was) and you say, "Bless your heart." Oh, Little Bunny, how glorious that is! And rare.

On top of all that, there's #25: You like Anthetics. I can't tell you how happy this makes me. To have my wife by my side in this great work. Oh, Kathy! I love you so.

And then (#26) you live in the wonderful city of Lafayette (with those great restaurants, fine people, etc. — low crime; warm climate. And it never gets hot (!), nor does it rain much(!).

How about #27: You have a rich, lush, gentle Southern accent. Oh, my!

Well, then, there's #28: You produce large quantities of nice tasty delicious goopy cream from your dear vagina for me to lap up, eat, and swallow down. Oh, how I love to eat the cream from your cunt! You produce much more than other girls. Yummm! Slurp!

And then -- #29: You have a dear Mama who loves you and blesses our union, and who loves me, and gives me permission to go down on you and eat your delicious pussy.

Well, there are more, a bunch here in #30: You don't smoke, drink, take drugs, etc.

How about #31: You are refined, not coarse, though there is a nice naughty coarse side of you I love. Another paradox.

Here's another: #32: You easily come to orgasm. How satisfying that is. However, it deprives me of the opportunity to eat your cunt longer. But your comes are so good to commingle myself with.

Then: we share the same desires in activities: mostly to be together, in each other's arms. But also to go to seminars, conferences, the APA convention, etc. That's #33.

Also, our taste in home furnishings is close enough: #34. Restaurants, too.

For another thing, we dislike the same things: opera, hiking, camping, ballet, concerts, museums, long shopping trips. #35.

A minor thing, this #36, but you are shorter than I am.

Number 37 is your willingness to give me extravagance lessons.

And you are considerably younger than I--#38.

Well, Little Bunny, these are just some of the reasons I love you, want to marry you, would never leave you, find you the ideal woman for me, my choice above, far above, all other women — no one can hold a candle to you.

There's also #39: we share a sense of humor.

And #40: We are soul mates, twins, counterparts.

And #41: We complement each other. You are softer, gentler; I am more confrontive, blunter.

Well, I guess the only thing for us is to get married. To live together, love each other, be joyous together, cry together, help each other with glitches. Sleep in our marriage bed, with our marriage comforter. Wake up in the middle of the night and cling together. Reach for each other in the morning when we wake up. Touch the most intimate parts of each other's psyche and body, with gentleness and caring and reverence. I guess those are the things we are destined to do.

In addition to creating our masterpieces.

WEDNESDAY, JUNE 28, 1989 7:00 PM

Beloved, bearded lover!

I celebrate you! I glory in us! Oh, we are something! Everything, everything we're experiencing we are using to bring us closer together. Oh, Jim, I love you. Now for a meditation on your beard: I love its dappled color—grey and (yes!) brown. Golden brown. I love its crinkly soft texture on my hand; on my face (no razor burn, hooray!). I also love the way your beard holds the smell of your Aramis soap throughout the day. So kisses are even more wonderful. God, I love you. It's huge. I'm floating in it. Upon it. Feeling its waves surge and support me with a cresting rush. You are absolutely perfect for me, you honey lover. Yes, you're my honey lover — like a man who's soaked himself in bee honey — full of sweetness- and so edible! I want to eat you up. I want to feast on you, and I know you welcome me.

And for your spiritual rightness for me, I say again, you are my spiritual head. The only man I would risk that relationship with. You are perfect for me — mature, wise, God-loving, cracked open to God's love, free. Oh, God, I am again overwhelmed with love for you.

Honey, Jim and Kathy Elliott (oh my, my stomach just leaped writing that) have a new telephone number. Jim, we're in business! Our life is taking off, catapulting in a great trajectory of glory and love; compatibility and harmony; synchrony and mutual challenge. You can tell I'm overcome — in the poetic mode.

Oh, theoretically speaking (isn't it fun jumping from topic to topic — high-voltage does that, you know) what do you think of hypnosis as a therapeutic technique? Have you experienced it, used it? I think it can be useful. I've never been hypnotized. I love you (oops, that just popped in).

Well, my love, may the force be with you — the spirit of the peach panties, I mean! Pack, pack, pack, pack. I'm waiting.

I adore you, honey man of mine,

your Kathy

WEDNESDAY, JUNE 28, 1989 1:55 PM

Dearest Kitty Kat,

I feel closer to you, more in love with you, than ever before. I think that writing about all those gaps (even though you felt bad) was helpful; if I can tell you about the gaps, and you still love me, it deepens my love for you; I feel I can trust you more, and if I can trust you with the negative stuff, then I can also trust you with the positive feelings more than ever.

In any case, I feel your presence more strongly than ever, even than my post-Asilomar kythe of you. Not only are you inside my head looking out (which I have not felt for a few months) but your perfume is with me, as are your other smells, and your voice speaks to me of love, and I kythed not just your face but your whole body — its voluptuousness en-folds me.

4 pm — I have just hung up after calling you. Kathy! We have a telephone number! Our marriage becomes more and more solid: first the comforter, then this.

About Leah. I want to say again that as you become more and more connected with me, you will break some of the connections you have with others, and it will indeed be painful. Kathy, I am the way to a new level of life for you. (And you for me.) We must be true to that new life; it must come first. I don't know exactly where it will lead, but it will produce more than one masterpiece. I want you with me. I want to give up any connections that will be impediments to that new life. I know you are willing to. You must also be prepared for the fact that some people, formerly your close friends, may vigorously dislike the path you will be on, may feel outraged and indignant and as self-righteous as a loyal Chinese party member. We, you and I, have noble work to do, and nothing must stop us. We will be side by side, giving each other support. I call you to this, from my position as your head.

Dear Kathy, as we individuate (as our relationship individuates), we will differentiate. This will bring us closer together. Nice, huh?

I love you so much my little Kitty Kat. I want us to stand against the world, if need be. You are my sole defender, as I am yours, in this precipitous night. Soon we will be together, my darling. Husband and wife. I can't wait.

Bah-bah, Little Bunny,

THURSDAY, JUNE 29, 1989 11:35 AM

My darling Kitty Kat,

I'm still feeling some vulnerability after our phone call this morning re: your answer (automatic) to Cali's question, but I want you to know that our love is strong and can handle any mistakes either of us might make. The powerful commitments we have to each other will handle anything that might come up. I love you still, even more than before, as I hear your movement away from Cali and toward me. I was glad for our sexual connection after processing the stuff that came up. I felt very close to you again when I came.

Kathy, I love you! I am firmly committed to you, come what may. I loved the fierceness with which you said you would hang on to me, even pursue me. That's very important to me, and I hope never to have it happen. As you can see, I did not withdraw from you. I never will, sweet Kitty Kat.

I am enclosing some pictures of me. The little one was taken by a commercial photo service. All are on or around the date of my graduation from Cal State Hayward. Right afterward, I headed for the hors d'oeuvres table, as usual, and gorged on little sandwiches; that's me about to eat one, I guess. The little thing on my tassel is the date: 88. The next one is me, just having gotten up to stand in line to get my symbolic diploma. Pale blue, I think, was for Educational Psychology. In the next one, I'm walking past a tent on the way to the diploma-giver. Then the next one shows me back at my chair. Finally, there are two taken in Tiburon.

(4:05pm) I am going nuts right now with pressures: the hearing aid man wants me to pick it up; I've got to pack; I'm having trouble getting airline reservations; I'm having trouble getting a moving company to return my calls. Thank you for listening to me when I called earlier. I know you will call me at 8 this evening, and that feels good. I want to get this letter in the mail to you soon. I love you, Little Bunny. Thank you for being there for me. Things are getting to a crucial stage now and I've got to coordinate a lot of things. And I wonder if I can get an extension on my time here in this office, and what to do if I can't.

Well, I just feel stressed now, not very rhapsodic;
But I know once I get to my new home I'll be okay.
I love you very much.

SATURDAY, JULY 1, 1989 1:10 PM

My darling wife,

Yes, you are. I can't wait for the wedding. I name you wife right now. And I name myself husband. And I name us married. So now let's go through the ritual and seal it.

The bookstore man came today and carted off half the books: 15 boxes. He'll come back Monday for the rest. So things are happening.

Your bear card came today. Thank you for loving me.

I'm still frazzled—in the middle of packing—wondering if everything is going to happen on schedule. I'll know for sure Tuesday afternoon when the moving woman comes to give me an estimate.

Here's an article I wrote; any comments?

Got to go now and throw out another carload of paper.

What a non-rhapsodic letter!

I love you and am determined to marry you. And play in our marriage bed with you. Celebrate our union. Kiss all parts of your body, especially the naughty ones. Touch you all over. (Maybe I'm getting a little rhapsodic, huh?) Lick you. Hold you very tightly, all interwoven with you. Talk in our special way, mouth to mouth, breathing each other's breath. Play with your hair.

Thank you for not wanting to let me go.

I love you, little Bunny,

MONDAY, JULY 3, 1989 12:15 PM

My dearest Kitty Kat,

You are having a hard time right now with me and my money fears, and I want to tell you of my strong love for you in response to your patience with me and your indulgence of me and your understanding of my panic. This means a whole lot to me. I know it's my stuff, and it is happening on top of my other fears: fear of not finding a mover, fear of not getting an airplane ticket, fear of having to move out before I'm ready, fear of not getting packed—ever. I have many catastrophic expectations. Thank you, Kitty Kat, for being so understanding. I'm not sure that God provides money for us, but I know he does provide an enfolding and guiding presence within which we can get the money we need. It's a benign context for us. But my belief is that we have to co-create: we must take the initiative to do things that will provide money. Like doing Inner Critic Workshops. Which, I will already have told you, I would like to schedule (the next one, that is) for Saturday, August 5.

Now about my theory. It is, as I mentioned, that our relationship is not just our preference; it is a model for others. Others, that is, approximate to it in varying degrees but few, if any, reach it. Not that we are perfect; we are still learning. But we have the right methods, values, and goals. We want maximum closeness: spiritual, intellectual, emotion-al, physical, sexual. An archetype of unification drives us to merge, but still retaining our identities. An Anthetic relationship. This dyad we have created seems to be a basic building block in the drive of humanity to become one. It must be accomplished first. The thing that will interest me, then, is how we will relate Anthetically to other couples (and to individuals, too). Let's create something good here.

As you can see from the prosaicness of this letter, I am bogged down in machinery. Do not doubt however that I love you very much. You are the goal I am working toward: going to you; marrying you; playing in bed with you; going on our honeymoon together; living with you. All those things will inevitably happen; all we need to do is wait for one day after another to go by, and then we will have the bliss we are working toward. Until then, I will be somewhat frazzled. Thank you again, Little Bunny, for understanding.

The support you give me melts me. I think of you always throughout the day: your sweet face, your soothing body, your dear breasts, your panties. They are with me, as is your voice whispering in my ear of love as I deal with one crisis after another. Oh, I love you so!

"Nothing in the world is single," writes Shelley. "All things by a law divine in one spirit meet and mingle." "The mountains kiss the heaven," he says. "The waves clasp one another."

(I am near tears as I read this).

"The sunlight clasps the earth. The moonbeams kiss the sea."

Oh, Kathy, isn't that sweet? Oh, Little Bunny! I want to cry when I think of what you mean to me, how much I love you, how much you love me! Soon we will lie naked in our marriage bed, and I will hold you close and put my masculine hand between your dear legs.

And we will sleep like that. And awaken in the night like that, turning to each other with little cries of love.

I love you, sweet Kitty Kat,

WEDNESDAY, JULY 5, 1989 11:40 AM

My darling girl,

Yes, I love you! More than ever. (I thought I'd begin with that thought since you might be wondering.) As I walk around, packing, sorting, etc., I see your sweet face before me, your whole body in fact. Clothed, right now.

The man from the moving company is in the group room figuring how much weight I have to move. In a few minutes he'll give me an estimate.

Your card came today — the scorched pantyhose one. How delightful! You write me exactly the right things — the things I want to read. "You are my best lover." And "ready to receive your tongue." And "I am wild for you." And "I like for a boy to eat my pussy." And "I'll let you do it." Also: "Mama said it was okay. She said I should let you do it." And your request to suck me off and eat my semen. (Oh, Little Bunny!) "And swallow it all down." (Oh, Kathy dear!) And "The minx is wild and playful and ready for you."

Thank you, thank you for saying and writing these things — things that give me so many thrills.

(1:30 pm) The moving company man has come and gone, and he quoted me a price of $4400, but I think it's a bit high. Another moving company person is coming at 3:30, and I think she'll be lower. In addition, I'm going to ship some books by 4th class mail, book rate. Well, we'll see.

But, darling Kathy! Know what? I have an airline reservation for the nineteenth. Surely I'll be able to pack by then. (?????). Well, I have overcome my moving date fear and my new-tenant-moving-in fear. Now I've got to work on my two-weeks-to-move fear. Two-weeks-to-pack, that is. Oh, me!

I'm really frazzled again. I may not be very effusive in this letter. But I feel good about having a travel date. I'll leave no matter what.

I'm enclosing—(I was going to say, "I'm enclosing a check," but I don't know what amount to write yet, or which check(s) to use; and the second moving person is here, a woman, who is now [3:25pm] figuring out the weight and will soon give me a proposal.)

Ah, proposals. Remember when I proposed to you? You accepted! And now, dear Kitty Kat, we will be married! I never thought: That I would get married again. That I would be living in Louisiana. That I would be going on my honeymoon to Mississippi. That I would find, ever, exactly the right girl!

Oh, I love you!

Kathy, guess what? (What, my love?) We'll be together on the 19th! For good.

This is a disjointed letter, because today is a disjointed day. Tomorrow will be better; I won't be having any appointments, I think. God, I wish this was over.

Well, Sweetheart, there may or may not be a check in this letter. If there is, please deposit it as quickly as possible so it will clear. What I'd like you to do is have it in your account so you can write a check against it (certified) when the movers come.

I love you. I'm working hard to fly to you quickly,

MONDAY, JULY 10, 1989 9:30 AM

Dearest Little Bunny,

I have been feeling great surges of love for you lately — brought on I think by the fact that you are living alone now (in our new home), and you can speak freely and expressively, and really be with me when I jack off (dare I write that?) or play with myself, and be very expressive, which I love so much. You dear little Kitty Kat!

Yesterday I got a lot of packing done; today will be taken up with errands mostly but some packing, too. This is Day 9; I think I can get all this done in nine days. Easily. I hope.

(11:30am) Somehow I lost my address book and notebook; as I was tossing out paper at the recycling place? Oh, well. It's replaceable. They must have fallen out of my pocket when I bent over. But I have no recollection of bending over and no need to. Oh, well.

(12:30pm, Tuesday). I'm getting movophobia again: fear of not getting packed in time for the movers to pick up everything. I'm working today on going through piles of papers and putting them into small boxes. I have three areas to work on: the middle office, the front office, and the rear building. It seems even more interminable than the other packing I've done. Every piece of paper has to be processed. It must come to an end, Kathy. Right? Oh, me! This is Day 8. I think I can do it. One day for this task: little things into little boxes. Maybe an extra day for it. Then two days for packing the little boxes into big ones. Then two days for packing books. That's five days.

With three days left over. Oh, I hope I can do it!

Anyway, here are two checks. Please deposit them as soon as possible so we can write a certified check against the funds.

I love you, Kathy. Thank you for the nice, ecstatic sexual communion last night. You thrill me. Sigh. (More rhapsodicness later.)

I love you, Little Bunny,

FRIDAY (JIM'S DIARY) JULY 21, 1989

Airport van—6:10—(alarm clock went off 15 min. late, so I'm rushed, beard untrimmed, not room for everything, but I'm here—on way to airport). Will airplane crash? Some fear. A DC-10 just crashed over Iowa. But no—my destiny is to marry Kathy, my treasure. How strange my life has become and will be! Moving to Louisiana. Getting married. Superficially it feels risky—each one—until I think about them—and then they seem exactly the right thing to do. The time for bold decisions has come. Large sums of money are available and now must be committed. Without holding back.

The result—my new life
—Kathy. My beloved wife by my side.
—Lafayette.
—Ph.D.
—Sabotage book
—A fully-staffed office

Enough money. Fame and recognition. New friends. Happiness—at last.

Any possible problems? None that I can see.

8 am—I am in the plane now. Aisle seat, center section—all section to myself. A milk run.

1:05 p.m.—We are on the ground at Dallas. I am feeling sexually wild for my darling girl who awaits me in her pink and white striped dress.

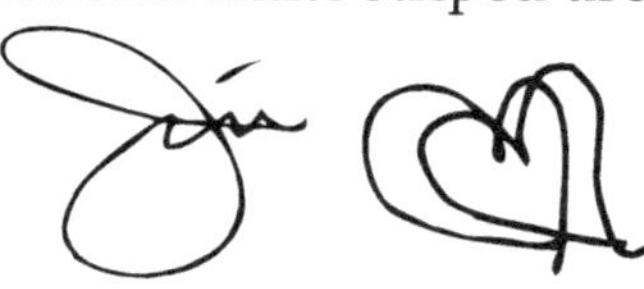

Jim & Kathy's Wedding
July 28, 1989 at 7:00pm

Setting: Kathy's friend, Minette's lovely home. Kathy's Peace Time friends had decorated inside and out—Outside: Caladiums, begonias, balloons, swaths of white cloth, garlands of ivy and pink roses over the front door. Inside: Gorgeous, lush flower arrangements, pink crape myrtle, banana flowers, caladium leaves, roses; masses of candles burning on the mantle above us as we stood in front of the fireplace. Dining Room: Dining table set with silver tureens of food they'd prepared; side buffet table set with our three tiered fresh banana-flavored wedding cake, made by Margaret our favorite baker at Piccadilly Cafeteria, and decorated with orchids and crape myrtle blossoms.

Living room before the fireplace filled with folding chairs and the sofa, packed with people, laughing and talking.

Photography: Cali with cameras for still shots (she had volunteered). Lexie with video camera.

Enter minister, in white alb with hood and yellow stole, then Kevin, Carol, Jim, Caroline, Lorraine, and Kathryn. A hush falls on the crowd.

Jim and Kathy face each other.

Jim reads Phyllis McGinley's poem, "Midcentury Love Letter" (the poem he had read the first night at Pawling, our first sexual communion).

Stay near me, speak my name.

Oh, do not wander by a thought's span, heart's impulse from the light we kindle here.

You are my sole defender, as I am yours, in this precipitous night which over earth so common landmarks alter is falling, without stars and bitter cold.

We two have but our burning selves for shelter.

Huddle against me. So might two climbers lost in mountain weather on a high slope, desperate in the darkness cling together under one cloak and breathe each other warm.

Stay near me, spirit perishable as bone through no such winter can survive alone.

Kathy: (Smiles at him, nodding)

Kathy reads poem to Jim (also from the first night at Pawling):

There was never such a summer for roses in spite of the ruinous weather, ochre and crimson and sugar pink they have flared and flaunted in the scalding hours before storm and the long sly drizzle, streaming out flat in the sharp sudden winds from every quarter, cold, damp, petal spilling, or a tepid, devouring airstream, a northern scirroco.

And still they have flowered wave upon wave of brilliance, though sometimes the hideous rain has clotted their petals and rotted them, sapping their color to bunches of paper.

And yet with a desperate urgency, almost as though, dear heart, they knew of our troubles. And meant to show us that strength may lie in a colored passion, blindly fountaining up from the soil of nature.

They have budded again and flowered and kept on flowering, for the rain has nourished the roots. The infanticidal world chilling winds in spring held back the bloom until the last date of frost was past, so that when the sun came at last, broken, briefly, with a kaleidoscope's minute crash, they all burst together, as love bursts.

And note that the blight was powerless, the fly a failure, and the roses triumphed, as we shall.

Jim, nodding.

Minister: Friends, we are here together in the sight of God and in the presence of these witnesses to join together Jim and Kathy in marriage, which is an honorable estate, not to be entered unadvisedly, but reverently. And knowing the power of God's presence, it's into this holy state that these two persons come now to be joined. They've reached a point in the development of their love when Kathy and Jim, feeling incomplete alone, have discovered that something special in them, something about the way they're made that enables them to find more fulfillment together than they could ever have hoped to have found apart. And having discovered that, they wish to sanctify this union and give it a unique meaning and significance in your presence and with God's blessing.

Jim and Kathy have shared two sources of inspiration, and I have two also in terms of scripture. The first comes from Paul's letter in 1 Corinthians, Chapter 13. Paul defines what love is: Without love I am nothing. Love is patient and kind, keeps no score of wrongs. There is nothing love cannot face. There is no limit to its faith, its hope, and its endurance. Love never ends. And from Song of Songs, Chapter 8, verse 6: Wear me as a seal upon your heart, as a seal upon your arm, for love is strong as death, passion cruel as the grave. It blazes up like blazing fire, fiercer than any flame. Many waters cannot quench love. No flood can keep it away.

Now, what lies ahead for these two is not certain, but they've reached a time in their lives today, a time for tying a knot in the rope of days and saying, "We will not slip backward from here. We are going forward." It's a time for taking vows, for facing the uncertainty with the things with which they are certain. That is that they love one another, and that whatever the future brings, they'll face it together.

And you and I are here to celebrate it with them, perhaps to derive some strength in future days for our having been here when they took this important step. We have our vows to make as well as they. By being here we're involved with them in their future: When they cry, it's ours to weep. When they hurt, it's ours to give comfort. Will you who are here to witness these vows do all in your power to support and uphold this marriage in the years to come? If so, answer, we will.

Crowd: We will!

Minister: We will hear from Ida, who will share the gift of music.

Ida (Singing, "Looking through the Eyes of Love" to piano accompaniment): Please, don't let this feeling end. It's everything I am; everything I want to be. I can see you're mine now; finding out what's true, since I found you. And now I do believe that even in our storms we'll find sunlight. Knowing you're beside me, I'm alright. Please don't let this feeling end, it may not come again, and I want to remember how it feels to touch you; how I feel so much, since I found you. Looking through the eyes of love.

Minister: Jim and Kathy have asked two special

people, Lorraine and Caroline to share a few words at this time.

Lorraine: Kathy and Jim, you have my warmest love and richest blessing. May God grant you a long life and much happiness. Peace. Gentleness. (Pause.) And wonder. And remember: When love and skill work together, it creates a masterpiece.

Caroline: Jim and Kathy, I bless you. With spontaneity. And sustained passion. And friendship. And travel. All these I wish for you.

Minister: It is in the tradition of the Northwest Indians, that when they set up their homes, they set up totems, as symbols of their lives, past, present, and future. It is at this time Kathy and Jim would like to share with you some of the totems in their lives.

Jim: (with little stuffed sea lion) This is a baby sea lion that I gave Kathy at Asilomar. Kathy and I sat on the rocks and watched the sea lions playing. It is a token of the beginning of our relationship, what I hoped would be.

Kathy: (holding sea lion) Jim, when I got this, I knew that there was a sensitivity in you. And that there was a recognition of a childlikeness in me. That had to be in you too. Also it represents the place where we met — the California Oceanside and the breaking of the waves on the rocks.

Jim: (with stuffed tiger) This is a tiger. (Crowd laughs). This is a symbol, as I see it, of defending our relationship against words of people who are cynical about love. One person said to me a couple years ago, "Why get married? You don't need to get married." And we found that we needed to defend ourselves against cynical people.

Kathy: (with tiger) Part of the work I've had to do on myself is to learn personal boundaries, especially boundaries against people's negativity, cynicism, too. Jim has come to me with a tiger's spirit to defend our relationship. He fulfills the masculine role of defending who we are — and our great risk in loving each other and marrying each other. (To Jim) So I claim you as my — Daddy Tiger! (Crowd laughs loudly.)

Lorraine (sotto voce): Love it, love it, love it.

Jim (Holding a crystal compote of strawberries and cream): This is simply strawberries and cream. And this represents the deliciousness of our love and our sexual relationship. (He feeds Kathy). (Then Kathy feeds him.) (He nods and moves to return to the original spot in front of the fireplace; then turns back and nods again. Raucous laughter from people.)

Minister: At this time I invite Jim and Kathy to exchange their vows.

Jim to Lorraine: Before I talk about my vows, I want to say thanks to you, Lorraine, for raising such a sweet, loving, sensitive, caring daughter. You've done a beautiful job.

Lorraine: I just ask that you always love and take care of her.

Jim: I will.

Jim (to Kathy): Kathy — out of all the women in the world, I choose you. I hold you above all others — way above. I forsake all others and cling to you. I survey your mind, your body, and your soul, and over all I see, I cast my strong male look of approval. I promise to attend to your slightest qualm. As you submit to me, I surrender to me. I want to spend the rest of my life pleasing you. I will take your hand and hold it tightly as we explore deeper and deeper into the primal levels of our being. I have a map. I offer you the bright, fierce flame of my love. So we can get closer, to as intense closeness as possible.

Kathy (to Jim): Jim, I tell you today before these witnesses that I choose you. I forsake all others and cling to you. I will be kind to you. I will cosset you when you are hurting. I give my body and my spirit to have its calming influence upon you. I reach into your core and gently touch the hurting and wondrous things that I find there. And I apply my feminine Kathy balm. (Crowd: Mmm). I lay myself open to you for a deep rich communion to heal you and comfort you. I commit to working on stuff, to talk through everything, to stand with the pain until we get through to the other side. I tell you my willingness to talk; to initiate communication, to bring up ideas that will enrich our relationship. I bring to our marriage a wonderful model of love—my mom and dad, who married not for financial provision but for the close, loving communion that supported them through 30 years of marriage. Jim, I invite you to be my spiritual head. I gladly submit to your headship. And Jim, I want to be with you when you die; to see you through that passage; to hold you in my arms and place you in the arms of God.

Minister: Jim, will you have Kathy to be your wife?

Jim: (Nodding) I will.

Minister: Kathy, will you have Jim to be your husband?

Kathy: I will.

Minister: (to crowd) Now that seems like a funny question, doesn't it? They've said all that, but they still wanted to say, I will. (Crowd laughs.) May I have the wedding rings?

The wedding ring is an outward and visible sign of an inward and spiritual grace, signifying unto all the uniting of Jim and Kathy. We bless these rings as a symbol of the vows they are making. Lord, bless these rings that they who wear them may abide in your peace and continue in your favor. Amen.

Jim: (Putting ring on Kathy's finger) Kathy, I give you this ring as a symbol of my commitment to this marriage and to our love. And as a sign to everyone that you are mine. (Kisses ring on Kathy's finger)

Kathy: (Putting ring on Jim's finger) Jim, I give you this ring as a sign of our love and a sign to others that you are mine.

Minister: And now that Jim and Kathy have given themselves each to the other by solemn vows, the giving and receiving of rings, I pronounce that they are husband and wife together. (Jim looks at his watch: 7:30 pm) And may Almighty God, the father of us all, what God has joined together, let no one put asunder.

Let us each offer our prayers for these two; that the days ahead may be filled with thy grace.

Let us pray. (Jim and Kathy holding hands, and minister covering their joined hands with his.) O eternal God, the creator and preserver of all life, we ask your blessing upon this marriage as Kathy and Jim begin their new life together. May this moment bear fruit in new added devotion and new inner strength and a new sense of the sacredness of all life. We pray they learn and grow through all experiences of sorrow and trial; that they find life good and worth celebrating. As they approach life together that they be equipped to forgive, to laugh and to enjoy; to see the worth of each other. And let them in the measure of time that is theirs find much joy in many small things. Look graciously upon them that they may love, honor, and cherish each other, and so live together in faithfulness and patience; in wisdom and true godliness that their home may be a haven of blessing and a place of peace. Now draw them together and to you, Lord. Amen.

Now, Jim and Kathy Elliott! It's really done! (Enthusiastic applause, joy, and laughter from the crowd. Jim and Kathy throw back their heads in abandoned laughter.)

(Jim turns and hugs Kevin.)

Minister (to crowd): Usually the bride and groom kiss each other!

Jim takes Kathy's face in his hands, slowly kissing her.

Minister: You may come and greet them and share your blessing with them.

Part 6

Epilogue

The next day, we shared an early breakfast with Kevin, Carol, and their families. Then, we were off on our honeymoon in our red Honda Accord hatchback. Carol had affixed a JUST MARRIED sign on our back window and placed a box of Red Hots candy on our dashboard. For us, it was the best honeymoon ever. When we returned from our trip to the Gulf Coast, Jim had to fly back to California to finish packing.

FRIDAY, AUGUST 11, 1989 4:30 PM

My darling wife,

Not wife-to-be, but wife. Real wife. True wife. My wife. How I love you, my wife. I just had a nap and am beginning to come back to normal after being out of whack because of the airplane trip and the Chevron group. I feel optimistic, but I dread the thought of all the things I have to do. I wish they could be done magically.

Can I complain? Okay. I don't want to be in this place. I want to be with you. With my wife. In bed. I'm spoiled. I think I'll never be able to do routine clerical work again.

Okay, that's enough complaining.

Here I have to write letters to you again, dammit— not be with you (one more complaint)!

Oh, Kathy Elliott, how I love you!

Let me express. What I must do is pick up each piece of paper, each non-paper item, and deal with it. Pack it somewhere. Or put it somewhere so it can be packed. Throw it out. Or write something about it and mail it, or call someone. There are a finite number of items. The job will be done. Right now it feels endless, even though I have done a lot of it already.

Yes, I can do it.

My 8-millimmeter wedding band gleams as I type. It constantly reminds me of you. Kathy, I'm a married man!

I've got to buy some sealing tape and put this letter in the mail.

I love you, Kathy. I adore you. More solidly now. Great solid strength. Joined to you forever. Adoring you forever. Pouring out my love to you forever. Letting God's flow through me. Drinking in the God you flow forth from you to me.

Enclosed is an announcement you might use to think about your next spirituality lecture.

I need grounding. Not panty-grounding, but talking with you. Not much longer till 8pm.

I love you so much, my Little bunny,

SATURDAY, AUGUST 12, 1989 2:15 PM

My darling precious wife,

I just finished talking with Kevin; it was an excellent conversation. We talked about the wedding; he liked it, but he does not have our expressiveness.

I want you to know how secure I feel, how I feel "fitted in" to something greater, by virtue of our being husband and wife. I am no longer a single, sole, solitary person; I am connected to someone — very intimately connected, merged at times; I have a life partner, an intermingler, a companion at so many levels (sexual, intellectual, collegial, emotional, therapeutic, and more). Kathy, we would be sensational as couple therapists! I love you.

My packing is going well; I'm organizing my thinking, my "packing attitude," and it all seems quite easy and attainable now, whereas yesterday I didn't know what to do with anything I picked up. I feel quite confident I can make the August 24th flight.

Let's have a big celebration in New Orleans — that this will all be behind us. A mini-honeymoon. An advanced honeymoon? You cute thing; I see you smiling.

Kathy, my wife, I want to call forth your intellectual and conceptual powers. I want to discuss spirituality with you, concepts — then do our peer days — and develop my own ideas of spirituality. I'm so looking forward to discussing Amy Fisher's work with you. I want us to be the best, better than she, and so we will be. We are an unbeatable combination. Masterpieces!

I have been so busy exploring our sexual and

emotional and love-expressive levels that I have not considered all the others, but I mean to. Let us study together. Oh, Kathy Jo, how much I adore you!

Love,

Your husband,

WEDNESDAY, AUGUST 16, 1989 3:15 PM

Dear Little Bunny Wife,

I'm making rapid progress in packing; thoughts of pink panties fill my mind, driving me forward. Thoughts of your lush body, too. Your pink tongue. Your wonderfully accepting love of me. Well, this will be the last time we will have to yearn for each other; from now on, we'll be able to reach out and fondle whatever part of each other we want. Right there in bed. The hard parts as well as the soft parts. (Do you feel something poking you in the back?)

Sweet Bunny, my typewriter clacks hollowly now, because things are being (or have been) taken out of this room; the bare walls echo. I guess I am making progress. I bought my ticket today.

Eastern, August 24

Flt 74, leaves SF 12:45 pm (lunch)

Arrives Atlanta 8:30pm

Flt 667, leaves Atlanta 9:40pm

Arrives New Orleans 10:05pm

Flt Lovebird Special, leaves New Orleans 10:06pm

Arrives motel 10:07pm

Clothes off by 10:08pm

Insertion 10:09pm

Please keep your tray tables and other organs in

an upright position in preparation for landing.

It may be a bit bumpy.

Let's fly united next time.

I love you, my darling wife.

Oh, how I love you!

We talked with Little Kathy last night; I love her, too. I want to protect her and comfort her. And I want her to express whatever she wants, so we can comfort her even more, so she won't have to go around with some dark secret. But in her own time.

I love you, my Kitty Kat.

Your husband,

Acknowledgements

This book has been called into being. Many special people in our lives have been part of that calling, and we want to thank them here. The first memory I (Kathryn) have of those who evoked this book were the special women who took such intimate and devoted care of Jim during the three years following his stroke. Thank you, especially, LaRae, Rocquelle, Janelle, April, and Wendy, for beholding our love, and for issuing the first call as you heard me read the love letters aloud to Jim. Your exclamations of wonder and your tears when moved, along with your words, "You have to publish these letters!" were the impetus for this book coming to life. Another special thank you to LaRae, who while watching over Jim in the wee hours, organized and collated the letters so that I could convert them to digital form. A special thank you to Jim's nurse (and I regret I can't remember your name) during one hospital stay, whose 3 am comment to me while Jim slept and I told you about our love letters, named the book, "Why, you have a self-help romance!" Your insightful comment helped us see how our letters, once published, could contribute to readers.

Our deep gratitude to Donna, writer who walked beside us. The many e-mails we exchanged, in which you asked questions about our love story and we answered, evoked this book into being. Your lovely words of encouragement saw us through many challenging days. Thank you for reading the great volume of our work I sent you and for encouraging and loving us. Without you, I would not have begun blogging. Without the soulmate-skills blog, I would not have developed the perspective that formed The Finding portion of this book. You have the gift, and I can never thank you enough for sharing it with us.

Our heartfelt thanks to Marianne and Linnette, soul-friends who love us and who love Anthetics. You have never faltered. You have valued us so highly, and it has fed our souls. Tearful, overflowing love to you for all you have done to care for Jim and for me. Marianne, a special thank you to you for treasuring the soulmate-skills blog and for keeping it safe in print, so that when the website crashed, it was not lost.

Amy and Andrew, our loving thanks for reading the rough draft; for giving us your beautiful feedback; and for believing in the power of this book. Your love for each other inspires and blesses us.

To our family, children and grandchildren, thank you so much for loving both of us and for supporting our relationship from the very beginning. Carol, thank you heart and soul for caring for your dad and for loving me so devotedly. Mama, thank you for praying Jim into my life and for loving and supporting us as you did.

A special thank you to our gifted granddaughter, Jocelyne. Not only did you design our first website, soulmateskills, but you did it while caring for your grandfather. When formatting this book became overwhelming to me, you stepped in with your skills and carried the book forward to print. Deepest gratitude for being there to design the beautiful cover. Words cannot express what your loving contributions have meant to us.

To our staff at Anthetic Psychology Center, we thank you with full hearts. Misty, yours and Pat's loving devotion to us, to our relationship, and to our work, have blessed and upheld us. Scott, yours and Crystal's love for us and your belief in Anthetics have been a solid source of comfort and strength. Sara, your love for us and Anthetics continues to bless us. I hold in my heart your special reading of the letters to me on that long drive so I could hear their power anew. Tamra, yours and Jacob's valuing of both our relationship and our work as an inspiration and model to you is a great gift.

To all our clients and students, thank you for valuing and loving us and our work. Your requests for our stories confirmed to us that the love letters would have an eager audience when published. A special thank you to April, my graduate assistant, who sat with me as Jim went through those touch-and-go initial days following his stroke. Love to my graduate assistant, Beth, for enfolding me with love as the blog and this book were being born. To Tiffany, thank you deeply for loving and honoring and "getting" us.

We owe this book to all of you. We hold you in our hearts; in fact, with hearts entwined.

About the Authors

Kathryn Elliott, Ph.D. and James Elliott, Ph.D., are authors of Disarming Your Inner Critic. Kathryn is Director of Anthetic Psychology Center in Lafayette, Louisiana. James is originator of Anthetic Therapy. Prior to James's death in 2011, James and Kathryn spent 22 years doing therapy, publishing professional journal articles, and presenting at dozens of professional conferences. They have been featured on "NPR: All Things Considered," and in Modern Bride, Good Housekeeping, and WebMD.